NON SANZ DROICT.

The Winters Tale.

Decorative headband and title of the earliest printed version of *The Winter's Tale*, in the First Folio (1623)

William Shakespeare

The Winter's Tale

With New and Updated Critical Essays and a Revised Bibliography

Edited by Frank Kermode

THE SIGNET CLASSIC SHAKESPEARE
General Editor: Sylvan Barnet

A SIGNET CLASSIC

SIGNET CLASSIC
Published by New American Library, a division of
Penguin Putnam Inc., 375 Hudson Street, New York, New York 10014,
U.S.A.
Penguin Books Ltd, 27 Wrights Lane, London W8 5TZ, England
Penguin Books Australia Ltd, Ringwood, Victoria, Australia
Penguin Books Canada Ltd, 10 Alcorn Avenue, Toronto, Ontario,
Canada M4V 3B2
Penguin Books (N.Z.) Ltd, 182–190 Wairau Road, Auckland 10, New
Zealand

Penguin Books Ltd, Registered Offices:
Harmondsworth, Middlesex, England

Published by Signet Classic, an imprint of New American Library,
a division of Penguin Putnam Inc.

First Signet Classic Printing, 1963
First Signet Classic Printing (Second Revised Edition), November 1998
20 19 18 17 16 15 14 13

Library of Congress Catalog Card Number: 97-62215

Printed in the United States of America

Contents

Shakespeare: An Overview

Biographical Sketch

Between the record of his baptism in Stratford on 26 April 1564 and the record of his burial in Stratford on 25 April 1616, some forty official documents name Shakespeare, and many others name his parents, his children, and his grandchildren. Further, there are at least fifty literary references to him in the works of his contemporaries. More facts are known about William Shakespeare than about any other playwright of the period except Ben Jonson. The facts should, however, be distinguished from the legends. The latter, inevitably more engaging and better known, tell us that the Stratford boy killed a calf in high style, poached deer and rabbits, and was forced to flee to London, where he held horses outside a playhouse. These traditions are only traditions; they may be true, but no evidence supports them, and it is well to stick to the facts.

Mary Arden, the dramatist's mother, was the daughter of a substantial landowner; about 1557 she married John Shakespeare, a tanner, glove-maker, and trader in wool, grain, and other farm commodities. In 1557 John Shakespeare was a member of the council (the governing body of Stratford), in 1558 a constable of the borough, in 1561 one of the two town chamberlains, in 1565 an alderman (entitling him to the appellation of "Mr."), in 1568 high bailiff—the town's highest political office, equivalent to mayor. After 1577, for an unknown reason he drops out of local politics. What *is* known is that he had to mortgage his wife's property, and that he was involved in serious litigation.

The birthday of William Shakespeare, the third child and the eldest son of this locally prominent man, is unrecorded, but the Stratford parish register records that the infant was baptized on 26 April 1564. (It is quite possible that he was born on 23 April, but this date has probably been assigned by tradition because it is the date on which, fifty-two years later, he died, and perhaps because it is the feast day of St. George, patron saint of England.) The attendance records of the Stratford grammar school of the period are not extant, but it is reasonable to assume that the son of a prominent local official attended the free school—it had been established for the purpose of educating males precisely of his class—and received substantial training in Latin. The masters of the school from Shakespeare's seventh to fifteenth years held Oxford degrees; the Elizabethan curriculum excluded mathematics and the natural sciences but taught a good deal of Latin rhetoric, logic, and literature, including plays by Plautus, Terence, and Seneca.

On 27 November 1582 a marriage license was issued for the marriage of Shakespeare and Anne Hathaway, eight years his senior. The couple had a daughter, Susanna, in May 1583. Perhaps the marriage was necessary, but perhaps the couple had earlier engaged, in the presence of witnesses, in a formal "troth plight" which would render their children legitimate even if no further ceremony were performed. In February 1585, Anne Hathaway bore Shakespeare twins, Hamnet and Judith.

That Shakespeare was born is excellent; that he married and had children is pleasant; but that we know nothing about his departure from Stratford to London or about the beginning of his theatrical career is lamentable and must be admitted. We would gladly sacrifice details about his children's baptism for details about his earliest days in the theater. Perhaps the poaching episode is true (but it is first reported almost a century after Shakespeare's death), or perhaps he left Stratford to be a schoolmaster, as another tradition holds; perhaps he was moved (like Petruchio in *The Taming of the Shrew*) by

> Such wind as scatters young men through the world,
> To seek their fortunes farther than at home
> Where small experience grows.   (1.2.49–51)

In 1592, thanks to the cantankerousness of Robert Greene, we have our first reference, a snarling one, to Shakespeare as an actor and playwright. Greene, a graduate of St. John's College, Cambridge, had become a playwright and a pamphleteer in London, and in one of his pamphlets he warns three university-educated playwrights against an actor who has presumed to turn playwright:

> There is an upstart crow, beautified with our feathers, that with his *tiger's heart wrapped in a player's hide* supposes he is as well able to bombast out a blank verse as the best of you, and being an absolute Johannes-factotum [i.e., jack-of-all-trades] is in his own conceit the only Shake-scene in a country.

The reference to the player, as well as the allusion to Aesop's crow (who strutted in borrowed plumage, as an actor struts in fine words not his own), makes it clear that by this date Shakespeare had both acted and written. That Shakespeare is meant is indicated not only by *Shake-scene* but also by the parody of a line from one of Shakespeare's plays, *3 Henry VI*: "O, tiger's heart wrapped in a woman's hide" (1.4.137). If in 1592 Shakespeare was prominent enough to be attacked by an envious dramatist, he probably had served an apprenticeship in the theater for at least a few years.

In any case, although there are no extant references to Shakespeare between the record of the baptism of his twins in 1585 and Greene's hostile comment about "Shake-scene" in 1592, it is evident that during some of these "dark years" or "lost years" Shakespeare had acted and written. There are a number of subsequent references to him as an actor. Documents indicate that in 1598 he is a "principal comedian," in 1603 a "principal tragedian," in 1608 he is one of the "men players." (We do not have, however, any solid information about which roles he may have played; later traditions say he played Adam in *As You Like It* and the ghost in *Hamlet*, but nothing supports the assertions. Probably his role as dramatist came to supersede his role as actor.) The profession of actor was not for a gentleman, and it occasionally drew the scorn of university men like Greene who resented writing speeches for persons less educated than themselves, but it was respectable enough; players, if prosperous, were in effect members of the bourgeoisie, and there is nothing to suggest that Stratford considered William Shakespeare less than a solid citizen. When, in 1596, the Shakespeares were granted a coat of arms—i.e., the right to be considered gentlemen—the grant was made to Shakespeare's father, but probably William Shakespeare had arranged the matter on his own behalf. In subsequent transactions he is occasionally styled a gentleman.

Although in 1593 and 1594 Shakespeare published two narrative poems dedicated to the Earl of Southampton, *Venus and Adonis* and *The Rape of Lucrece*, and may well have written most or all of his sonnets in the middle nineties, Shakespeare's literary activity seems to have been almost entirely devoted to the theater. (It may be significant that the two narrative poems were written in years when the plague closed the theaters for several months.) In 1594 he was a charter member of a theatrical company called the Chamberlain's Men, which in 1603 became the royal company, the King's Men, making Shakespeare the king's playwright. Until he retired to Stratford (about 1611, apparently), he was with this remarkably stable company. From 1599 the company acted primarily at the Globe theater, in which Shakespeare held a one-tenth interest. Other Elizabethan dramatists are known to have acted, but no other is known also to have been entitled to a share of the profits.

Shakespeare's first eight published plays did not have his name on them, but this is not remarkable; the most popular play of the period, Thomas Kyd's *The Spanish Tragedy*, went through many editions without naming Kyd, and Kyd's authorship is known only because a book on the profession of acting happens to quote (and attribute to Kyd) some lines on the interest of Roman emperors in the drama. What is remarkable is that after 1598 Shakespeare's name commonly appears on printed plays—some of which are not his. Presumably his name was a drawing card, and publishers used it to attract potential buyers. Another indication of his popularity comes from Francis Meres, author of *Palladis Tamia: Wit's Treasury* (1598). In this anthology of snippets accompanied by an essay on literature, many playwrights are mentioned, but Shakespeare's name occurs more often than any other, and Shakespeare is the only playwright whose plays are listed.

From his acting, his play writing, and his share in a playhouse, Shakespeare seems to have made considerable money. He put it to work, making substantial investments in Stratford real estate. As early as 1597 he bought New Place, the second-largest house in Stratford. His family moved in soon afterward, and the house remained in the family until a granddaughter died in 1670. When Shakespeare made his will in 1616, less than a month before he died, he sought to leave his property intact to his descendants. Of small bequests to relatives and to friends (including three actors, Richard Burbage, John Heminges, and Henry Condell), that to his wife of the second-best bed has provoked the most comment. It has sometimes been taken as a sign of an unhappy marriage (other supposed signs are the apparently hasty marriage, his wife's seniority of eight years, and his residence in London without his family). Perhaps the second-best bed was the bed the couple had slept in, the best bed being reserved for visitors. In any case, had Shakespeare not excepted it, the bed would have gone (with the rest of his household possessions) to his daughter and her husband.

On 25 April 1616 Shakespeare was buried within the chancel of the church at Stratford. An unattractive monument to his memory, placed on a wall near the grave, says that he died on 23 April. Over the grave itself are the lines, perhaps by Shakespeare, that (more than his literary fame) have kept his bones undisturbed in the crowded burial ground where old bones were often dislodged to make way for new:

> Good friend, for Jesus' sake forbear
> To dig the dust enclosed here.
> Blessed be the man that spares these stones
> And cursed be he that moves my bones.

A Note on the Anti-Stratfordians, Especially Baconians and Oxfordians

Not until 1769—more than a hundred and fifty years after Shakespeare's death—is there any record of anyone expressing doubt about Shakespeare's authorship of the plays and poems. In 1769, however, Herbert Lawrence nominated Francis Bacon (1561–1626) in *The Life and Adventures of Common Sense*. Since then, at least two dozen other nominees have been offered, including Christopher Marlowe, Sir Walter Raleigh, Queen Elizabeth I, and Edward de Vere, 17th earl of Oxford. The impulse behind all anti-Stratfordian movements is the scarcely concealed snobbish opinion that "the man from Stratford" simply could not have written the plays because he was a country fellow without a university education and without access to high society. Anyone, the argument goes, who used so many legal terms, medical terms, nautical terms, and so forth, and who showed some familiarity with classical writing, must have attended a university, and anyone who knew so much about courtly elegance and courtly deceit must himself have moved among courtiers. The plays do indeed reveal an author whose interests were exceptionally broad, but specialists in any given field—law, medicine, arms and armor, and so on—soon find that the plays do not reveal deep knowledge in specialized matters; indeed, the playwright often gets technical details wrong.

The claim on behalf of Bacon, forgotten almost as soon as it was put forth in 1769, was independently reasserted by Joseph C. Hart in 1848. In 1856 it was reaffirmed by W. H. Smith in a book, and also by Delia Bacon in an article; in 1857 Delia Bacon published a book, arguing that Francis Bacon had directed a group of intellectuals who wrote the plays.

Francis Bacon's claim has largely faded, perhaps because it was advanced with such evident craziness by Ignatius Donnelly, who in *The Great Cryptogram* (1888) claimed to break a code in the plays that proved Bacon had written not only the plays attributed to Shakespeare but also other Renaissance works, for instance the plays of Christopher Marlowe and the essays of Montaigne.

Consider the last two lines of the Epilogue in *The Tempest*:

As you from crimes would pardoned be,
Let your indulgence set me free.

What was Shakespeare—sorry, Francis Bacon, Baron Verulam—*really* saying in these two lines? According to Baconians, the lines are an anagram reading, "Tempest of Francis Bacon, Lord Verulam; do ye ne'er divulge me, ye words." Ingenious, and it is a pity that in the quotation the letter *a* appears only twice in the cryptogram, whereas in the deciphered message it appears three times. Oh, no problem; just alter "Verulam" to "Verul'm" and it works out very nicely.

Most people understand that with sufficient ingenuity one can torture any text and find in it what one wishes. For instance: Did Shakespeare have a hand in the King James Version of the Bible? It was nearing completion in 1610, when Shakespeare was forty-six years old. If you look at the 46th Psalm and count forward for forty-six words, you will find the word *shake*. Now if you go to the end of the psalm and count backward forty-six words, you will find the word *spear*. Clear evidence, according to some, that Shakespeare slyly left his mark in the book.

Bacon's candidacy has largely been replaced in the twentieth century by the candidacy of Edward de Vere (1550–1604), 17th earl of Oxford. The basic ideas behind the Oxford theory, advanced at greatest length by Dorothy and Charlton Ogburn in *This Star of England* (1952, rev. 1955), a book of 1297 pages, and by Charlton Ogburn in *The Mysterious William Shakespeare* (1984), a book of 892 pages, are these: (1) The man from Stratford could not possibly have had the mental equipment and the experience to have written the plays—only a courtier could have written them; (2) Oxford had the requisite background (social position, education, years at Queen Elizabeth's court); (3) Oxford did not wish his authorship to be known for two basic reasons: writing for the public theater was a vulgar pursuit, and the plays show so much courtly and royal disreputable behavior that they would have compromised Oxford's position at court. Oxfordians offer countless details to support the claim. For example, Hamlet's phrase "that ever I was born to set it right" (1.5.89) barely conceals "E. Ver, I was born to set it right," an unambiguous announcement of de Vere's authorship, according to *This Star of England* (p. 654). A second example: Consider Ben

Jonson's poem entitled "To the Memory of My Beloved Master William Shakespeare," prefixed to the first collected edition of Shakespeare's plays in 1623. According to Oxfordians, when Jonson in this poem speaks of the author of the plays as the "swan of Avon," he is alluding not to William Shakespeare, who was born and died in Stratford-on-Avon and who throughout his adult life owned property there; rather, he is alluding to Oxford, who, the Ogburns say, used "William Shakespeare" as his pen name, and whose manor at Bilton was on the Avon River. Oxfordians do not offer any evidence that Oxford took a pen name, and they do not mention that Oxford had sold the manor in 1581, forty-two years before Jonson wrote his poem. Surely a reference to the Shakespeare who was born in Stratford, who had returned to Stratford, and who had died there only seven years before Jonson wrote the poem is more plausible. And exactly why Jonson, who elsewhere also spoke of Shakespeare as a playwright, and why Heminges and Condell, who had acted with Shakespeare for about twenty years, should speak of Shakespeare as the author in their dedication in the 1623 volume of collected plays is never adequately explained by Oxfordians. Either Jonson, Heminges and Condell, and numerous others were in on the conspiracy, or they were all duped—equally unlikely alternatives. Another difficulty in the Oxford theory is that Oxford died in 1604, and some of the plays are clearly indebted to works and events later than 1604. Among the Oxfordian responses are: At his death Oxford left some plays, and in later years these were touched up by hacks, who added the material that points to later dates. *The Tempest*, almost universally regarded as one of Shakespeare's greatest plays and pretty clearly dated to 1611, does indeed date from a period after the death of Oxford, but it is a crude piece of work that should not be included in the canon of works by Oxford.

The anti-Stratfordians, in addition to assuming that the author must have been a man of rank and a university man, usually assume two conspiracies: (1) a conspiracy in Elizabethan and Jacobean times, in which a surprisingly large number of persons connected with the theater knew that the actor Shakespeare did not write the plays attributed to him but for some reason or other pretended that he did; (2) a conspiracy of today's Stratfordians, the professors who teach Shakespeare in the colleges and universities, who are said to have a vested interest in preserving Shakespeare as the author of the plays they teach. In fact, (1) it is inconceivable that the secret of Shakespeare's non-authorship could have been preserved by all of the people who supposedly were in on the conspiracy, and (2) academic fame awaits any scholar today who can disprove Shakespeare's authorship.

The Stratfordian case is convincing not only because hundreds or even thousands of anti-Stratford arguments—of the sort that say "ever I was born" has the secret double meaning "E. Ver, I was born"—add up to nothing at all but also because irrefutable evidence connects the man from Stratford with the London theater and with the authorship of particular plays. The anti-Stratfordians do not seem to understand that it is not enough to dismiss the Stratford case by saying that a fellow from the provinces simply couldn't have written the plays. Nor do they understand that it is not enough to dismiss all of the evidence connecting Shakespeare with the plays by asserting that it is perjured.

The Shakespeare Canon

We return to William Shakespeare. Thirty-seven plays as well as some nondramatic poems are generally held to constitute the Shakespeare canon, the body of authentic works. The exact dates of composition of most of the works are highly uncertain, but evidence of a starting point and/or of a final limiting point often provides a framework for informed guessing. For example, *Richard II* cannot be earlier than 1595, the publication date of some material to which it is indebted; *The Merchant of Venice* cannot be later than 1598, the year Francis Meres mentioned it. Sometimes arguments for a date hang on an alleged topical allusion, such as the lines about the unseasonable weather in *A Midsummer Night's Dream*, 2.1.81–117, but such an allusion, if indeed it is an allusion to an event in the real world, can be variously interpreted, and in any case there is always the possibility that a topical allusion was inserted years later, to bring the play up to date. (The issue of alterations in a text between the time that Shakespeare drafted it and the time that it was printed—alterations due to censorship or playhouse practice or Shakespeare's own second thoughts—will be discussed in "The Play Text as a Collaboration" later in this overview.) Dates are often attributed on the basis of style, and although conjectures about style usually rest on other conjectures (such as Shakespeare's development as a playwright, or the appropriateness of lines to character), sooner or later one must rely on one's literary sense. There is no documentary proof, for example, that *Othello* is not as early as *Romeo and Juliet*, but one feels that *Othello* is a later, more mature work, and because the first record of its performance is 1604, one is glad enough to set its composition at that date and not push it back into Shakespeare's early years. (*Romeo and Juliet* was first published in 1597, but evidence suggests that it was written a little earlier.) The following chronology, then, is indebted not only to facts but also to informed guesswork and sensitivity. The dates, necessarily imprecise for some works, indicate something like a scholarly consensus concerning the time of original composition. Some plays show evidence of later revision.

Plays. The first collected edition of Shakespeare, published in 1623, included thirty-six plays. These are all accepted as Shakespeare's, though for one of them, *Henry VIII*, he is thought to have had a collaborator. A thirty-seventh play, *Pericles*, published in 1609 and attributed to Shakespeare on the title page, is also widely accepted as being partly by Shakespeare even though it is not included in the 1623 volume. Still another play not in the 1623 volume, *The Two Noble Kinsmen*, was first published in 1634, with a title page attributing it to John Fletcher and Shakespeare. Probably most students of the subject now believe that Shakespeare did indeed have a hand in it. Of the remaining plays attributed at one time or another to Shakespeare, only one, *Edward III*, anonymously published in 1596, is now regarded by some scholars as a serious candidate. The prevailing opinion, however, is that this rather simpleminded play is not Shakespeare's; at most he may have revised some passages, chiefly scenes with the Countess of

Salisbury. We include *The Two Noble Kinsmen* but do not include *Edward III* in the following list.

1588–94	*The Comedy of Errors*
1588–94	*Love's Labor's Lost*
1589–91	*2 Henry VI*
1590–91	*3 Henry VI*
1589–92	*1 Henry VI*
1592–93	*Richard III*
1589–94	*Titus Andronicus*
1593–94	*The Taming of the Shrew*
1592–94	*The Two Gentlemen of Verona*
1594–96	*Romeo and Juliet*
1595	*Richard II*
1595–96	*A Midsummer Night's Dream*
1596–97	*King John*
1594–96	*The Merchant of Venice*
1596–97	*1 Henry IV*
1597	*The Merry Wives of Windsor*
1597–98	*2 Henry IV*
1598–99	*Much Ado About Nothing*
1598–99	*Henry V*
1599	*Julius Caesar*
1599–1600	*As You Like It*
1599–1600	*Twelfth Night*
1600–1601	*Hamlet*
1601–1602	*Troilus and Cressida*
1602–1604	*All's Well That Ends Well*
1603–1604	*Othello*
1604	*Measure for Measure*
1605–1606	*King Lear*
1605–1606	*Macbeth*
1606–1607	*Antony and Cleopatra*
1605–1608	*Timon of Athens*
1607–1608	*Coriolanus*
1607–1608	*Pericles*
1609–10	*Cymbeline*
1610–11	*The Winter's Tale*
1611	*The Tempest*

1612–13	*Henry VIII*
1613	*The Two Noble Kinsmen*

Poems. In 1989 Donald W. Foster published a book in which he argued that "A Funeral Elegy for Master William Peter," published in 1612, ascribed only to the initials W.S., *may* be by Shakespeare. Foster later published an article in a scholarly journal, *PMLA* 111 (1996), in which he asserted the claim more positively. The evidence begins with the initials, and includes the fact that the publisher and the printer of the elegy had published Shakespeare's *Sonnets* in 1609. But such facts add up to rather little, especially because no one has found any connection between Shakespeare and William Peter (an Oxford graduate about whom little is known, who was murdered at the age of twenty-nine). The argument is based chiefly on statistical examinations of word patterns, which are said to correlate with Shakespeare's known work. Despite such correlations, however, many readers feel that the poem does not sound like Shakespeare. True, Shakespeare has a great range of styles, but his work is consistently imaginative and interesting. Many readers find neither of these qualities in "A Funeral Elegy."

1592–93	*Venus and Adonis*
1593–94	*The Rape of Lucrece*
1593–1600	*Sonnets*
1600–1601	*The Phoenix and the Turtle*

Shakespeare's English

1. Spelling and Pronunciation. From the philologist's point of view, Shakespeare's English is modern English. It requires footnotes, but the inexperienced reader can comprehend substantial passages with very little help, whereas for the same reader Chaucer's Middle English is a foreign language. By the beginning of the fifteenth century the chief grammatical changes in English had taken place, and the final unaccented -*e* of Middle English had been lost (though it survives even today in spelling, as in *name*); during the fifteenth century the dialect of London, the commercial and political center, gradually displaced the provincial dialects, at least in writing; by the end of the century, printing had helped to regularize and stabilize the language, especially spelling. Elizabethan spelling may seem erratic to us (there were dozens of spellings of *Shakespeare*, and a simple word like *been* was also spelled *beene* and *bin*), but it had much in common with our spelling. Elizabethan spelling was conservative in that for the most part it reflected an older pronunciation (Middle English) rather than the sound of the language as it was then spoken, just as our spelling continues to reflect medieval pronunciation—most obviously in the now silent but formerly pronounced letters in a word such as *knight*. Elizabethan pronunciation, though not identical with ours, was much closer to ours than to that of the Middle Ages. Incidentally, though no one can be certain about what Elizabethan English sounded like, specialists tend to believe it was rather like the speech of a modern stage Irishman (*time* apparently was pronounced *toime*, *old* pronounced *awld*, *day* pronounced *die*, and *join* pronounced *jine*) and not at all like the Oxford speech that most of us think it was.

An awareness of the difference between our pronunciation and Shakespeare's is crucial in three areas—in accent, or number of syllables (many metrically regular lines may look irregular to us); in rhymes (which may not look like rhymes); and in puns (which may not look like puns). Examples will be useful. Some words that were at least on occasion stressed differently from today are *aspèct*, *còmplete*, *fòrlorn*, *revènue*, and *sepùlcher*. Words that sometimes had an additional syllable are *emp[e]ress*, *Hen[e]ry*, *mon[e]th*, and *villain* (three syllables, *vil-lay-in*). An additional syllable is often found in possessives, like *moon*'s (pronounced *moones*) and in words ending in *-tion* or *-sion*. Words that had one less syllable than they now have are *needle* (pronounced *neel*) and *violet* (pronounced *vilet*). Among rhymes now lost are *one* with *loan*, *love* with *prove*, *beast* with *jest*, *eat* with *great*. (In reading, trust your sense of metrics and your ear, more than your eye.) An example of a pun that has become obliterated by a change in pronunciation is Falstaff's reply to Prince Hal's "Come, tell us your reason" in *1 Henry IV*: "Give you a reason on compulsion? If reasons were as plentiful as blackberries, I would give no man a reason upon compulsion, I" (2.4.237–40). The *ea* in *reason* was pronounced rather like a long *a*, like the *ai* in *raisin*, hence the comparison with blackberries.

Puns are not merely attempts to be funny; like metaphors they often involve bringing into a meaningful relationship areas of experience normally seen as remote. In *2 Henry IV*, when Feeble is conscripted, he stoically says, "I care not. A man can die but once. We owe God a death" (3.2.242–43), punning on *debt*, which was the way *death* was pronounced. Here an enormously significant fact of life is put into simple commercial imagery, suggesting its commonplace quality. Shakespeare used the same pun earlier in *1 Henry IV*, when Prince Hal says to Falstaff, "Why, thou owest God a death," and Falstaff replies, " 'Tis not due yet: I would be loath to pay him before his day. What need I be so forward with him that calls not on me?" (5.1.126–29).

Sometimes the puns reveal a delightful playfulness; sometimes they reveal aggressiveness, as when, replying to Claudius's "But now, my cousin Hamlet, and my son," Hamlet says, "A little more than kin, and less than kind!" (1.2.64–65). These are Hamlet's first words in the play, and we already hear him warring verbally against Claudius. Hamlet's "less than kind" probably means (1) Hamlet is not of Claudius's family or nature, *kind* having the sense it still has in our word *mankind*; (2) Hamlet is not kindly (affectionately) disposed toward Claudius; (3) Claudius is not naturally (but rather unnaturally, in a legal sense incestuously) Hamlet's father. The puns evidently were not put in as sops to the groundlings; they are an important way of communicating a complex meaning.

2. Vocabulary. A conspicuous difficulty in reading Shakespeare is rooted in the fact that some of his words are no longer in common use—for example, words concerned with armor, astrology, clothing, coinage, hawking, horsemanship, law, medicine, sailing, and war. Shakespeare had a large vocabulary—something near thirty thousand words— but it was not so much a vocabulary of big words as a vocabulary drawn from a wide range of life, and it is partly his ability to call upon a great body of concrete language that gives his plays the sense of being in close contact with life. When the right word did not already exist, he made it up. Among words thought to be his coinages are *accommodation, all-knowing, amazement, bare-faced, countless, dexterously, dislocate, dwindle, fancy-free, frugal, indistinguishable, lackluster, laughable, overawe, premeditated, sea change, star-crossed*. Among those that have not survived are the verb *convive*, meaning to feast together, and *smilet*, a little smile.

Less overtly troublesome than the technical words but more treacherous are the words that seem readily intelligible to us but whose Elizabethan meanings differ from their modern ones. When Horatio describes the Ghost as an "erring spirit," he is saying not that the ghost has sinned or made an error but that it is wandering. Here is a short list of some of the most common words in Shakespeare's plays that often (but not always) have a meaning other than their most usual modern meaning:

'a	he
abuse	deceive
accident	occurrence
advertise	inform
an, and	if
annoy	harm
appeal	accuse
artificial	skillful
brave	fine, splendid
censure	opinion
cheer	(1) face (2) frame of mind
chorus	a single person who comments on the events
closet	small private room
competitor	partner
conceit	idea, imagination
cousin	kinsman
cunning	skillful
disaster	evil astrological influence
doom	judgment
entertain	receive into service

envy	malice
event	outcome
excrement	outgrowth (of hair)
fact	evil deed
fancy	(1) love (2) imagination
fell	cruel
fellow	(1) companion (2) low person (often an insulting term if addressed to someone of approximately equal rank)
fond	foolish
free	(1) innocent (2) generous
glass	mirror
hap, haply	chance, by chance
head	army
humor	(1) mood (2) bodily fluid thought to control one's psychology
imp	child
intelligence	news
kind	natural, acting according to nature
let	hinder
lewd	base
mere(ly)	utter(ly)
modern	commonplace
natural	a fool, an idiot
naughty	(1) wicked (2) worthless
next	nearest
nice	(1) trivial (2) fussy
noise	music
policy	(1) prudence (2) stratagem
presently	immediately
prevent	anticipate
proper	handsome
prove	test
quick	alive
sad	serious
saw	proverb
secure	without care, incautious
silly	innocent

sensible	capable of being perceived by the senses
shrewd	sharp
so	provided that
starve	die
still	always
success	that which follows
tall	brave
tell	count
tonight	last night
wanton	playful, careless
watch	keep awake
will	lust
wink	close both eyes
wit	mind, intelligence

All glosses, of course, are mere approximations; sometimes one of Shakespeare's words may hover between an older meaning and a modern one, and as we have seen, his words often have multiple meanings.

3. Grammar. A few matters of grammar may be surveyed, though it should be noted at the outset that Shakespeare sometimes made up his own grammar. As E.A. Abbott says in *A Shakespearian Grammar,* "Almost any part of speech can be used as any other part of speech": a noun as a verb ("he childed as I fathered"); a verb as a noun ("She hath made compare"); or an adverb as an adjective ("a seldom pleasure"). There are hundreds, perhaps thousands, of such instances in the plays, many of which at first glance would not seem at all irregular and would trouble only a pedant. Here are a few broad matters.

Nouns: The Elizabethans thought the *-s* genitive ending for nouns (as in *man's*) derived from *his;* thus the line " 'gainst the count his galleys I did some service," for "the count's galleys."

Adjectives: By Shakespeare's time adjectives had lost the endings that once indicated gender, number, and case. About the only difference between Shakespeare's adjectives and ours is the use of the now redundant *more* or *most* with the comparative ("some more fitter place") or superlative

("This was the most unkindest cut of all"). Like double comparatives and double superlatives, double negatives were acceptable; Mercutio "will not budge for no man's pleasure."

Pronouns: The greatest change was in pronouns. In Middle English *thou, thy,* and *thee* were used among familiars and in speaking to children and inferiors; *ye, your,* and *you* were used in speaking to superiors (servants to masters, nobles to the king) or to equals with whom the speaker was not familiar. Increasingly the "polite" forms were used in all direct address, regardless of rank, and the accusative *you* displaced the nominative *ye*. Shakespeare sometimes uses *ye* instead of *you,* but even in Shakespeare's day *ye* was archaic, and it occurs mostly in rhetorical appeals.

Thou, thy, and *thee* were not completely displaced, however, and Shakespeare occasionally makes significant use of them, sometimes to connote familiarity or intimacy and sometimes to connote contempt. In *Twelfth Night* Sir Toby advises Sir Andrew to insult Cesario by addressing him as *thou:* "If thou thou'st him some thrice, it shall not be amiss" (3.2.46–47). In *Othello* when Brabantio is addressing an unidentified voice in the dark he says, "What are you?" (1.1.91), but when the voice identifies itself as the foolish suitor Roderigo, Brabantio uses the contemptuous form, saying, "I have charged thee not to haunt about my doors" (93). He uses this form for a while, but later in the scene, when he comes to regard Roderigo as an ally, he shifts back to the polite *you,* beginning in line 163, "What said she to you?" and on to the end of the scene. For reasons not yet satisfactorily explained, Elizabethans used *thou* in addresses to God—"O God, thy arm was here," the king says in *Henry V* (4.8.108)—and to supernatural characters such as ghosts and witches. A subtle variation occurs in *Hamlet*. When Hamlet first talks with the Ghost in 1.5, he uses *thou,* but when he sees the Ghost in his mother's room, in 3.4, he uses *you,* presumably because he is now convinced that the Ghost is not a counterfeit but is his father.

Perhaps the most unusual use of pronouns, from our point of view, is the neuter singular. In place of our *its, his* was often used, as in "How far that little candle throws *his* beams." But the use of a masculine pronoun for a neuter noun came to seem unnatural, and so *it* was used for the possessive as well as the nominative: "The hedge-sparrow fed the cuckoo so long / That it had it head bit off by it young." In the late sixteenth century the possessive form *its* developed, apparently by analogy with the *-s* ending used to indicate a genitive noun, as in *book*'s, but *its* was not yet common usage in Shakespeare's day. He seems to have used *its* only ten times, mostly in his later plays. Other usages, such as "you have seen Cassio and she together" or the substitution of *who* for *whom*, cause little problem even when noticed.

Verbs, Adverbs, and Prepositions: Verbs cause almost no difficulty: The third person singular present form commonly ends in *-s*, as in modern English (e.g., "He blesses"), but sometimes in *-eth* (Portia explains to Shylock that mercy "blesseth him that gives and him that takes"). Broadly speaking, the *-eth* ending was old-fashioned or dignified or "literary" rather than colloquial, except for the words *doth, hath,* and *saith.* The *-eth* ending (regularly used in the King James Bible, 1611) is very rare in Shakespeare's dramatic prose, though not surprisingly it occurs twice in the rather formal prose summary of the narrative poem *Lucrece.* Sometimes a plural subject, especially if it has collective force, takes a verb ending in *-s,* as in "My old bones aches." Some of our strong or irregular preterites (such as *broke*) have a different form in Shakespeare (*brake*); some verbs that now have a weak or regular preterite (such as *helped*) in Shakespeare have a strong or irregular preterite (*holp*). Some adverbs that today end in *-ly* were not inflected: "grievous sick," "wondrous strange." Finally, prepositions often are not the ones we expect: "We are such stuff as dreams are made on," "I have a king here to my flatterer."

Again, none of the differences (except meanings that have substantially changed or been lost) will cause much difficulty. But it must be confessed that for some elliptical passages there is no widespread agreement on meaning. Wise editors resist saying more than they know, and when they are uncertain they add a question mark to their gloss.

Shakespeare's Theater

In Shakespeare's infancy, Elizabethan actors performed wherever they could—in great halls, at court, in the courtyards of inns. These venues implied not only different audiences but also different playing conditions. The innyards must have made rather unsatisfactory theaters: on some days they were unavailable because carters bringing goods to London used them as depots; when available, they had to be rented from the innkeeper. In 1567, presumably to avoid such difficulties, and also to avoid regulation by the Common Council of London, which was not well disposed toward theatricals, one John Brayne, brother-in-law of the carpenter turned actor James Burbage, built the Red Lion in an eastern suburb of London. We know nothing about its shape or its capacity; we can say only that it may have been the first building in Europe constructed for the purpose of giving plays since the end of antiquity, a thousand years earlier. Even after the building of the Red Lion theatrical activity continued in London in makeshift circumstances, in marketplaces and inns, and always uneasily. In 1574 the Common Council required that plays and playing places in London be licensed because

> sundry great disorders and inconveniences have been found to ensue to this city by the inordinate haunting of great multitudes of people, specially youth, to plays, interludes, and shows, namely occasion of frays and quarrels, evil practices of incontinency in great inns having chambers and secret places adjoining to their open stages and galleries.

The Common Council ordered that innkeepers who wished licenses to hold performance put up a bond and make contributions to the poor.

The requirement that plays and innyard theaters be licensed, along with the other drawbacks of playing at inns and presumably along with the success of the Red Lion, led James Burbage to rent a plot of land northeast of the city walls, on property outside the jurisdiction of the city. Here he built England's second playhouse, called simply the Theatre. About all that is known of its construction is that it was wood. It soon had imitators, the most famous being the Globe (1599), essentially an amphitheater built across the Thames (again outside the city's jurisdiction), constructed with timbers of the Theatre, which had been dismantled when Burbage's lease ran out.

Admission to the theater was one penny, which allowed spectators to stand at the sides and front of the stage that jutted into the yard. An additional penny bought a seat in a covered part of the theater, and a third penny bought a more comfortable seat and a better location. It is notoriously difficult to translate prices into today's money, since some things that are inexpensive today would have been expensive in the past and vice versa—a pipeful of tobacco (imported, of course) cost a lot of money, about three pennies, and an orange (also imported) cost two or three times what a chicken cost—but perhaps we can get some idea of the low cost of the penny admission when we realize that a penny could also buy a pot of ale. An unskilled laborer made about five or sixpence a day, an artisan about twelve pence a day, and the hired actors (as opposed to the sharers in the company, such as Shakespeare) made about ten pence a performance. A printed play cost five or sixpence. Of course a visit to the theater (like a visit to a baseball game today) usually cost more than the admission since the spectator probably would also buy food and drink. Still, the low entrance fee meant that the theater was available to all except the very poorest people, rather as movies and most athletic events are today. Evidence indicates that the audience ranged from apprentices who somehow managed to scrape together the minimum entrance fee and to escape from their masters for a few hours, to prosperous members of the middle class and aristocrats who paid the additional fee for admission to the galleries. The exact proportion of men to women cannot be determined, but women of all classes certainly were present. Theaters were open every afternoon but Sundays for much of the year, except in times of plague, when they were closed because of fear of infection. By the way, no evidence suggests the presence of toilet facilities. Presumably the patrons relieved themselves by making a quick trip to the fields surrounding the playhouses.

There are four important sources of information about the

structure of Elizabethan public playhouses—drawings, a contract, recent excavations, and stage directions in the plays. Of drawings, only the so-called de Witt drawing (c. 1596) of the Swan—really his friend Aernout van Buchell's copy of Johannes de Witt's drawing—is of much significance. The drawing, the only extant representation of the interior of an Elizabethan theater, shows an amphitheater of three tiers, with a stage jutting from a wall into the yard or

Johannes de Witt, a Continental visitor to London, made a drawing of the Swan theater in about the year 1596. The original drawing is lost; this is Aernout van Buchell's copy of it.

center of the building. The tiers are roofed, and part of the stage is covered by a roof that projects from the rear and is supported at its front on two posts, but the groundlings, who paid a penny to stand in front of the stage or at its sides, were exposed to the sky. (Performances in such a playhouse were held only in the daytime; artificial illumination was not used.) At the rear of the stage are two massive doors; above the stage is a gallery.

The second major source of information, the contract for the Fortune (built in 1600), specifies that although the Globe (built in 1599) is to be the model, the Fortune is to be square, eighty feet outside and fifty-five inside. The stage is to be forty-three feet broad, and is to extend into the middle of the yard, i.e., it is twenty-seven and a half feet deep.

The third source of information, the 1989 excavations of the Rose (built in 1587), indicate that the Rose was fourteen-sided, about seventy-two feet in diameter with an inner yard almost fifty feet in diameter. The stage at the Rose was about sixteen feet deep, thirty-seven feet wide at the rear, and twenty-seven feet wide downstage. The relatively small dimensions and the tapering stage, in contrast to the rectangular stage in the Swan drawing, surprised theater historians and have made them more cautious in generalizing about the Elizabethan theater. Excavations at the Globe have not yielded much information, though some historians believe that the fragmentary evidence suggests a larger theater, perhaps one hundred feet in diameter.

From the fourth chief source, stage directions in the plays, one learns that entrance to the stage was by the doors at the rear (*"Enter one citizen at one door, and another at the other"*). A curtain hanging across the doorway—or a curtain hanging between the two doorways—could provide a place where a character could conceal himself, as Polonius does, when he wishes to overhear the conversation between Hamlet and Gertrude. Similarly, withdrawing a curtain from the doorway could "discover" (reveal) a character or two. Such discovery scenes are very rare in Elizabethan drama, but a good example occurs in *The Tempest* (5.1.171), where a stage direction tells us, *"Here Prospero discovers Ferdinand and Miranda playing at chess."* There was also some sort of playing space "aloft" or "above" to represent, for instance, the top of a city's walls or a room above the street. Doubtless each theater had its own peculiarities, but perhaps we can talk about a "typical" Elizabethan theater if we realize that no theater need exactly fit the description, just as no mother is the average mother with 2.7 children.

This hypothetical theater is wooden, round, or polygonal (in *Henry V* Shakespeare calls it a "wooden *O*") capable of holding some eight hundred spectators who stood in the yard around the projecting elevated stage—these spectators were the "groundlings"—and some fifteen hundred additional spectators who sat in the three roofed galleries. The stage, protected by a "shadow" or "heavens" or roof, is entered from two doors; behind the doors is the "tiring house" (attiring house, i.e., dressing room), and above the stage is some sort of gallery that may sometimes hold spectators but can be used (for example) as the bedroom from which Romeo—according to a stage direction in one text—"goeth down." Some evidence suggests that a throne can be low-ered onto the platform stage, perhaps from the "shadow"; certainly characters can descend from the stage through a trap or traps into the cellar or "hell." Sometimes this space beneath the stage accommodates a sound-effects man or musician (in *Antony and Cleopatra* "*music of the hautboys* [oboes] *is under the stage*") or an actor (in *Hamlet* the "*Ghost cries under the stage*"). Most characters simply walk on and off through the doors, but because there is no curtain in front of the platform, corpses will have to be car-ried off (Hamlet obligingly clears the stage of Polonius's corpse, when he says, "I'll lug the guts into the neighbor room"). Other characters may have fallen at the rear, where a curtain on a doorway could be drawn to conceal them.

Such may have been the "public theater," so called be-cause its inexpensive admission made it available to a wide range of the populace. Another kind of theater has been called the "private theater" because its much greater admission charge (sixpence versus the penny for general ad-mission at the public theater) limited its audience to the wealthy or the prodigal. The private theater was basically a large room, entirely roofed and therefore artificially illumi-nated, with a stage at one end. The theaters thus were dis-tinct in two ways: One was essentially an amphitheater that catered to the general public; the other was a hall that catered to the wealthy. In 1576 a hall theater was established in Blackfriars, a Dominican priory in London that had been suppressed in 1538 and confiscated by the Crown and thus was not under the city's jurisdiction. All the actors in this Blackfriars theater were boys about eight to thirteen years old (in the public theaters similar boys played female parts; a boy Lady Macbeth played to a man Macbeth). Near the end of this section on Shakespeare's theater we will talk at some length about possible implications in this convention of using boys to play female roles, but for the moment we should say that it doubtless accounts for the relative lack of female roles in Elizabethan drama. Thus, in *A Midsummer Night's Dream*, out of twenty-one named roles, only four are female; in *Hamlet*, out of twenty-four, only two (Gertrude and Ophelia) are female. Many of Shakespeare's characters have fathers but no mothers—for instance, King Lear's daughters. We need not bring in Freud to explain the disparity; a dramatic company had only a few boys in it.

To return to the private theaters, in some of which all of the performers were children—the "eyrie of . . . little eyases" (nest of unfledged hawks—2.2.347–48) which Rosencrantz mentions when he and Guildenstern talk with Hamlet. The theater in Blackfriars had a precarious existence, and ceased operations in 1584. In 1596 James Burbage, who had already made theatrical history by building the Theatre, began to construct a second Blackfriars theater. He died in 1597, and for several years this second Blackfriars theater was used by a troupe of boys, but in 1608 two of Burbage's sons and five other actors (including Shakespeare) became joint operators of the theater, using it in the winter when the open-air Globe was unsuitable. Perhaps such a smaller theater, roofed, artificially illuminated, and with a tradition of a wealthy audience, exerted an influence in Shakespeare's late plays.

Performances in the private theaters may well have had intermissions during which music was played, but in the public theaters the action was probably uninterrupted, flowing from scene to scene almost without a break. Actors would enter, speak, exit, and others would immediately enter and establish (if necessary) the new locale by a few properties and by words and gestures. To indicate that the scene took place at night, a player or two would carry a torch. Here are some samples of Shakespeare establishing the scene:

This is Illyria, lady.   (*Twelfth Night,* 1.2.2)

Well, this is the Forest of Arden.   (*As You Like It,* 2.4.14)

This castle has a pleasant seat; the air
Nimbly and sweetly recommends itself
Unto our gentle senses.   (*Macbeth,* 1.6.1–3)

The west yet glimmers with some streaks of day.
                                                (*Macbeth,* 3.3.5)

Sometimes a speech will go far beyond evoking the minimal setting of place and time, and will, so to speak, evoke the social world in which the characters move. For instance, early in the first scene of *The Merchant of Venice* Salerio suggests an explanation for Antonio's melancholy. (In the following passage, *pageants* are decorated wagons, floats, and *cursy* is the verb "to curtsy," or "to bow.")

Your mind is tossing on the ocean,
There where your argosies with portly sail—
Like signiors and rich burghers on the flood,
Or as it were the pageants of the sea—
Do overpeer the petty traffickers
That cursy to them, do them reverence,
As they fly by them with their woven wings.   (1.1.8–14)

Late in the nineteenth century, when Henry Irving produced the play with elaborate illusionistic sets, the first scene showed a ship moored in the harbor, with fruit vendors and dock laborers, in an effort to evoke the bustling and exotic life of Venice. But Shakespeare's words give us this exotic, rich world of commerce in his highly descriptive language when Salerio speaks of "argosies with portly sail" that fly with "woven wings"; equally important, through Salerio Shakespeare conveys a sense of the orderly, hierarchical society in which the lesser ships, "the petty trafflickers," curtsy and thereby "do . . . reverence" to their superiors, the merchant prince's ships, which are "Like signiors and rich burghers."

On the other hand, it is a mistake to think that except for verbal pictures the Elizabethan stage was bare. Although Shakespeare's Chorus in *Henry V* calls the stage an "unworthy scaffold" (Prologue 1.10) and urges the spectators to "eke out our performance with your mind" (Prologue 3.35), there was considerable spectacle. The last act of *Macbeth,* for instance, has five stage directions calling for *"drum and colors,"* and another sort of appeal to the eye is indicated by the stage direction *"Enter Macduff, with Macbeth's head."* Some scenery and properties may have been substantial; doubtless a throne was used, but the pillars supporting the roof would have served for the trees on which Orlando pins his poems in *As You Like It*.

Having talked about the public theater—"this wooden *O*"—at some length, we should mention again that Shakespeare's plays were performed also in other locales. Alvin Kernan, in *Shakespeare, the King's Playwright: Theater in the Stuart Court 1603–1613* (1995) points out that "several of [Shakespeare's] plays contain brief theatrical performances, set always in a court or some noble house. When Shakespeare portrayed a theater, he did not, except for the choruses in *Henry V*, imagine a public theater" (p. 195). (Examples include episodes in *The Taming of the Shrew, A Midsummer Night's Dream, Hamlet,* and *The Tempest*.)

A Note on the Use of Boy Actors in Female Roles

Until fairly recently, scholars were content to mention that the convention existed; they sometimes also mentioned that it continued the medieval practice of using males in female roles, and that other theaters, notably in ancient Greece and in China and Japan, also used males in female roles. (In classical Noh drama in Japan, males still play the female roles.) Prudery may have been at the root of the academic failure to talk much about the use of boy actors, or maybe there really is not much more to say than that it was a convention of a male-centered culture (Stephen Greenblatt's view, in *Shakespearean Negotiations* [1988]). Further, the very nature of a convention is that it is not thought about: Hamlet is a Dane and Julius Caesar is a Roman, but in Shakespeare's plays they speak English, and we in the audience never give this odd fact a thought. Similarly, a character may speak in the presence of others and we understand, again without thinking about it, that he or she is not heard by the figures on the stage (the aside); a character alone on the stage may speak (the soliloquy), and we do not take the character to be unhinged; in a realistic (box) set, the fourth wall, which allows us to see what is going on, is miraculously missing. The no-nonsense view, then, is that the boy actor was an accepted convention, accepted unthinkingly—just as today we know that Kenneth Branagh is not Hamlet, Al Pacino is not Richard III, and Denzel Washington is not the Prince of Aragon. In this view, the audience takes the performer for the role, and that is that; such is the argument we now make for race-free casting, in which African-Americans and Asians can play roles of persons who lived in medieval Denmark and ancient Rome. But gender perhaps is different, at least today. It is a matter of abundant academic study: The Elizabethan theater is now sometimes called a transvestite theater, and we hear much about cross-dressing.

Shakespeare himself in a very few passages calls attention to the use of boys in female roles. At the end of *As You Like It* the boy who played Rosalind addresses the audience, and says, "O men, . . . if I were a woman, I would kiss as many of you as had beards that pleased me." But this is in the Epilogue; the plot is over, and the actor is stepping out of the play and into the audience's everyday world. A second reference to the practice of boys playing female roles occurs in *Antony and Cleopatra*, when Cleopatra imagines that she and Antony will be the subject of crude plays, her role being performed by a boy:

> The quick comedians
> Extemporally will stage us, and present
> Our Alexandrian revels: Antony
> Shall be brought drunken forth, and I shall see
> Some squeaking Cleopatra boy my greatness.   (5.2.216–20)

In a few other passages, Shakespeare is more indirect. For instance, in *Twelfth Night* Viola, played of course by a boy, disguises herself as a young man and seeks service in the house of a lord. She enlists the help of a Captain, and (by way of explaining away her voice and her beardlessness) says,

> I'll serve this duke
> Thou shalt present me as an eunuch to him.   (1.2.55–56)

In *Hamlet*, when the players arrive in 2.2, Hamlet jokes with the boy who plays a female role. The boy has grown since Hamlet last saw him: "By'r Lady, your ladyship is nearer to heaven than when I saw you last by the altitude of a chopine" (a lady's thick-soled shoe). He goes on: "Pray God your voice . . . be not cracked" (434–38).

Exactly how sexual, how erotic, this material was and is, is now much disputed. Again, the use of boys may have been unnoticed, or rather not thought about—an unexamined convention—by most or all spectators most of the time, perhaps *all* of the time, except when Shakespeare calls the convention to the attention of the audience, as in the passages just quoted. Still, an occasional bit seems to invite erotic thoughts. The clearest example is the name that Rosalind takes in *As You Like It*, Ganymede—the beautiful youth whom Zeus abducted. Did boys dressed to play female roles carry homoerotic appeal for straight men (Lisa Jardine's view, in *Still Harping on Daughters* [1983]), or for gay men, or for some or all women in the audience? Further, when the boy actor played a woman who (for the purposes of the plot) disguised herself as a male, as Rosalind, Viola, and Portia do—so we get a boy playing a woman playing a man—what sort of appeal was generated, and for what sort of spectator?

Some scholars have argued that the convention empowered women by letting female characters display a freedom unavailable in Renaissance patriarchal society; the convention, it is said, undermined rigid gender distinctions. In this view, the convention (along with plots in which female characters for a while disguised themselves as young men) allowed Shakespeare to say what some modern gender critics say: Gender is a constructed role rather than a bio-logical given, something we make, rather than a fixed binary opposition of male and female (see Juliet Dusinberre, in *Shakespeare and the Nature of Women* [1975]). On the other hand, some scholars have maintained that the male disguise assumed by some female characters serves only to reaffirm traditional social distinctions since female characters who don male garb (notably Portia in *The Merchant of Venice* and Rosalind in *As You Like It*) return to their female garb and at least implicitly (these critics say) reaffirm the status quo. (For this last view, see Clara Claiborne Park, in an essay in *The Woman's Part*, ed. Carolyn Ruth Swift Lenz et al. [1980].) Perhaps no one answer is right for all plays; in *As You Like It* cross-dressing empowers Rosalind, but in *Twelfth Night* cross-dressing comically traps Viola.

Shakespeare's Dramatic Language: Costumes, Gestures and Silences; Prose and Poetry

Because Shakespeare was a dramatist, not merely a poet, he worked not only with language but also with costume, sound effects, gestures, and even silences. We have already discussed some kinds of spectacle in the preceding section, and now we will begin with other aspects of visual language; a theater, after all, is literally a "place for seeing." Consider the opening stage direction in *The Tempest*, the first play in the first published collection of Shakespeare's plays: *"A tempestuous noise of thunder and Lightning heard: Enter a Ship-master, and a Boteswain."*

Costumes: What did that shipmaster and that boatswain wear? Doubtless they wore something that identified them as, men of the sea. Not much is known about the costumes that Elizabethan actors wore, but at least three points are clear: (1) many of the costumes were splendid versions of contemporary Elizabethan dress; (2) some attempts were made to approximate the dress of certain occupations and of antique or exotic characters such as Romans, Turks, and Jews; (3) some costumes indicated that the wearer was supernatural. Evidence for elaborate Elizabethan clothing can be found in the plays themselves and in contemporary comments about the "sumptuous" players who wore the discarded clothing of noblemen, as well as in account books that itemize such things as "a scarlet cloak with two broad gold laces, with gold buttons down the sides."

The attempts at approximation of the dress of certain occupations and nationalities also can be documented from the plays themselves, and it derives additional confirmation from a drawing of the first scene of Shakespeare's *Titus Andronicus*—the only extant Elizabethan picture of an identifiable episode in a play. (See pp. xxxviii–xxxix.) The drawing, probably done in 1594 or 1595, shows Queen Tamora pleading for mercy. She wears a somewhat medieval-looking robe and a crown; Titus wears a toga and a wreath, but two soldiers behind him wear costumes fairly close to Elizabethan dress. We do not know, however, if the drawing represents an actual stage production in the public theater, or perhaps a private production, or maybe only a reader's visualization of an episode. Further, there is some conflicting evidence: In *Julius Caesar* a reference is made to Caesar's doublet (a close-fitting jacket), which, if taken literally, suggests that even the protagonist did not wear Roman clothing; and certainly the lesser characters, who are said to wear hats, did not wear Roman garb.

It should be mentioned, too, that even ordinary clothing can be symbolic: Hamlet's "inky cloak," for example, sets him apart from the brightly dressed members of Claudius's court and symbolizes his mourning; the fresh clothes that are put on King Lear partly symbolize his return to sanity. Consider, too, the removal of disguises near the end of some plays. For instance, Rosalind in *As You Like It* and Portia and Nerissa in *The Merchant of Venice* remove their male attire, thus again becoming fully themselves.

Gestures and Silences: Gestures are an important part of a dramatist's language. King Lear kneels before his daughter Cordelia for a benediction (4.7.57–59), an act of humility that contrasts with his earlier speeches banishing her and that contrasts also with a comparable gesture, his ironic

kneeling before Regan (2.4.153–55). Northumberland's failure to kneel before King Richard II (3.3.71–72) speaks volumes. As for silences, consider a moment in *Coriolanus*: Before the protagonist yields to his mother's entreaties (5.3.182), there is this stage direction: *"Holds her by the hand, silent."* Another example of "speech in dumbness" occurs in *Macbeth*, when Macduff learns that his wife and children have been murdered. He is silent at first, as Malcolm's speech indicates: "What, man! Ne'er pull your hat upon your brows. Give sorrow words" (4.3.208–09). (For a discussion of such moments, see Philip C. McGuire's *Speechless Dialect: Shakespeare's Open Silences* [1985].)

Of course when we think of Shakespeare's work, we think primarily of his language, both the poetry and the prose.

Prose: Although two of his plays (*Richard II* and *King John*) have no prose at all, about half the others have at least one quarter of the dialogue in prose, and some have notably more: *1 Henry IV* and *2 Henry IV*, about half; *As You Like It*

and *Twelfth Night*, a little more than half; *Much Ado About Nothing*, more than three quarters; and *The Merry Wives of Windsor*, a little more than five sixths. We should remember that despite Molière's joke about M. Jourdain, who was amazed to learn that he spoke prose, most of us do not speak prose. Rather, we normally utter repetitive, shapeless, and often ungrammatical torrents; prose is something very different—a sort of literary imitation of speech at its most coherent.

Today we may think of prose as "natural" for drama; or even if we think that poetry is appropriate for high tragedy we may still think that prose is the right medium for comedy. Greek, Roman, and early English comedies, however, were written in verse. In fact, prose was not generally considered a literary medium in England until the late fifteenth century; Chaucer tells even his bawdy stories in verse. By the end of the 1580s, however, prose had established itself on the English comic stage. In tragedy, Marlowe made some use of prose, not simply in the speeches of clownish servants but even in the speech of a tragic hero, Doctor Faustus. Still, before Shakespeare, prose normally was used in the theater only for special circumstances: (1) letters and proclamations, to set them off from the poetic dialogue; (2) mad characters, to indicate that normal thinking has become disordered; and (3) low comedy, or speeches uttered by clowns even when they are not being comic. Shakespeare made use of these conventions, but he also went far beyond them. Sometimes he begins a scene in prose and then shifts into verse as the emotion is heightened; or conversely, he may shift from verse to prose when a speaker is lowering the emotional level, as when Brutus speaks in the Forum.

Shakespeare's prose usually is not prosaic. Hamlet's prose includes not only small talk with Rosencrantz and Guildenstern but also princely reflections on "What a piece of work is a man" (2.2.312). In conversation with Ophelia, he shifts from light talk in verse to a passionate prose denunciation of women (3.1.103), though the shift to prose here is perhaps also intended to suggest the possibility of madness. (Consult Brian Vickers, *The Artistry of Shakespeare's Prose* [1968].)

Poetry: Drama in rhyme in England goes back to the Middle Ages, but by Shakespeare's day rhyme no longer dominated poetic drama; a finer medium, blank verse (strictly speaking, unrhymed lines of ten syllables, with the stress on every second syllable) had been adopted. But before looking at unrhymed poetry, a few things should be said about the chief uses of rhyme in Shakespeare's plays. (1) A couplet (a pair of rhyming lines) is sometimes used to convey emotional heightening at the end of a blank verse speech; (2) characters sometimes speak a couplet as they leave the stage, suggesting closure; (3) except in the latest plays, scenes fairly often conclude with a couplet, and sometimes, as in *Richard II*, 2.1.145–46, the entrance of a new character within a scene is preceded by a couplet, which wraps up the earlier portion of that scene; (4) speeches of two characters occasionally are linked by rhyme, most notably in *Romeo and Juliet*, 1.5.95–108, where the lovers speak a sonnet between them; elsewhere a taunting reply occasionally rhymes with the previous speaker's last line; (5) speeches with sententious or gnomic remarks are sometimes in rhyme, as in the duke's speech in *Othello* (1.3.199–206); (6) speeches of sardonic mockery are sometimes in rhyme—for example, Iago's speech on women in *Othello* (2.1.146–58)—and they sometimes conclude with an emphatic couplet, as in Bolingbroke's speech on comforting words in *Richard II* (1.3.301–2); (7) some characters are associated with rhyme, such as the fairies in *A Midsummer Night's Dream*; (8) in the early plays, especially *The Comedy of Errors* and *The Taming of the Shrew*, comic scenes that in later plays would be in prose are in jingling rhymes; (9) prologues, choruses, plays-within-the-play, inscriptions, vows, epilogues, and so on are often in rhyme, and the songs in the plays are rhymed.

Neither prose nor rhyme immediately comes to mind when we first think of Shakespeare's medium: It is blank verse, unrhymed iambic pentameter. (In a mechanically exact line there are five iambic feet. An iambic foot consists of two syllables, the second accented, as in *away*; five feet make a pentameter line. Thus, a strict line of iambic pentameter contains ten syllables, the even syllables being stressed more heavily than the odd syllables. Fortunately, Shakespeare usually varies the line somewhat.) The first speech in *A Midsummer Night's Dream*, spoken by Duke Theseus to his betrothed, is an example of blank verse:

> Now, fair Hippolyta, our nuptial hour
> Draws on apace. Four happy days bring in
> Another moon; but, O, methinks, how slow
> This old moon wanes! She lingers my desires,
> Like to a stepdame, or a dowager,
> Long withering out a young man's revenue. (1.1.1–6)

As this passage shows, Shakespeare's blank verse is not mechanically unvarying. Though the predominant foot is the iamb (as in *apace* or *desires*), there are numerous variations. In the first line the stress can be placed on "fair," as the regular metrical pattern suggests, but it is likely that "Now" gets almost as much emphasis; probably in the second line "Draws" is more heavily emphasized than "on," giving us a trochee (a stressed syllable followed by an unstressed one); and in the fourth line each word in the phrase "This old moon wanes" is probably stressed fairly heavily, conveying by two spondees (two feet, each of two stresses) the oppressive tedium that Theseus feels.

In Shakespeare's early plays much of the blank verse is end-stopped (that is, it has a heavy pause at the end of each line), but he later developed the ability to write iambic pentameter verse paragraphs (rather than lines) that give the illusion of speech. His chief techniques are (1) enjambing, i.e., running the thought beyond the single line, as in the first three lines of the speech just quoted; (2) occasionally replacing an iamb with another foot; (3) varying the position of the chief pause (the caesura) within a line; (4) adding an occasional unstressed syllable at the end of a line, traditionally called a feminine ending; (5) and beginning or ending a speech with a half line.

Shakespeare's mature blank verse has much of the rhythmic flexibility of his prose; both the language, though richly figurative and sometimes dense, and the syntax seem natural. It is also often highly appropriate to a particular character. Consider, for instance, this speech from *Hamlet*, in which Claudius, King of Denmark ("the Dane"), speaks to Laertes:

> And now, Laertes, what's the news with you?
> You told us of some suit. What is't, Laertes?
> You cannot speak of reason to the Dane
> And lose your voice. What wouldst thou beg, Laertes,
> That shall not be my offer, not thy asking?   (1.2.42–46)

Notice the short sentences and the repetition of the name "Laertes," to whom the speech is addressed. Notice, too, the shift from the royal "us" in the second line to the more intimate "my" in the last line, and from "you" in the first three lines to the more intimate "thou" and "thy" in the last two lines. Claudius knows how to ingratiate himself with Laertes.

For a second example of the flexibility of Shakespeare's blank verse, consider a passage from *Macbeth*. Distressed by the doctor's inability to cure Lady Macbeth and by the imminent battle, Macbeth addresses some of his remarks to the doctor and others to the servant who is arming him. The entire speech, with its pauses, interruptions, and irresolution (in "Pull't off, I say," Macbeth orders the servant to remove the armor that the servant has been putting on him), catches Macbeth's disintegration. (In the first line, *physic* means "medicine," and in the fourth and fifth lines, *cast the water* means "analyze the urine.")

> Throw physic to the dogs, I'll none of it.
> Come, put mine armor on. Give me my staff.
> Seyton, send out.—Doctor, the thanes fly from me.—
> Come, sir, dispatch. If thou couldst, doctor, cast
> The water of my land, find her disease
> And purge it to a sound and pristine health,
> I would applaud thee to the very echo,
> That should applaud again.—Pull't off, I say.—
> What rhubarb, senna, or what purgative drug,
> Would scour these English hence? Hear'st thou of them?
>
> (5.3.47–56)

Blank verse, then, can be much more than unrhymed iambic pentameter, and even within a single play Shakespeare's blank verse often consists of several styles, depending on the speaker and on the speaker's emotion at the moment.

The Play Text as a Collaboration

Shakespeare's fellow dramatist Ben Jonson reported that the actors said of Shakespeare, "In his writing, whatsoever he penned, he never blotted out line," i.e., never crossed out material and revised his work while composing. None of Shakespeare's plays survives in manuscript (with the possible exception of a scene in *Sir Thomas More*), so we cannot fully evaluate the comment, but in a few instances the published work clearly shows that he revised his manuscript. Consider the following passage (shown here in facsimile) from the best early text of *Romeo and Juliet*, the Second Quarto (1599):

Ro. Would I were ſleepe and peace ſo ſweet to reſt
The grey eyde morne ſmiles on the frowning night,
Checkring the Eaſterne Clouds with ſtreaks of light,
And darkneſſe fleckted like a drunkard reeles,
From ſorth daies pathway, made by *Tytans* wheeles.
Hence will I to my ghoſtly Friers cloſe cell,
His helpe to craue, and my deare hap to tell.

                                                        Exit.

Enter Frier alone with a baſket.   (night,
Fri. The grey-eyed morne ſmiles on the frowning
Checking the Eaſterne clowdes with ſtreaks of light:
And fleckeld darkneſſe like a drunkard reeles,
From ſorth daies path, and *Titans* burning wheeles:
Now ere the ſun aduance his burning eie,

Romeo rather elaborately tells us that the sun at dawn is
dispelling the night (morning is smiling, the eastern clouds
are checked with light, and the sun's chariot—Titan's
wheels—advances), and he will seek out his spiritual father,
the Friar. He exits and, oddly, the Friar enters and says pretty
much the same thing about the sun. Both speakers say that
"the gray-eyed morn smiles on the frowning night," but there
are small differences, perhaps having more to do with the
business of printing the book than with the author's
composition: For Romeo's "checkring," "fleckted," and
"pathway," we get the Friar's "checking," "fleckeld," and
"path." (Notice, by the way, the inconsistency in Elizabethan
spelling: Romeo's "clouds" become the Friar's "clowdes.")
   Both versions must have been in the printer's copy, and it
seems safe to assume that both were in Shakespeare's manuscript. He must have written one version—let's say he first
wrote Romeo's closing lines for this scene—and then he
decided, no, it's better to give this lyrical passage to the
Friar, as the opening of a new scene, but he neglected to
delete the first version. Editors must make a choice, and they
may feel that the reasonable thing to do is to print the text as
Shakespeare intended it. But how can we know what he
intended? Almost all modern editors delete the lines from

Romeo's speech, and retain the Friar's lines. They don't do this because they know Shakespeare's intention, however. They give the lines to the Friar because the first published version (1597) of *Romeo and Juliet* gives only the Friar's version, and this text (though in many ways inferior to the 1599 text) is thought to derive from the memory of some actors, that is, it is thought to represent a performance, not just a script. Maybe during the course of rehearsals Shakespeare—an actor as well as an author—unilaterally decided that the Friar should speak the lines; if so (remember that we don't know this to be a fact) his final intention was to give the speech to the Friar. Maybe, however, the actors talked it over and settled on the Friar, with or without Shakespeare's approval. On the other hand, despite the 1597 version, one might argue (if only weakly) on behalf of giving the lines to Romeo rather than to the Friar, thus: (1) Romeo's comment on the coming of the daylight emphasizes his separation from Juliet, and (2) the figurative language seems more appropriate to Romeo than to the Friar. Having said this, in the Signet edition we have decided in this instance to draw on the evidence provided by earlier text and to give the lines to the Friar, on the grounds that since Q1 reflects a production, in the theater (at least on one occasion) the lines were spoken by the Friar.

A playwright sold a script to a theatrical company. The script thus belonged to the company, not the author, and author and company alike must have regarded this script not as a literary work but as the basis for a play that the actors would create on the stage. We speak of Shakespeare as the author of the plays, but readers should bear in mind that the texts they read, even when derived from a single text, such as the First Folio (1623), are inevitably the collaborative work not simply of Shakespeare with his company—doubtless during rehearsals the actors would suggest alterations—but also with other forces of the age. One force was governmental censorship. In 1606 parliament passed "an Act to restrain abuses of players," prohibiting the utterance of oaths and the name of God. So where the earliest text of *Othello* gives us "By heaven" (3.3.106), the first Folio gives "Alas," presumably reflecting the compliance of stage practice with the law. Similarly, the 1623 version of *King Lear* omits the oath "Fut" (probably from "By God's foot") at 1.2.142, again presumably reflecting the line as it was spoken on the stage. Editors who seek to give the reader the play that Shakespeare initially conceived—the "authentic" play conceived by the solitary Shakespeare—probably will restore the missing oaths and references to God. Other editors, who see the play as a collaborative work, a construction made not only by Shakespeare but also by actors and compositors and even government censors, may claim that what counts is the play as it was actually performed. Such editors regard the censored text as legitimate, since it is the play that was (presumably) finally put on. A performed text, they argue, has more historical reality than a text produced by an editor who has sought to get at what Shakespeare initially wrote. In this view, the text of a play is rather like the script of a film; the script is not the film, and the play text is not the performed play. Even if we want to talk about the play that Shakespeare "intended," we will find ourselves talking about a script that he handed over to a company with the intention that it be implemented by actors. The "intended" play is the one that the actors—we might almost say "society"—would help to construct.

Further, it is now widely held that a play is also the work of readers and spectators, who do not simply receive meaning, but who create it when they respond to the play. This idea is fully in accord with contemporary post-structuralist critical thinking, notably Roland Barthes's "The Death of the Author," in *Image-Music-Text* (1977) and Michel Foucault's "What Is an Author?," in *The Foucault Reader* (1984). The gist of the idea is that an author is not an isolated genius; rather, authors are subject to the politics and other social structures of their age. A dramatist especially is a worker in a collaborative project, working most obviously with actors—parts may be written for particular actors—but working also with the audience. Consider the words of Samuel Johnson, written to be spoken by the actor David Garrick at the opening of a theater in 1747:

> The stage but echoes back the public voice;
> The drama's laws, the drama's patrons give,
> For we that live to please, must please to live.

The audience—the public taste as understood by the playwright—helps to determine what the play is. Moreover, even members of the public who are not part of the playwright's immediate audience may exert an influence through censorship. We have already glanced at governmental censorship, but there are also other kinds. Take one of Shakespeare's most beloved characters, Falstaff, who appears in three of Shakespeare's plays, the two parts of *Henry IV* and *The Merry Wives of Windsor*. He appears with this name in the earliest printed version of the first of these plays, *1 Henry IV*, but we know that Shakespeare originally called him (after an historical figure) Sir John Oldcastle. Oldcastle appears in Shakespeare's source (partly reprinted in the Signet edition of *1 Henry IV*), and a trace of the name survives in Shakespeare's play, 1.2.43–44, where Prince Hal punningly addresses Falstaff as "my old lad of the castle." But for some reason—perhaps because the family of the historical Oldcastle complained—Shakespeare had to change the name. In short, the play as we have it was (at least in this detail) subject to some sort of censorship. If we think that a text should present what we take to be the author's intention, we probably will want to replace *Falstaff* with *Oldcastle*. But if we recognize that a play is a collaboration, we may welcome the change, even if it was forced on Shakespeare. Somehow *Falstaff*, with its hint of *false-staff*, i.e., inadequate prop, seems just right for this fat knight who, to our delight, entertains the young prince with untruths. We can go as far as saying that, at least so far as a play is concerned, an insistence on the author's original intention (even if we could know it) can sometimes impoverish the text.

The tiny example of Falstaff's name illustrates the point that the text we read is inevitably only a version—something in effect produced by the collaboration of the playwright with his actors, audiences, compositors, and editors—of a fluid text that Shakespeare once wrote, just as the *Hamlet* that we see on the screen starring Kenneth Branagh is not the *Hamlet* that Shakespeare saw in an open-air playhouse starring Richard Burbage. *Hamlet* itself, as we shall note in a moment, also exists in several versions. It is not surprising that there is now much talk about the *instability* of Shakespeare's texts.

Because he was not only a playwright but was also an actor and a shareholder in a theatrical company, Shakespeare probably was much involved with the translation of the play from a manuscript to a stage production. He may or may not have done some rewriting during rehearsals, and he may or may not have been happy with cuts that were made. Some plays, notably *Hamlet* and *King Lear*, are so long that it is most unlikely that the texts we read were acted in their entirety. Further, for both of these plays we have more than one early text that demands consideration. In *Hamlet*, the Second Quarto (1604) includes some two hundred lines not found in the Folio (1623). Among the passages missing from the Folio are two of Hamlet's reflective speeches, the "dram of evil" speech (1.4.13–38) and "How all occasions do inform against me" (4.4.32–66). Since the Folio has more numerous and often fuller stage directions, it certainly looks as though in the Folio we get a theatrical version of the play, a text whose cuts were probably made—this is only a hunch, of course—not because Shakespeare was changing his conception of Hamlet but because the playhouse demanded a modified play. (The problem is complicated, since the Folio not only cuts some of the Quarto but adds some material. Various explanations have been offered.)

Or take an example from *King Lear*. In the First and Second Quarto (1608, 1619), the final speech of the play is given to Albany, Lear's surviving son-in-law, but in the First Folio version (1623), the speech is given to Edgar. The Quarto version is in accord with tradition—usually the highest-ranking character in a tragedy speaks the final words. Why does the Folio give the speech to Edgar? One possible answer is this: The Folio version omits some of Albany's speeches in earlier scenes, so perhaps it was decided (by Shakespeare? by the players?) not to give the final lines to so pale a character. In fact, the discrepancies are so many between the two texts, that some scholars argue we do not simply have texts showing different theatrical productions. Rather, these scholars say, Shakespeare substantially revised the play, and we really have two versions of *King Lear* (and of *Othello* also, say some)—two different plays—not simply two texts, each of which is in some ways imperfect.

In this view, the 1608 version of *Lear* may derive from Shakespeare's manuscript, and the 1623 version may derive from his later revision. The Quartos have almost three hundred lines not in the Folio, and the Folio has about a hundred lines not in the Quartos. It used to be held that all the texts were imperfect in various ways and from various causes—some passages in the Quartos were thought to have been set from a manuscript that was not entirely legible, other passages were thought to have been set by a compositor who was new to setting plays, and still other passages were thought to have been provided by an actor who misremembered some of the lines. This traditional view held that an editor must draw on the Quartos and the Folio in order to get Shakespeare's "real" play. The new argument holds (although not without considerable strain) that we have two authentic plays, Shakespeare's early version (in the Quarto) and Shakespeare's—or his theatrical company's—revised version (in the Folio). Not only theatrical demands but also Shakespeare's own artistic sense, it is argued, called for extensive revisions. Even the titles vary: Q1 is called *True Chronicle Historie of the life and death of King Lear and his three Daughters*, whereas the Folio text is called *The Tragedie of King Lear*. To combine the two texts in order to produce what the editor thinks is the play that Shakespeare intended to write is, according to this view, to produce a text that is false to the history of the play. If the new view is correct, and we do have texts of two distinct versions of *Lear* rather than two imperfect versions of one play, it supports in a textual way the poststructuralist view that we cannot possibly have an unmediated vision of (in this case) a play by Shakespeare; we can only recognize a plurality of visions.

Editing Texts

Though eighteen of his plays were published during his lifetime, Shakespeare seems never to have supervised their publication. There is nothing unusual here; when a playwright sold a play to a theatrical company he surrendered his ownership to it. Normally a company would not publish the play, because to publish it meant to allow competitors to acquire the piece. Some plays did get published: Apparently hard-up actors sometimes pieced together a play for a publisher; sometimes a company in need of money sold a play; and sometimes a company allowed publication of a play that no longer drew audiences. That Shakespeare did not concern himself with publication is not remarkable; of his contemporaries, only Ben Jonson carefully supervised the publication of his own plays.

In 1623, seven years after Shakespeare's death, John Heminges and Henry Condell (two senior members of Shakespeare's company, who had worked with him for about twenty years) collected his plays—published and unpublished—into a large volume, of a kind called a folio. (A folio is a volume consisting of large sheets that have been folded once, each sheet thus making two leaves, or four pages. The size of the page of course depends on the size of the sheet—a folio can range in height from twelve to sixteen inches, and in width from eight to eleven; the pages in the 1623 edition of Shakespeare, commonly called the First Folio, are approximately thirteen inches tall and eight inches wide.) The eighteen plays published during Shakespeare's lifetime had been issued one play per volume in small formats called quartos. (Each sheet in a quarto has been folded twice, making four leaves, or eight pages, each page being about nine inches tall and seven inches wide, roughly the size of a large paperback.)

Heminges and Condell suggest in an address "To the great variety of readers" that the republished plays are presented in better form than in the quartos:

> Before you were abused with diverse stolen and surreptitious copies, maimed and deformed by the frauds and stealths of injurious impostors that exposed them; even those, are now offered to your view cured and perfect of their limbs, and all the rest absolute in their numbers, as he [i.e., Shakespeare] conceived them.

There is a good deal of truth to this statement, but some of the quarto versions are better than others; some are in fact preferable to the Folio text.

Whoever was assigned to prepare the texts for publication

in the first Folio seems to have taken the job seriously and yet not to have performed it with uniform care. The sources of the texts seem to have been, in general, good unpublished copies or the best published copies. The first play in the collection, *The Tempest*, is divided into acts and scenes, has unusually full stage directions and descriptions of spectacle, and concludes with a list of the characters, but the editor was not able (or willing) to present all of the succeeding texts so fully dressed. Later texts occasionally show signs of carelessness: in one scene of *Much Ado About Nothing* the names of actors, instead of characters, appear as speech prefixes, as they had in the Quarto, which the Folio reprints; proofreading throughout the Folio is spotty and apparently was done without reference to the printer's copy; the pagination of *Hamlet* jumps from 156 to 257. Further, the proofreading was done while the presses continued to print, so that each play in each volume contains a mix of corrected and uncorrected pages.

Modern editors of Shakespeare must first select their copy; no problem if the play exists only in the Folio, but a considerable problem if the relationship between a Quarto and the Folio—or an early Quarto and a later one—is unclear. In the case of *Romeo and Juliet*, the First Quarto (Q1), published in 1597, is vastly inferior to the Second (Q2), published in 1599. The basis of Q1 apparently is a version put together from memory by some actors. Not surprisingly, it garbles many passages and is much shorter than Q2. On the other hand, occasionally Q1 makes better sense than Q2. For instance, near the end of the play, when the parents have assembled and learned of the deaths of Romeo and Juliet, in Q2 the Prince says (5.3.208–9),

Come, *Montague;* for thou art early vp
To see thy sonne and heire, now earling downe.

The last three words of this speech surely do not make sense, and many editors turn to Q1, which instead of "now earling downe" has "more early downe." Some modern editors take only "early" from Q1, and print "now early down"; others take "more early," and print "more early down." Further, Q1 (though, again, quite clearly a garbled and abbreviated text) includes some stage directions that are not found in Q2, and today many editors who base their text on Q2 are glad to add these stage directions, because the directions help to give us a sense of what the play looked like on Shakespeare's stage. Thus, in 4.3.58, after Juliet drinks the potion, Q1 gives us this stage direction, not in Q2: *"She falls upon her bed within the curtains."*

In short, an editor's decisions do not end with the choice of a single copy text. First of all, editors must reckon with Elizabethan spelling. If they are not producing a facsimile, they probably modernize the spelling, but ought they to preserve the old forms of words that apparently were pronounced quite unlike their modern forms—*lanthorn, alablaster*? If they preserve these forms are they really preserving Shakespeare's forms or perhaps those of a compositor in the printing house? What is one to do when one finds *lanthorn* and *lantern* in adjacent lines? (The editors of this series in general, but not invariably, assume that words should be spelled in their modern form, unless, for instance, a rhyme is involved.) Elizabethan punctuation, too, presents problems. For example, in the First Folio, the only text for the play, Macbeth rejects his wife's idea that he can wash the blood from his hand (2.2.60–62):

> No: this my Hand will rather
> The multitudinous Seas incarnardine,
> Making the Greene one, Red.

Obviously an editor will remove the superfluous capitals, and will probably alter the spelling to "incarnadine," but what about the comma before "Red"? If we retain the comma, Macbeth is calling the sea "the green one." If we drop the comma, Macbeth is saying that his bloody hand will make the sea ("the Green") *uniformly* red.

An editor will sometimes have to change more than spelling and punctuation. Macbeth says to his wife (1.7.46–47):

> I dare do all that may become a man,
> Who dares no more, is none.

For two centuries editors have agreed that the second line is unsatisfactory, and have emended "no" to "do": "Who dares do more is none." But when in the same play (4.2.21–22) Ross says that fearful persons

> Floate vpon a wilde and violent Sea
> Each way, and moue,

need we emend the passage? On the assumption that the compositor misread the manuscript, some editors emend "each way, and move" to "and move each way"; others emend "move" to "none" (i.e., "Each way and none"). Other editors, however, let the passage stand as in the original. The editors of the Signet Classic Shakespeare have restrained themselves from making abundant emendations. In their minds they hear Samuel Johnson on the dangers of emendation: "I have adopted the Roman sentiment, that it is more honorable to save a citizen than to kill an enemy." Some departures (in addition to spelling, punctuation, and lineation) from the copy text have of course been made, but the original readings are listed in a note following the play, so that readers can evaluate the changes for themselves.

Following tradition, the editors of the Signet Classic Shakespeare have prefaced each play with a list of characters, and throughout the play have regularized the names of the speakers. Thus, in our text of *Romeo and Juliet*, all speeches by Juliet's mother are prefixed "Lady Capulet," although the 1599 Quarto of the play, which provides our copy text, uses at various points seven speech tags for this one character: *Capu. Wi.* (i.e., Capulet's wife), *Ca. Wi., Wi., Wife, Old La.* (i.e., Old Lady), *La.,* and *Mo.* (i.e., Mother). Similarly, in *All's Well That Ends Well*, the character whom we regularly call "Countess" is in the Folio (the copy text) variously identified as *Mother, Countess, Old Countess, Lady,* and *Old Lady.* Admittedly there is some loss in regularizing, since the various prefixes may give us a hint of the way Shakespeare (or a scribe who copied Shakespeare's manuscript) was thinking of the character in a particular scene—for instance, as a mother, or as an old lady. But too much can be made of these differing prefixes, since the social relationships implied are *not* always relevant to the given scene.

We have also added line numbers and in many cases act and scene divisions as well as indications of locale at the beginning of scenes. The Folio divided most of the plays into acts and some into scenes. Early eighteenth-century editors increased the divisions. These divisions, which provide a convenient way of referring to passages in the plays, have been retained, but when not in the text chosen as the basis for the Signet Classic text they are enclosed within square brackets, [ ], to indicate that they are editorial additions. Similarly, though no play of Shakespeare's was equipped with indications of the locale at the heads of scene divisions, locales have here been added in square brackets for the convenience of readers, who lack the information that costumes, properties, gestures, and scenery afford to spectators. Spectators can tell at a glance they are in the throne room, but without an editorial indication the reader may be puzzled for a while. It should be mentioned, incidentally, that there are a few authentic stage directions—perhaps Shakespeare's, perhaps a prompter's—that suggest locales, such as *"Enter Brutus in his orchard,"* and *"They go up into the Senate house."* It is hoped that the bracketed additions in the Signet text will provide readers with the sort of help provided by these two authentic directions, but it is equally hoped that the reader will remember that the stage was not loaded with scenery.

Shakespeare on the Stage

Each volume in the Signet Classic Shakespeare includes a brief stage (and sometimes film) history of the play. When we read about earlier productions, we are likely to find them eccentric, obviously wrongheaded—for instance, Nahum Tate's version of *King Lear*, with a happy ending, which held the stage for about a century and a half, from the late seventeenth century until the end of the first quarter of the nineteenth. We see engravings of David Garrick, the greatest actor of the eighteenth century, in eighteenth-century garb as King Lear, and we smile, thinking how absurd the production must have been. If we are more thoughtful, we say, with the English novelist L. P. Hartley, "The past is a foreign country: they do things differently there." But if the eighteenth-century staging is a foreign country, what of the plays of the late sixteenth and seventeenth centuries? A foreign language, a foreign theater, a foreign audience.

Probably all viewers of Shakespeare's plays, beginning with Shakespeare himself, at times have been unhappy with the plays on the stage. Consider three comments about production that we find in the plays themselves, which suggest Shakespeare's concerns. The Chorus in *Henry V* complains that the heroic story cannot possibly be adequately staged:

> But pardon, gentles all,
> The flat unraisèd spirits that hath dared
> On this unworthy scaffold to bring forth
> So great an object. Can this cockpit hold
> The vasty fields of France? Or may we cram
> Within this wooden *O* the very casques
> That did affright the air at Agincourt?
> . . . .
> Piece out our imperfections with your thoughts.
>
> (Prologue 1.8–14,23)

Second, here are a few sentences (which may or may not represent Shakespeare's own views) from Hamlet's longish lecture to the players:

> Speak the speech, I pray you, as I pronounced it to you, trippingly on the tongue. But if you mouth it, as many of our players do, I had as lief the town crier spoke my lines. . . . O, it offends me to the soul to hear a robustious periwig-pated fellow tear a passion to tatters, to very rags, to split the ears of the groundlings. . . . And let those that play your clowns speak no more than is set down for them, for there be of them that will themselves laugh, to set on some quantity of barren spectators to laugh too, though in the meantime some necessary question of the play be then to be considered. That's villainous and shows a most pitiful ambition in the fool that uses it. (3.2.1–47)

Finally, we can quote again from the passage cited earlier in this introduction, concerning the boy actors who played the female roles. Cleopatra imagines with horror a theatrical version of her activities with Antony:

> The quick comedians
> Extemporally will stage us, and present
> Our Alexandrian revels: Antony
> Shall be brought drunken forth, and I shall see
> Some squeaking Cleopatra boy my greatness
> I' th' posture of a whore.
>
> (5.2.216–21)

It is impossible to know how much weight to put on such passages—perhaps Shakespeare was just being modest about his theater's abilities—but it is easy enough to think that he was unhappy with some aspects of Elizabethan production. Probably no production can fully satisfy a playwright, and for that matter, few productions can fully satisfy *us;* we regret this or that cut, this or that way of costuming the play, this or that bit of business.

One's first thought may be this: Why don't they just do "authentic" Shakespeare, "straight" Shakespeare, the play as Shakespeare wrote it? But as we read the plays—words written to be performed—it sometimes becomes clear that we do not know *how* to perform them. For instance, in *Antony and Cleopatra* Antony, the Roman general who has succumbed to Cleopatra and to Egyptian ways, says, "The nobleness of life / Is to do thus" (1.1.36–37). But what is "thus"? Does Antony at this point embrace Cleopatra? Does he embrace and kiss her? (There are, by the way, very few scenes of kissing on Shakespeare's stage, possibly because boys played the female roles.) Or does he make a sweeping gesture, indicating the Egyptian way of life?

This is not an isolated example; the plays are filled with lines that call for gestures, but we are not sure what the gestures should be. *Interpretation* is inevitable. Consider a passage in *Hamlet*. In 3.1, Polonius persuades his daughter, Ophelia, to talk to Hamlet while Polonius and Claudius eavesdrop. The two men conceal themselves, and Hamlet encounters Ophelia. At 3.1.131 Hamlet suddenly says to her, "Where's your father?" Why does Hamlet, apparently out of nowhere—they have not been talking about Polonius—ask this question? Is this an example of the "antic disposition" (fantastic behavior) that Hamlet earlier (1.5.172) had told Horatio and others—including us—he would display? That is, is the question about the whereabouts of her father a seemingly irrational one, like his earlier question (3.1.103) to Ophelia, "Ha, ha! Are you honest?" Or, on the other hand, has Hamlet (as in many productions) suddenly glimpsed Polonius's foot protruding from beneath a drapery at the rear? That is, does Hamlet ask the question because he has suddenly seen something suspicious and now is testing Ophelia? (By the way, in productions that do give Hamlet a physical cue, it is almost always Polonius rather than Claudius who provides the clue. This itself is an act of interpretation on the part of the director.) Or (a third possibility) does Hamlet get a clue from Ophelia, who inadvertently betrays the spies by nervously glancing at their place of hiding? This is the interpretation used in the BBC television version, where Ophelia glances in fear toward the hiding place just after Hamlet says "Why wouldst thou be a breeder of sinners?" (121–22). Hamlet, realizing that he is being observed, glances here and there *before* he asks "Where's your father?" The question thus is a climax to what he has been doing while speaking the preceding lines. Or (a fourth interpretation) does Hamlet suddenly, without the aid of any clue whatsoever, intuitively (insightfully, mysteriously, wonderfully) sense that someone is spying? Directors must decide, of course—and so must readers.

Recall, too, the preceding discussion of the texts of the plays, which argued that the texts—though they seem to be before us in permanent black on white—are unstable. The Signet text of *Hamlet*, which draws on the Second Quarto (1604) and the First Folio (1623) is considerably longer than any version staged in Shakespeare's time. Our version, even if spoken very briskly and played without any intermission, would take close to four hours, far beyond "the two hours' traffic of our stage" mentioned in the Prologue to *Romeo and Juliet*. (There are a few contemporary references to the duration of a play, but none mentions more than three hours.) Of Shakespeare's plays, only *The Comedy of Errors*, *Macbeth*, and *The Tempest* can be done in less than three hours without cutting. And even if we take a play that exists only in a short text, *Macbeth*, we cannot claim that we are experiencing the very play that Shakespeare conceived, partly because some of the Witches' songs almost surely are non-Shakespearean additions, and partly because we are not willing to watch the play performed without an intermission and with boys in the female roles.

Further, as the earlier discussion of costumes mentioned, the plays apparently were given chiefly in contemporary, that is, in Elizabethan dress. If today we give them in the costumes that Shakespeare probably saw, the plays seem not contemporary but curiously dated. Yet if we use our own dress, we find lines of dialogue that are at odds with what we see; we may feel that the language, so clearly not our own, is inappropriate coming out of people in today's dress. A common solution, incidentally, has been to set the plays in the nineteenth century, on the grounds that this attractively distances the plays (gives them a degree of foreignness, allowing for interesting costumes) and yet doesn't put them into a museum world of Elizabethan England.

Inevitably our productions are adaptations, *our* adaptations, and inevitably they will look dated, not in a century but in twenty years, or perhaps even in a decade. Still, we cannot escape from our own conceptions. As the director Peter Brook has said, in *The Empty Space* (1968):

> It is not only the hair-styles, costumes and make-ups that look dated. All the different elements of staging—the shorthands of behavior that stand for emotions; gestures, gesticulations and tones of voice—are all fluctuating on an invisible stock exchange all the time. . . . A living theatre that thinks it can stand aloof from anything as trivial as fashion will wilt. (p. 16)

As Brook indicates, it is through today's hairstyles, costumes, makeup, gestures, gesticulations, tones of voice— this includes our *conception* of earlier hairstyles, costumes, and so forth if we stage the play in a period other than our own—that we inevitably stage the plays.

It is a truism that every age invents its own Shakespeare, just as, for instance, every age has invented its own classical world. Our view of ancient Greece, a slave-holding society in which even free Athenian women were severely circumscribed, does not much resemble the Victorians' view of ancient Greece as a glorious democracy, just as, perhaps, our view of Victorianism itself does not much resemble theirs. We cannot claim that the Shakespeare on our stage is the true Shakespeare, but in our stage productions we find a Shakespeare that speaks to us, a Shakespeare that our ancestors doubtless did not know but one that seems to us to be the true Shakespeare—at least for a while.

Our age is remarkable for the wide variety of kinds of staging that it uses for Shakespeare, but one development deserves special mention. This is the now common practice of race-blind or color-blind or nontraditional casting, which allows persons who are not white to play in Shakespeare. Previously blacks performing in Shakespeare were limited to a mere three roles, Othello, Aaron (in *Titus Andronicus*), and the Prince of Morocco (in *The Merchant of Venice*), and there were no roles at all for Asians. Indeed, African-Americans rarely could play even one of these three roles, since they were not welcome in white companies. Ira Aldridge (c.1806–1867), a black actor of undoubted talent, was forced to make his living by performing Shakespeare in England and in Europe, where he could play not only Othello but also—in whiteface—other tragic roles such as King Lear. Paul Robeson (1898–1976) made theatrical history when he played Othello in London in 1930, and there was some talk about bringing the production to the United States, but there was more talk about whether American audiences would tolerate the sight of a black man—a real black man, not a white man in blackface—kissing and then killing a white woman. The idea was tried out in summer stock in 1942, the reviews were enthusiastic, and in the following year Robeson opened on Broadway in a production that ran an astounding 296 performances. An occasional all-black company sometimes performed Shakespeare's plays, but otherwise blacks (and other minority members) were in effect shut out from performing Shakespeare. Only since about 1970 has it been common for nonwhites to play major roles along with whites. Thus, in a 1996–97 production of *Antony and Cleopatra*, a white Cleopatra, Vanessa Redgrave, played opposite a black Antony, David Harewood.

Multiracial casting is now especially common at the New York Shakespeare Festival, founded in 1954 by Joseph Papp, and in England, where even siblings such as Claudio and Isabella in *Measure for Measure* or Lear's three daughters may be of different races. Probably most viewers today soon stop worrying about the lack of realism, and move beyond the color of the performers' skin to the quality of the performance.

Nontraditional casting is not only a matter of color or race; it includes sex. In the past, occasionally a distinguished woman of the theater has taken on a male role—Sarah Bernhardt (1844–1923) as Hamlet is perhaps the most famous example—but such performances were widely regarded as eccentric. Although today there have been some performances involving cross-dressing (a drag *As You Like It* staged by the National Theatre in England in 1966 and in the United States in 1974 has achieved considerable fame in the annals of stage history), what is more interesting is the casting of women in roles that traditionally are male but that need not be. Thus, a 1993–94 English production of *Henry V* used a woman—*not* cross-dressed—in the role of the governor of Harfleur. According to Peter Holland, who reviewed the production in *Shakespeare Survey* 48 (1995), "having a female Governor of Harfleur feminized the city and provided a direct response to the horrendous threat of rape and murder that Henry had offered, his language and her body in direct connection and opposition" (p. 210). Ten years from now the device may not play so effectively, but today it speaks to us. Shakespeare, born in the Elizabethan Age, has been dead nearly four hundred years, yet he is, as Ben Jonson said, "not of an age but for all time." We must understand, however, that he is "for all time" precisely because each age finds in his abundance something for itself and something of itself.

And here we come back to two issues discussed earlier in this introduction—the instability of the text and, curiously, the Bacon/Oxford heresy concerning the authorship of the plays. *Of course* Shakespeare wrote the plays, and we should daily fall on our knees to thank him for them—and yet there is something to the idea that he is not their only author. Every editor, every director and actor, and every reader to some degree shapes them, too, for when we edit, direct, act, or read, we inevitably become Shakespeare's collaborator and re-create the plays. The plays, one might say, are so cunningly contrived that they guide our responses, tell us how we ought to feel, and make a mark on us, but (for better or for worse) we also make a mark on them.

—SYLVAN BARNET
Tufts University

Introduction

The Winter's Tale is a very late work of Shakespeare's, probably the last he wrote without a collaborator except for *The Tempest*; and it is universally supposed to be closely associated with *Cymbeline*, *The Tempest*, and *Pericles* (though this last play probably contains the work of another hand) in a grouping of comedies commonly called the "Romances." I have no intention of trying to overthrow this supposition; but it is worth recalling that the friends of Shakespeare who compiled the First Folio in 1623, far from thinking these plays should be read as a group, allowed them to be separated from each other to the limits of physical possibility. *The Tempest* is the first play in the Folio, heading the section of comedies; *The Winter's Tale* is the last of the comedies, and almost got left out altogether; *Cymbeline* comes last among the *tragedies*, and is the final play of the Folio; *Pericles* they did not include at all, and it was left to the editors of the Third Folio (1664) to insert it, together with six other plays that nobody now attributes to Shakespeare. But the long labors of the chronologists have brought together these scattered cousins; it is another "triumph of time," like *The Winter's Tale* itself. And this has prepared the way for much interesting comment on the group and the relations between its members. Still, the indifference or imperceptiveness of Heminges and Condell may at least serve as a caution. Much as the Romances resemble one another, they also exhibit striking differences; under the family resemblance, each has its private, personal life. The warning is so obvious as to be often ignored, and some intemperate commentary has resulted. *The Winter's Tale* has suffered with the others.

There is, for instance, the view—less common nowadays, but still to be met with—that these plays share a sort of calm or detached simplicity, as if the author had sought in Romance relief from the evils and disasters of the tragedies. Now, the idea of romance, properly understood, implies passion and catastrophe, storm and violence; and Shakespeare's romances not only contain such elements, but often enact them with much turbulence both in the action and in the language. The verse frequently registers not a gentle detachment but rather a remarkable activity of mind. Thus the jealousy of Leontes may in the last analysis be a less complex matter than that of Othello; but it is less simply expressed. The language that embodies it combines hysterical grossness with suggestions of a mind once habituated to clarity but no longer quite able to declare itself clearly because of emotional pressure:

> Ha' you not seen, Camillo—
> But that's past doubt, you have, or your eyeglass
> Is thicker than a cuckold's horn—or heard—
> For to a vision so apparent, rumor
> Cannot be mute—or thought—for cogitation
> Resides not in that man that does not think—
> My wife is slippery?   (1.2.267–73)

The evidence of Hermione's adultery is so overwhelming, so disgusting, that an intelligent friend's failure to notice it is an additional cause for anger. Leontes, accustomed to putting his thoughts clearly, organizes what he has to say in terms of sight, hearing, and reflection; but it would be equally loathsome to hear Camillo fawningly agree or disagree in order to dissuade him from the course of self-torture to which he has committed himself. Thus contempt and fear join with sexual disgust and an intolerable sense of his own indignity to crowd and crush the speech, and neither Elizabethan nor modern punctuation can cope with its jolting syntax and distorted argument. Measure it against the grave and by no means ill-written opening of Greene's *Pandosto*: ". . . whoso seeks by friendly counsel to raze out this hellish passion, it forthwith suspecteth that he giveth this advice to cover his own guiltiness. Yea, whoso is pained with this restless torment doubteth all, distrusteth himself, is always frozen with fear and fired with suspicion. . . ." Leontes in the play is ablaze with the passion of which Greene merely speaks. Or compare the same speech with Othello's after his fall into the same hell of sexual shock, reduced, when his agony is greatest, to broken exclamations: "O blood, blood, blood!" "Goats and monkeys!" Othello is not credited, as Leontes is, with an articulateness that matches his sense of self-destruction; he makes the great gestures appropriate to a noble understanding of what it means for a hero's life to be broken— "Man but a rush against Othello's breast, / And he retires"—but escapes the more intellectual torments of Leontes.[1]

Nor is this tumult of passionate meaning confined to moments of agony. It is a fair criticism of *Cymbeline* that there are places in it where the language is unnecessarily opaque, where—to quote Coleridge's definition of "mental bombast"—there are "thoughts and images too great for the subject." When Prospero tells Miranda, in *The Tempest*, of his brother's treachery, he can scarcely compress his meaning in his excited utterance. In *The Winter's Tale* we feel the pressure of excited intelligence in many other speakers, as well as in Leontes, notably in Perdita and Florizel; their language breaks bounds in the quest for completeness of statement.

> What you do
> Still betters what is done. When you speak, sweet,

[1] I am not suggesting that *The Winter's Tale* has the stature of *Othello*. The tragedy has a different and perhaps a greater design; its focus is on the hero and the ideas by which he animates and gives value to his world; whereas the hero of *The Winter's Tale* is Time; or you might prefer to say that its heroine is Nature. The difference of emphasis may be suggested by one small indication. The word "honor" occurs with great frequency in *The Winter's Tale* to show that its characters are all necessarily concerned with this public acceptance of their own integrity; but the *idea* of honor is not at all stressed, as of course it is in *Othello*, and I myself had not noticed the frequent occurrence of the word until I gave the text slow editorial scrutiny. The main interests of the play lie in such a way that "honor" is a marginal, though necessary, consideration.

I'd have you do it ever; when you sing,
I'd have you buy and sell so; so give alms,
Pray so; and for the ord'ring your affairs,
To sing them too. When you do dance, I wish you
A wave o' th' sea, that you might ever do
Nothing but that—move still, still so,
And own no other function. Each your doing,
So singular in each particular,
Crowns what you are doing in the present deeds,
That all your acts are queens.

                                        (4.4.135–46)

Florizel begins a catalogue of beauties, each more amorously and extravagantly expressed than its predecessor, and all related to action: "do," "done," "do," "doing," "function," "doing," "acts." He is drunk with the exquisite activity of Perdita. But he has a rhetorical scheme, and persists in it: Each act is in itself perfect, yet each surpasses the other. This lover's hyperbole might ring out frigidly from the pages of Greene's novella, but here the whole scheme is transformed by the figure of the wave, a rich metaphor that the verse enacts rhythmically: "move still, still so"; until, at the end, the rhetorician's wit glows with imaginative solemnity, for "queens" not only concludes the prescribed scheme but moves us out beyond it, into the sphere where Perdita, singing and dancing, queen of the feast and dressed as a goddess of spring's renewal, assumes the power to end by her action the hard grip of winter on the lives of her parents.

Such verse makes ridiculous the notion of an author grown vaguely benign with old age; and it is to be found in all the Romances. There are other common features. In every play there is a discovery of lost royalty, princesses who are represented as of almost divine virtue and beauty; characters near death are restored to life; the breach in some prince's life is mended, years after the disaster which caused it, by the agency of young, beautiful, and innocent people; there are scenes of a pastoral character. All this is of the nature of Romance, and the plays could well be called romantic tragicomedies. Edwin Greenlaw long ago pointed out that they derive ultimately from the Greek novel, especially perhaps from *Daphnis and Chloe*. This is the world of lost princesses, great storms that sunder families, lifetimes spent in wandering or suffering, babies put to sea in little boats (an experience that belonged to Perdita, in the source story, though Shakespeare saved it for Miranda) and later recognized by a mole or a jewel. Greene's *Pandosto*, on which Shakespeare based his *Winter's Tale*, is a typical Elizabethan novel in the same tradition. And these plays are dramatic versions of such stories.

Shakespeare had used elements of romance plot as early as *The Comedy of Errors*; in returning to it he handles it with a new simplicity, especially in *The Winter's Tale*. He has no more compunction than a novelist might have in allowing sixteen years to pass in the middle of the story. But this is not because he couldn't help it, because his technique had gone soft. Stories of this kind are in their nature somewhat primitive, and if profundities are to be found in them it will be by the writer who respects their nature. It required much lucidity and experience to design *The Winter's Tale* so simply. "Shakespeare," Northrop Frye has said, "arrived in his last period at the bedrock of drama, the romantic spectacle out of which all the more specialized forms of drama, such as tragedy and social comedy, have come, and to which they recurrently return." Of course there are very bad romance plays, some of them in the repertory of Shakespeare's company at this period. Merely using an archaic narrative ensures no big bonus of significance. That is the reward of genius, and of a lifetime of intelligent practice. I daresay Shakespeare might have been surprised to read in Frye that his Hermione is a "Proserpine figure," but not to hear that he had told his story in such a way that we see human life renewing itself, as spring follows winter. He even suggests the relevance of the well-known Proserpine myth in Perdita's flower speech. He is writing, with very conscious art, about the destruction and renewal of life, and finds in these romance stories the pattern he needs; it is his craft to elicit and enlarge their relevance.

It is perfectly consistent to add that Shakespeare was probably writing to meet a specific public demand (as the revival of an old and bad romance, *Mucedorus*, suggests). With similar opportunism, he probably used in the fourth act dances that his company had performed under grander circumstances at court. He may also have had in mind the Blackfriars, his company's new indoor theater, where from about 1609 they enjoyed the advantages of a smaller house with better music, good artificial lighting, scenes and machines, and an audience willing to pay six times the price of the cheapest place at the Globe. This was the time of the spectacular masques at the court of James I; Shakespeare's company were the King's Men; never had relations between court and stage been closer than now. They continued to play in the great outdoor theater; but possibly the Blackfriars, where some of the courtly spectacle could be reproduced, had something to do with the vogue for extravagant romance stories.

Yet this is not the most important clue to the nature of *The Winter's Tale*. For that we should turn to the greatest works in prose and verse of the period, Sidney's *Arcadia* and Spenser's *Faerie Queene*. It is no reflection on Greene to say that his novel cannot live with such romances as these; for they are in intention and performance the profoundest and most serious art of the period (Spenser's book, to risk a comparison for the modern reader, is as complex in plan as *Ulysses*). They nevertheless use romantic themes. They are concerned less with psychological realism than with supernaturally sanctioned reality under human appearances. Shakespeare knew them both, and used them, especially Spenser. Marina is his Florimel, Perdita his Pastorella; in *The Winter's Tale* he transforms Fawnia, Greene's royal changeling, and does so to make her like Spenser's noble shepherdess. And insofar as *The Winter's Tale* is philosophical it is Spenserian too; like Spenser, Shakespeare is preoccupied by Time as destroyer and renewer, that which ruins the work of men but is the father of truth. Just as the sea appears to be aimlessly destructive, tearing apart father and child, husband and wife, but is in the end seen to be "merciful" because it finally brings them together and restores their happiness, so Time only seems to change things because it must renew their truth.

> All things steadfastness do hate
> And changed be: yet being rightly weighed
> They are not changed from their first estate,
> But by their change their being do dilate,
> And turning to themselves at length again,
> Do work their own perfection so by fate.

Whatever else may be added on the point, this is the "philosophy" of *The Winter's Tale* as well as of the Mutability Cantos of Spenser. And Greene, to give him his due, called the novel on which Shakespeare based his play *Pandosto: or, The Triumph of Time.*

One more point before we turn from the romances in general to the specific qualities of *The Winter's Tale*: stories of this kind create for the dramatist peculiar technical problems. Characteristically, they require that there be treated the initial disaster by which the plot gains movement; the intermediate period where people suffer under the consequent wrongs and sorrows; and finally the restoration of happiness, the *recognition*, where all, by the work of time, "turns to itself at length again." Dramatically, the focus of such stories will tend to be the recognition; in *Pericles*, a very straggling play, this climax was what overwhelmingly interested Shakespeare, and he made it a kind of prototype of all the others. In *Cymbeline* he attempted a multiple recognition scene so extraordinary as to be without theatrical parallel. In *The Tempest* he concentrates the whole action at the moment of climax, merely recalling the initial treachery of Antonio. In *The Winter's Tale* he approaches the problem quite differently by dividing the story into three parts: first the Sicilian disaster, the destruction of happiness by Leontes' diseased passion; then the "green world" in which Perdita demonstrates renewed beauty and nobility (these two parts being equally balanced as to length); and finally an act of recognition. Though the great scene in *Pericles* is the ancestor of them all, the recognition scenes of these plays are all very different, and this of course contributes to their individuality, the sense we have that each grows its own imaginative and philosophical atmosphere. And nowhere is this atmosphere more distinctive, nowhere is the recognition more daringly conceived, than in *The Winter's Tale*.

Some indication of the dramatist's intention, both in this and in other aspects of the play, may be derived from a consideration of the changes he made in his source. A large part of Greene's *Pandosto* is printed at the end of this volume, and the reader may see for himself the extent of both debt and deviation; a few editorial words on the matter are prefixed to the extracts. But on the crucial matter of the great final act something must be said here. The statue scene is without parallel in *Pandosto*; at some stage Shakespeare made the momentous decision to keep Hermione alive, and invented the *motif* of the statue. It is possible that he did so in the course of writing; as Coleridge early pointed out, it would have been simple enough to provide for her survival by some ambiguity in the oracle, but Shakespeare does not do so, and it is a remarkable instance, the only one in Shakespeare or perhaps in the whole drama of the period, of the playwright's concealing so material a circumstance from the audience. Simon Forman, reporting on a performance of 1611 when the play was still fairly new, did not include in his account of the plot any allusion to the statue scene, so the play may have been without it in its first form. Having preserved Hermione alive, Shakespeare had of course greatly increased his technical problem at the end of the play. Had he followed Greene, the climactic moment would have been the discovery of Perdita's identity, and the scene would have had to be very like that of the reunion of Pericles and Marina. He could hardly have followed this with another scene of rapt verse and music for the reunion of Leontes and his wife; so he boldly throws away the Perdita recognition in a scene of gentlemanly chatter, and saves the great effects for the reunion of father, mother, and daughter at the end. Thus he avoids the anticlimactic conclusion of *Pericles*, where the reunion with Thaisa cannot make much effect after the great scene that precedes it. So Shakespeare solved his technical problem; the question remains, why did he need to create it by forsaking Greene and keeping Hermione alive? Why should the climax of the play be not the restoration of Perdita to her inheritance but the restoration of the Queen to life? No one can answer that without looking at the play as a whole.

The whole work is as unorthodox structurally as the final scene. The first part, up to the end of 3.2, is dominated by the insane and tyrannous passion of Leontes. The Sicilian court has been a world of courtesy and innocence; these are virtues of Hermione and also of Polixenes, whose opening speech, with its pastoral figures, merely establishes an intelligent harmony that will be broken by the power of the diseased king. Polixenes remembers the innocence of his childhood friendship with Leontes, and says it resembled that of man before the Fall, when passion overthrew reason; and with the onset of the King's jealousy this overthrow is re-enacted. It is clumsy to treat this as pure allegory, though that is a modern fashion; Shakespeare knew very well that there was implied in this narrative an analogy with the Fall, and he lived in an age when Biblical typology and allegory were as familiar as they now seem outlandish. But this should lead us to the conclusion, not that he was writing allegory, but that he was recognizing the *typical* quality of this, as of any other story. A powerful mind is disturbed by a passion it is unwilling to control; suddenly the clear world of honor and courtesy darkens; friends can be Judases, good counselors traitors; what seems to be virtuous is in truth vicious; the gods themselves are liars. Here as elsewhere Shakespeare associates this profound perturbation, this infection of a world with the disease of one mind, with a specifically sexual misery. For Leontes—the word tolls out through these scenes—is diseased, and the air around him is infected, as if by a plague-bearing planet. His very language is hectic. That there is another and purer air we learn from the brief, beautifully placed 3.1, when Cleomenes and Dion speak of the delicate climate and sweet air of Apollo's temple. And when, sixteen years later, we breathe the air of Perdita's pastoral Bohemia we recognize once more a purity associated with pure sexuality; as when Perdita wishes her lover "quick, and in mine arms." The country, its healing herbs and prophylactic flowers, is the antithesis of the plague-stricken city. And later, when Perdita arrives in Sicily, Leontes remembers the days of the great infection and prays accordingly:

> The blessèd gods
> Purge all infection from our air whilst you
> Do climate here! (5.1.168–70)

In the dark opening phase, the part of Hermione is that of the victim, Leontes that of the tyrant. Tyranny begins, as Milton says, "when upstart passions catch the government." But he considers and rejects the idea that he is behaving tyrannously; she, at her trial (which must recall the trial of Katherine in *Henry VIII*), argues that he is. His rejection of the oracle is a tyrannous act (Greene's *Pandosto* accepts it), and he at once suffers the traditional fate of the tyrant, the sudden exemplary punishment of heaven. His son dies, his queen dies; henceforth his life must be only repentance and obloquy. Or so it seems. At the end of 3.2, halfway through the play, we have reached what is practically a full tragic close, and if Leontes were to stab himself at that point there would be little sense of dramatic illogic. He has thrown away the pearl richer than all his tribe. Only the hint of the oracle ("*if* that which is lost be not found") and the fact that in romance castaway children always turn up, exist to make a faint suggestion of a happy issue.

The next scene, 3.3, is crucial and again extraordinary; Antigonus, having had a vision of the *dead* Hermione, is sacrificed in order to move the play into a fantastic realm; the clown and his father show us how different is the world we have entered by the unconcerned calm of their talk on the sinking of the ship and the bear's consumption of Antigonus. Then the old man speaks the famous line: "Now bless thyself; thou met'st with things dying, I with things new born." We pass from the world in which happiness and prosperity are destroyed by the storm of passion, to the world where nature—great creating Nature, as Shakespeare calls the presiding figure of the Mutability Cantos—re-establishes love and human continuance and proves that time and change are her servants, agents not only of change but of perpetuity, redeemers as well as destroyers.

The central action of Act 4 is not complicated, but it is a very long act, and must have been the longer for the various diversions, the "nest of antics" ridiculed by Jonson, the catches and songs. The mood is of innocence (even Autolycus contributes to this, partly by establishing rustic virtues as opposed to those of the court—an old pastoral theme, and one paralleled by the debates between Corin and Touchstone in *As You Like It*), and Shakespeare wanted this part of the play to have mass enough to balance the Sicilian opening. Essentially, this act establishes a world in which Perdita's inborn nobility can display itself.

Although Shakespeare accepts some of the assumptions of the pastoral genre, it was clearly his effort to avoid urban condescension and sentimentality in this scene. These shepherds and shepherdesses are not the graceful figures of Spenser and Sidney; the young clown has his meanness, the old one his strong sense of self-preservation; Polixenes is charmed by the feast and by Perdita's beauty, but when the holiday is over his exposure of the girl and his judgment of his son are extremely tough. Against this infused realism, the insistence upon Perdita's superiority, her innate nobility and godlike beauty, becomes more remarkable. It is, considered merely as a narrative device, part of the tradition, but it occupied Shakespeare at a very deep level. There are signs of his interest in it at an earlier stage in his career, but in the Romances he turned upon it the same deepening attention as we observe him giving such conventions as the twin plot—that which was first only a dramaturgical device becomes an issue for mature meditation. Marina in the brothel, Cymbeline's sons in the Welsh cave have the virtue of high birth, and their hereditary cultivation will show itself even in unfavorable circumstances. In *The Tempest* Caliban is the base natural stock, Miranda (educated with him) has, as part of her inheritance, that "better nature" which places her on the side

of mankind toward the gods, as he is on the side toward
the beasts.[2] Perdita, like all the Romance heroines mistaken for a goddess, is, very remarkably, made the occasion for Shakespeare's fullest exposition of the idea. It is
characteristic of Shakespeare's economy that her flower
piece, which could have been a moment of pastoral pretti-
ness, modulates into this quasi-philosophical debate with
Polixenes:

Perdita.   Sir, the year growing ancient,
    Not yet on summer's death nor on the birth
    Of trembling winter, the fairest flow'rs o' th' season
    Are our carnations, and streaked gillyvors,
    Which some call Nature's bastards; of that kind
    Our rustic garden's barren; and I care not
    To get slips of them.

Polixenes.   Wherefore, gentle maiden,
    Do you neglect them?

Perdita.   For I have heard it said,
    There is an art, which in their piedness shares
    With great creating Nature.

Polixenes.   Say there be;
    Yet Nature is made better by no mean,
    But Nature makes that mean; so over that art,
    Which you say adds to Nature, is an art
    That Nature makes. You see, sweet maid, we marry
    A gentler scion to the wildest stock,
    And make conceive a bark of baser kind
    By bud of nobler race. This is an art
    Which does mend Nature, change it rather; but
    The art itself is Nature.

Perdita.   So it is.

Polixenes. Then make your garden rich in gillyvors,
    And do not call them bastards.

Perdita.   I'll not put

[2]This point is discussed and documented in my Arden edition of *The
Tempest* (6th ed. rev.). Cambridge, Mass.: Harvard University Press; London: Methuen & Co., Ltd., 1958.

The dibble in earth, to set one slip of them;
No more than were I painted, I would wish
This youth should say 'twere well, and only therefore
Desire to breed by me.

                                                    (4.4.79–103)

In this disagreement Polixenes only *seems* to win, though
he has the general weight of contemporary thought on his
side; the art of the gardener in improving wild natural stocks
was treated as a figure of the distinctive human power to im-
prove and civilize the environment, and it was customary to
add that in so doing Art was nevertheless the agent of Nature. Perdita does not know she is herself noble, and is only
playing at being a queen, though the audience has already
noted strong suggestions of her royalty, indeed of her semi-
divinity; and there is a purely dramatic irony in the discussion, since Polixenes is to oppose the union of his noble son
with a supposedly base-born girl, this contradicting his own
philosophy; whereas she, base-born and hoping to marry a
prince, resists his horticultural analogy. Her case is precisely
that of Marvell in his poem "The Mower against Gardens,"
in which the gardener is called not an improver of nature but
a pander; but Perdita, unable to answer the argument from
gardening, produces one from cosmetics ("the gillyvors are
like painted women") and so tacitly rejects the implied resemblance between herself and "barks of baser kind." Leaving aside the purely dramatic ironies, this debate is one on
which the arguments on both sides were well known, and
Shakespeare's purpose is not to identify himself with one or
other side so much as to tell the audience that the great topic
of the relations between art and nature are relevant to his
purposes; to establish in every word as well as every action
the "better nature" of Perdita, and to prepare the way for a
climactic scene in which, when the statue proves to be powerful and beautiful beyond the scope of art, we shall see finally the incomparable work of "great creating Nature."
Whenever he includes discussion of this kind—as he does,
for example, in *The Merchant of Venice*, in *Troilus and
Cressida*, in *Measure for Measure*—we may expect it to

have its repercussions on the action. In this play we find them in the last act.

The pattern of this act is determined, as we have seen, by the need for a double recognition, but nothing at the level of plot required the dramatist to bring Hermione back into the play as a statue. Admittedly the scene lends itself to that tone of exalted joy which distinguishes these late plays of reunion, and is magnificently theatrical; having once committed himself to the situation the old master makes the most of the chance, holds us to the long moment of Hermione's immobility, and when it is over, concludes the play with what must appear, unless the producer has the necessary sensitivity and tact, unseemly haste. But as usual he makes theatrical effect compatible with thematic interest. Paulina soaks her guests in art by taking them on an extended tour round the gallery before she lets them see the statue. They praise it for its naturalness, its "life," while she protests that the color is still wet and calls it a "poor image." "What was he that did make it?" asks Leontes in unconscious tribute to the god of nature. The work is so "alive," he says, "that we are mocked with art." Slowly the statue moves out of the possibilities of art: "what fine chisel / Could ever yet cut breath?" Then it moves indeed, and the hypothesis that this is art can only be defended by calling that art magic. Finally it speaks, and blesses Perdita, and this no work of art, but only those of great creating nature, can do.

In its identification of the thematic and the theatrical, this is a true work of Shakespeare's. It is, of course, more complex than my account suggests. The survival of Hermione authenticates Perdita's beauty; time, which has seemed the destroyer, is a redeemer. At one masterly moment Perdita herself stands like a statue beside the supposed statue of her mother, to remind us that created things work their own perfection and continuance in time, as well as suffer under it. And in the end the play seems to say (I borrow the language of Yeats) that "whatever is begotten, born and dies" is nobler than "monuments of unageing intellect"—and also, when truly considered, more truly lasting.

Such a formula may justly attract the complaint that it is

partial and moralizing. The play is a great one, with a natural energy that supports all it says about natural power; its scheme is deep-laid and its language fertile in suggestion. It will not be trapped by the historian, though he can speak of the vogue of tragicomic romance and compare Perdita with Pastorella. It will not, either, be caught in the net of allegory. To say that Hermione suffers, dies, and is restored to life, is not to suggest a parallel that the author missed, but equally not to hit his true intention. All truths, he might argue, are related to the Truth; all good stories will have—to use the term of Erich Auerbach—a "figural" quality. *The Winter's Tale*, like many other stories, deals with sin and forgiveness, and with the triumph of time—also a Christian theme. But we value it not for some hidden truth, but for its power to realize experience, to show something of life that could only be shown by the intense activity of intellect and imagination in the medium of a theatrical form. It is not a great allegory or a great argument, but a great play.

—FRANK KERMODE
Fellow of the British Academy

The Winter's Tale

Dramatis Personae

Leontes, King of Sicilia
Mamillius, young Prince of Sicilia
Camillo ⎫
Antigonus ⎬ four Lords of Sicilia
Cleomenes ⎪
Dion ⎭
Hermione, Queen to Leontes
Perdita, daughter to Leontes and Hermione
Paulina, wife to Antigonus
Emilia, a Lady [attending on Hermione]
Polixenes, King of Bohemia
Florizel, Prince of Bohemia
Old Shepherd, reputed father of Perdita
Clown, his son
Autolycus, a rogue
Archidamus, a Lord of Bohemia
[A Mariner]
[A Jailer]
[Mopsa ⎫shepherdesses]
Dorcas ⎭
Other Lords and Gentlemen, [Ladies, Officers of the
   Court,] and Servants
Shepherds and Shepherdesses
[Time, as Chorus]
            [*Scene:* Sicilia and Bohemia]

The Winter's Tale

ACT 1

Scene 1. [*Sicilia, the Court of Leontes.*]

Enter Camillo and Archidamus.

Archidamus. If you shall chance, Camillo, to visit
Bohemia, on the like occasion whereon my services
are now on foot, you shall see, as I have said, great
difference betwixt our Bohemia and your Sicilia.

Camillo. I think this coming summer the King of   5
Sicilia means to pay Bohemia the visitation which he
justly owes him.

Archidamus. Wherein our entertainment shall shame us
we will be justified in our loves;° ¹for indeed——

Camillo. Beseech you——   10

Archidamus. Verily I speak it in the freedom of my
knowledge: we cannot with such magnificence—
in so rare—I know not what to say.... We will
give you sleepy drinks, that your senses, unintel-
ligent° of our insufficience, may, though they cannot   15
praise us, as little accuse us.

---

¹The degree sign (°) indicates a footnote, which is keyed to the text by the line
number. Text references are printed in **boldface** type; the annotation follows
in roman type. 1.1.8–9 **Wherein ... loves** our entertainment may fall short of
yours, but we shall make up for it by the strength of our affection   14–15 **un-
intelligent** unaware

Camillo. You pay a great deal too dear for what's
given freely.

Archidamus. Believe me, I speak as my understanding
20   instructs me, and as mine honesty puts it to utterance.

Camillo. Sicilia cannot show himself overkind to Bohemia. They were trained together in their child-
hoods; and there rooted betwixt them then such
25   an affection, which cannot choose but branch° now.
Since their more mature dignities and royal necessities made separation of their society,° their encounters, though not personal, have been royally
attorneyed° with interchange of gifts, letters, lov-
30   ing embassies, that they have seemed to be together,
though absent: shook hands, as over a vast;° and
embraced as it were from the ends of opposed winds.
The heavens continue their loves!

Archidamus. I think there is not in the world either
35   malice or matter to alter it. You have an unspeakable
comfort of your young Prince Mamillius; it is a gentleman of the greatest promise that ever came into
my note.

Camillo. I very well agree with you in the hopes of
40   him. It is a gallant child; one that, indeed, physics
the subject,° makes old hearts fresh; they that went
on crutches ere he was born desire yet their life to
see him a man.

Archidamus. Would they else be content to die?

45   *Camillo.* Yes, if there were no other excuse why they
should desire to live.

Archidamus. If the King had no son, they would desire
to live on crutches till he had one.

                                          Exeunt.

---

25 **branch** i.e., flourish   27 **society** companionship   29 **attorneyed** supplied
by substitutes   31 **vast** desolate space   40–41 **physics the subject** is good
medicine for the people

Scene 2. [*The Court of Leontes.*]

Enter Leontes, Hermione, Mamillius, Polixenes,
Camillo, [and Attendants].

Polixenes. Nine changes of the wat'ry star° hath been
  The shepherd's note since we have left our throne
  Without a burden: time as long again
  Would be filled up, my brother, with our thanks,
  And yet we should for perpetuity   *5*
  Go hence in debt. And therefore, like a cipher,
  Yet standing in rich place, I multiply
  With one "We thank you," many thousands moe°
  That go before it.°

Leontes.   Stay your thanks awhile,
  And pay them when you part.

Polixenes.   Sir, that's tomorrow.   *10*
  I am questioned by my fears of what may chance
  Or breed upon our absence, that may blow
  No sneaping winds at home, to make us say,
  "This is put forth too truly."° Besides, I have stayed
  To tire your royalty.

Leontes.   We are tougher, brother,   *15*
  Than you can put us to 't.°

1.2.1 **wat'ry star** i.e., the moon   8 **moe** more   3–9 **time as long . . . before**
it it would take us the same length of time to thank you, and even then we
should leave here forever your debtors. So I offer you one more thank-you,
which, though it is in itself nothing, works like a zero on the end of a number
and multiplies all the thanks I've given you before (instead of merely adding
to them)   11–14 **I am questioned . . . too truly** i.e., I'm worried about what
may happen at home, perhaps as a result of my absence—worried in case
blighting influences may not be at work which we shall regret, saying "We
went away only too well"   16 **put us to 't** drive us to extremities

Polixenes.   No longer stay.

Leontes. One sev'night longer.

Polixenes.   Very sooth, tomorrow.

Leontes. We'll part the time between 's then; and in that
    I'll no gainsaying.°

Polixenes.   Press me not, beseech you, so.
20   There is no tongue that moves, none, none i' th' world
    So soon as yours could win me; so it should now,
    Were there necessity in your request, although
    'Twere needful I denied it. My affairs
    Do even drag me homeward; which to hinder
25   Were, in your love, a whip to me;° my stay,
    To you a charge and trouble: to save both,
    Farewell, our brother.

Leontes.   Tongue-tied, our Queen? Speak you.

Hermione. I had thought, sir, to have held my peace until
    You had drawn oaths from him not to stay. You, sir,
30   Charge him too coldly. Tell him you are sure
    All in Bohemia's well; this satisfaction,
    The bygone day proclaimed. Say this to him,
    He's beat from his best ward.°

Leontes.   Well said, Hermione.

Hermione. To tell he longs to see his son were strong;
35   But let him say so then, and let him go;
    But let him swear so, and he shall not stay,
    We'll thwack him hence with distaffs.
    Yet of your royal presence, I'll adventure
    The borrow of a week. When at Bohemia
40   You take my lord, I'll give him my commission

---

19 **I'll no gainsaying** I'll not accept a refusal   25 **Were . . . to me** i.e., though
doing it out of love, you would be tormenting me by making me stay in these
circumstances   33 **ward** defensive posture in fencing

To let him there a month behind the gest°
Prefixed for 's parting, yet, good deed,° Leontes,
I love thee not a jar° o' th' clock behind
What lady she° her lord. You'll stay?

Polixenes.   No, madam.

Hermione. Nay, but you will?

Polixenes.   I may not, verily.   45

Hermione. Verily?
You put me off with limber° vows; but I,
Though you would seek t' unsphere the stars with
   oaths,
Should yet say, "Sir, no going." Verily,
You shall not go; a lady's "Verily" is   50
As potent as a lord's. Will you go yet?
Force me to keep you as prisoner,
Not like a guest; so you shall pay your fees°
When you depart, and save your thanks. How say
   you?
My prisoner or my guest? By your dread "Verily,"   55
One of them you shall be.

Polixenes.   Your guest, then, madam:
To be your prisoner should import offending;°
Which is for me less easy to commit,
Than you to punish.

Hermione.   Not your jailer, then,
But your kind hostess. Come, I'll question you   60
Of my lord's tricks, and yours, when you were boys:
You were pretty lordings then?

Polixenes.   We were, fair Queen,
Two lads that thought there was no more behind°
But such a day tomorrow as today,
And to be boy eternal.

Hermione.   Was not my lord   65
The verier wag o' th' two?

41 **gest** stage of royal progress; time allocated to one place on the route
42 **good deed** indeed, in very deed   43 **jar** tick   44 **lady she** gentlewoman
47 **limber** limp   53 **fees** (which were always due from prisoner to jailer)
57 **import offending** mean that I had committed some crime   63 **behind**
to come

Polixenes. We were as twinned lambs, that did frisk i'
        th' sun,
        And bleat the one at th' other; what we changed°
        Was innocence for innocence; we knew not
70   The doctrine of ill-doing, nor dreamed
        That any did; had we pursued that life,
        And our weak spirits ne'er been higher reared
        With stronger blood, we should have answered
            heaven
        Boldly, "not guilty"; the imposition cleared,
        Hereditary ours.°

75 *Hermione.*   By this we gather
        You have tripped since.

        Polixenes.   O my most sacred lady,
        Temptations have since then been born to 's, for
        In those unfledged days was my wife a girl;
        Your precious self had then not crossed the eyes
        Of my young playfellow.

80 *Hermione.*   Grace to boot!°
        Of this make no conclusion,° lest you say
        Your queen and I are devils. Yet go on,
        Th' offenses we have made you do we'll answer,
        If you first sinned with us, and that with us
        You did continue fault, and that you slipped not
        With any but with us.

85 *Leontes.*   Is he won yet?

    Hermione. He'll stay, my lord.

    Leontes.   At my request he would not.
        Hermione, my dearest, thou never spok'st
        To better purpose.

    Hermione.   Never?

---

68 **changed** exchanged 72–75 **our weak spirits ... Hereditary ours** i.e.,
had the weakness of our animal spirits not been fortified by the passionate
blood of maturity, our wills would never have been corrupted, and we should
have been able to claim exemption from the taint of original sin. 80 **Grace
to boot!** Heaven help me! 81 **make no conclusion** don't pursue that line of
argument

Leontes.   Never but once.

Hermione. What! Have I twice said well? When was 't
    before?   90
  I prithee tell me; cram 's with praise, and make 's
  As fat as tame things: one good deed, dying tongue-
    less,
  Slaughters a thousand waiting upon that.
  Our praises are our wages—you may ride 's
  With one soft kiss a thousand furlongs, ere   95
  With spur we heat an acre.° But to th' goal:
  My last good deed was to entreat his stay.
  What was my first? It has an elder sister,
  Or I mistake you; O, would her name were Grace!
  But once before I spoke to th' purpose? When?   100
  Nay, let me have 't; I long.

Leontes.   Why, that was when
  Three crabbèd months had soured themselves to
    death,
  Ere I could make thee open thy white hand
  And clap° thyself my love; then didst thou utter
  "I am yours forever."

Hermione.   'Tis Grace indeed.   105
  Why, lo you now, I have spoke to th' purpose twice:
  The one forever earned a royal husband;
  Th' other, for some while a friend.

Leontes.   [*Aside*] Too hot, too hot!
  To mingle friendship far is mingling bloods.
  I have tremor cordis° on me; my heart dances,   110
  But not for joy, not joy. This entertainment
  May a free face put on, derive a liberty
  From heartiness, from bounty, fertile bosom,°
  And well become the agent—'t may, I grant;
  But to be paddling palms and pinching fingers,   115
  As now they are, and making practiced smiles
  As in a looking glass; and then to sigh, as 'twere

---

96 **heat an acre** race over a furlong   104 **clap** offer the handclasp that seals a
bargain   110 **tremor cordis** palpitation of the heart   113 **fertile bosom** generous affection

The mort o' th' deer°—oh, that is entertainment
My bosom likes not, nor my brows.° Mamillius,
Art thou my boy?

Mamillius.   Ay, my good lord.

120 *Leontes.*   I' fecks!°
Why, that's my bawcock.° What, hast smutched thy
    nose?
They say it is a copy out of mine. Come, Captain,
We must be neat—not neat,° but cleanly, Captain:
And yet the steer, the heifer, and the calf,
125 Are all called neat. Still virginaling°
Upon his palm? How now, you wanton calf,
Art thou my calf?

Mamillius.   Yes, if you will, my lord.

Leontes. Thou want'st a rough pash,° and the shoots
    that I have
To be full like me: yet they say we are
130 Almost as like as eggs; women say so,
That will say anything. But were they false
As o'er-dyed blacks,° as wind, as waters; false
As dice are to be wished, by one that fixes
No bourn° 'twixt his and mine—yet were it true
135 To say this boy were like me. Come, Sir Page,
Look on me with your welkin° eye. Sweet villain,
Most dear'st, my collop!° Can thy dam,° may 't be?
Affection!° Thy intention° stabs the center.°
Thou dost make possible things not so held,
140 Communicat'st with dreams—how can this be?—
With what's unreal thou coactive art,

117–18 **as 'twere/The mort o' th' deer** like the horn call signifying the death
of the deer   119 **brows** (alluding to the myth of the horns that grow on the fore-
heads of cuckolds)   120 **fecks** (a mild oath, derived from "i' faith")   121 **bawcock** fine fellow (Fr. *beau coq*)   123 **neat** (Leontes rejects the word because it
also means "horned cattle")   125 **virginaling** i.e., as if playing the virginals (a
small keyboard instrument)   128 **pash** head   132 **o'er-dyed blacks** black garments worn out by too much dyeing   134 **bourn** boundary   136 **welkin** blue
(like the sky)   137 **collop** a cut off his own flesh   137 **dam** mother (Leontes'
thoughts still run on cattle)   138 **Affection** passion   138 **intention** purpose   138 **center** i.e., of the world (?) of my heart (?)

And fellow'st nothing. Then 'tis very credent°
Thou mayst co-join with something, and thou dost,
And that beyond commission, and I find it,
And that to the infection of my brains,   *145*
And hardening of my brows.°

Polixenes.   What means Sicilia?

Hermione. He something seems unsettled.

Polixenes.   How, my lord?

Leontes. What cheer? How is 't with you, best brother?

Hermione.   You look
As if you held a brow of much distraction;
Are you moved, my lord?

Leontes.   No, in good earnest.   *150*
How sometimes Nature will betray its folly,
Its tenderness, and make itself a pastime
To harder bosoms! Looking on the lines
Of my boy's face, methoughts I did recoil
Twenty-three years, and saw myself unbreeched,   *155*
In my green velvet coat; my dagger muzzled,
Lest it should bite its master, and so prove,
As ornaments oft do, too dangerous.
How like, methought, I then was to this kernel,
This squash,° this gentleman. Mine honest friend,   *160*
Will you take eggs for money?°

Mamillius. No, my lord, I'll fight.

Leontes. You will? Why, happy man be 's dole!° My
    brother,

---

142 **credent** credible   138-46 **Affection ... brows** (may be corrupt. Para-
phrase: "Passion! Your desire for fulfillment can pierce to the heart of things.
You deal with matters normally thought of as illusory—with dreams and fantasies, impossible as that sounds. You collaborate with the unreal; so it isn't
improbable that you should do so with what really exists; this is what has happened, as my mental disturbance and cuckold's horns indicate." The passion is
jealousy; Leontes recognizes that it is sometimes baseless, but argues that it is
not so in his case)   160 **squash** unripe peapod (young person)   161 **take
eggs for money** allow yourself to be imposed upon   163 **happy man be 's
dole** may it be his lot to be a happy man

Are you so fond of your young prince as we
Do seem to be of ours?

165 *Polixenes.*   If at home, sir,
He's all my exercise, my mirth, my matter;
Now my sworn friend, and then mine enemy;
My parasite, my soldier, statesman, all.
He makes a July's day short as December,
170 And with his varying childness, cures in me
Thoughts that would thick my blood.°

Leontes.   So stands this squire
Officed with me.° We two will walk, my lord,
And leave you to your graver steps. Hermione,
How thou lov'st us, show in our brother's welcome;
175 Let what is dear in Sicily, be cheap;
Next to thyself and my young rover, he's
Apparent° to my heart.

Hermione.   If you would seek us,
We are yours i' th' garden; shall's attend you there?

Leontes. To your own bents dispose you; you'll be
found,
180 Be you beneath the sky. [*Aside*] I am angling° now,
Though you perceive me not how I give line.
Go to, go to!
How she holds up the neb,° the bill to him!
And arms her with the boldness of a wife
To her allowing° husband!

                [*Exeunt Polixenes, Hermione, and Attendants.*]

                                   Gone already!
185
Inch-thick, knee-deep, o'er head and ears a forked°
one!
Go play, boy, play: thy mother plays, and I
Play too—but so disgraced a part, whose issue°
Will hiss me to my grave; contempt and clamor

---

171 **thick my blood** make me melancholy   171–72 **So stands ... me** My son
has a similar post in my household   177 **Apparent** heir apparent   180 **an-
gling** giving them scope, "playing" them   183 **neb** beak   185 **allowing** ap-
proving   186 **forked** (alluding to the branching cuckold's horns)   188 **issue**
exit (following the idea of the actor not capable of his part)

Will be my knell. Go play, boy, play. There have
    been,　　　　　　　　　　　　　　　　　　　　*190*
Or I am much deceived, cuckolds ere now,
And many a man there is, even at this present,
Now, while I speak this, holds his wife by th' arm,
That little thinks she has been sluiced in 's absence,
And his pond fished by his next neighbor, by　　*195*
Sir Smile, his neighbor, nay, there's comfort in 't,
Whiles other men have gates, and those gates
    opened,
As mine, against their will. Should all despair,
That have revolted° wives, the tenth of mankind
Would hang themselves. Physic for 't there's none;　*200*
It is a bawdy planet, that will strike
Where 'tis predominant;° and 'tis powerful, think it,
From east, west, north, and south. Be it concluded,
No barricado for a belly. Know 't
It will let in and out the enemy,　　　　　　　　*205*
With bag and baggage. Many thousand on 's
Have the disease, and feel 't not. How now, boy!

Mamillius. I am like you, they say.

Leontes.　　　　　　　　　Why, that's some comfort.
What! Camillo there?

Camillo. Ay, my good lord.　　　　　　　　　　*210*

Leontes. Go play, Mamillius; thou 'rt an honest man.

　　　　　　　　　　　　　　　[*Exit Mamillius.*]

Camillo, this great sir will yet stay longer.

Camillo. You had much ado to make his anchor hold;
When you cast out, it still came home.

Leontes.　　　　　　　　　　Didst note it?

Camillo. He would not stay at your petitions, made　*215*
His business more material.

Leontes.　　　　　　　　　Didst perceive it?

---

199 **revolted** unfaithful　202 **predominant** in the ascendant (a technical term
in astrology)

[*Aside*] They're here° with me already: whispering,
          rounding:°
"Sicilia is a so-forth":° 'tis far gone,
When I shall gust° it last. How came 't, Camillo,
That he did stay?

220 *Camillo.*   At the good Queen's entreaty.

Leontes. "At the Queen's" be 't: "Good" should be
          pertinent,
But so it is, it is not. Was this taken°
By any understanding pate but thine?
For thy conceit is soaking,° will draw in
225 More than the common blocks.° Not noted, is 't,
But of the finer natures? By some severals°
Of headpiece extraordinary? Lower messes°
Perchance are to this business purblind? Say.

Camillo. Business, my lord? I think most understand
          Bohemia stays here longer.

Leontes.   Ha?

230 *Camillo.*   Stays here longer.

Leontes. Ay, but why?

Camillo. To satisfy your Highness, and the entreaties
          Of our most gracious mistress.

Leontes.   Satisfy
Th' entreaties of your mistress? Satisfy?
235 Let that suffice. I have trusted thee, Camillo,
With all the nearest things to my heart, as well
My chamber-counsels,° wherein, priestlike, thou
Hast cleansed my bosom—ay, from thee departed
Thy penitent reformed; but we have been
240 Deceived in thy integrity, deceived
In that which seems so.

---

217 **They're here** They (onlookers) have already caught on to my situation
217 **rounding** speaking in secret   218 **so-forth** i.e., they slyly avoid the word
"cuckold"   219 **gust** taste, hear of   222 **taken** observed   224 **conceit is soaking** intelligence is absorbent   225 **blocks** blockheads   226 **severals** individuals
227 **Lower messes** inferior people ("mess" in the sense of a group who dine together and would be of the same—low—rank)   237 **chamber-counsels** confes-
sions of secret sins

Camillo.   Be it forbid, my lord!

Leontes. To bide° upon 't. Thou art not honest; or
　If thou inclin'st that way, thou art a coward,
　Which hoxes° honesty behind, restraining
　From course required; or else thou must be counted   *245*
　A servant, grafted in my serious trust,
　And therein negligent; or else a fool,
　That seest a game played home, the rich stake
　　drawn,°
　And tak'st it all for jest.

Camillo.   My gracious lord,
　I may be negligent, foolish, and fearful,   *250*
　In every one of these no man is free
　But that his negligence, his folly, fear,
　Among the infinite doings of the world,
　Sometime puts forth.° In your affairs, my lord,
　If ever I were willful negligent,   *255*
　It was my folly; if industriously
　I played the fool, it was my negligence,
　Not weighing well the end: if ever fearful
　To do a thing, where I the issue doubted,
　Whereof the execution did cry out   *260*
　Against the nonperformance, 'twas a fear
　Which oft infects the wisest. These, my lord,
　Are such allowed infirmities, that honesty
　Is never free of. But beseech your Grace,
　Be plainer with me, let me know my trespass   *265*
　By its own visage;° if I then deny it,
　'Tis none of mine.

Leontes.   Ha' not you seen, Camillo—
　But that's past doubt, you have, or your eyeglass°
　Is thicker than a cuckold's horn—or heard—
　For to a vision so apparent, rumor   *270*
　Cannot be mute—or thought—for cogitation
　Resides not in that man that does not think—

---

242 **bide** insist 244 **hoxes** hamstrings 248 **played home … stake drawn**
played earnestly, great stakes being won 254 **puts forth** shows itself
266 **by its own visage** under its true name 268 **eyeglass** the lens of the eye

My wife is slippery?° If thou wilt confess,
Or else be impudently negative,
275 To have nor eyes, nor ears, nor thought, then say
My wife's a hobbyhorse,° deserves a name
As rank as any flax-wench,° that puts to
Before her troth-plight; say 't, and justify 't.

Camillo. I would not be a stander-by to hear
280 My sovereign mistress clouded so, without
My present° vengeance taken; 'shrew my heart,
You never spoke what did become you less
Than this; which to reiterate, were sin
As deep as that, though true.°

Leontes.   Is whispering nothing?
285 Is leaning cheek to cheek? Is meeting noses?
Kissing with inside lip? Stopping the career°
Of laughter with a sigh (a note infallible
Of breaking honesty°)? Horsing foot on foot?
Skulking in corners? Wishing clocks more swift?
290 Hours, minutes? Noon, midnight? And all eyes
Blind with the pin and web,° but theirs; theirs only,
That would unseen be wicked? Is this nothing?
Why, then the world and all that's in 't is nothing,
The covering sky is nothing. Bohemia nothing,
295 My wife is nothing, nor nothing have these nothings,
If this be nothing.

Camillo.   Good my lord, be cured
Of this diseased opinion, and betimes,
For 'tis most dangerous.

Leontes.   Say it be, 'tis true.

Camillo. No, no, my lord.

Leontes.   It is; you lie, you lie.

267–73 **Ha' not you ... slippery?** Have you not seen—you must have, or your sight is grossly thick—or heard—as you must, since Hermione's conduct is so open that there must be gossip about it—or thought—and unless you have you can't think at all—that my wife is unfaithful? 276 **hobbyhorse** loose woman 277 **flax-wench** low-bred girl 281 **present** immediate 284 **As deep as that, though true** i.e., as wicked as her adultery if it were a fact, which it is not 286 **career** gallop 288 **honesty** chastity 291 **pin and web** cataract

I say thou liest, Camillo, and I hate thee,   *300*
Pronounce thee a gross lout, a mindless slave,
Or else a hovering° temporizer, that
Canst with thine eyes at once see good and evil,
Inclining to them both. Were my wife's liver°
Infected as her life, she would not live   *305*
The running of one glass.°

Camillo.   Who does infect her?

Leontes. Why, he that wears her like her medal,°
    hanging
About his neck, Bohemia, who, if I
Had servants true about me, that bare eyes
To see alike mine honor as their profits,   *310*
Their own particular thrifts,° they would do that
Which should undo more doing. Ay, and thou,
His cupbearer, whom I from meaner form
Have benched° and reared to worship, who mayst
    see
Plainly as heaven sees earth, and earth see heaven,   *315*
How I am gallèd, mightst bespice a cup,
To give mine enemy a lasting wink;°
Which draught to me were cordial.°

Camillo.   Sir, my lord,
I could do this, and that with no rash potion,
But with a lingering dram° that should not work   *320*
Maliciously, like poison; but I cannot
Believe this crack to be in my dread mistress,
So sovereignly being honorable.
I have loved thee——°

Leontes. Make that thy question, and go rot!°   *325*

302 **hovering** vacillating   304 **liver** (since this was the seat of the passions, it presumably was infected; transposition of "liver" and "life" has been proposed)   306 **glass** hourglass   307 **medal** (here a portrait miniature worn about the neck)   311 **particular thrifts** special gains   314 **benched** i.e., raised to place of dignity   317 **give ... lasting wink,** i.e., close his eyes forever   318 **cordial** medicine   320 **lingering dram** slow-working dose   324 **I have loved thee** (difficult to explain: Camillo may be about to protest his long loyalty, or threaten withdrawal of his love, but he would hardly address the King as "thou." Some editors give the words to Leontes, which hardly helps)   325 **Make ... rot** i.e., if you doubt the Queen's infidelity, go to hell

Dost think I am so muddy, so unsettled,
To appoint° myself in this vexation? Sully
The purity and whiteness of my sheets—
Which to preserve is sleep; which being spotted,
330   Is goads, thorns, nettles, tails of wasps—
Give scandal to the blood o' th' prince, my son,
Who I do think is mine, and love as mine,
Without ripe° moving to 't? Would I do this?
Could man so blench?°

Camillo.   I must believe you, sir;
335   I do, and will fetch off Bohemia for 't:
Provided that when he's removed, your Highness
Will take again your queen as yours at first,
Even for your son's sake, and thereby for sealing
The injury of tongues, in courts and kingdoms
Known and allied to yours.

340 *Leontes.*   Thou dost advise me,
Even so as I mine own course have set down.
I'll give no blemish to her honor, none.

Camillo. My lord,
Go then; and with a countenance as clear
345   As friendship wears at feasts, keep with Bohemia,
And with your queen: I am his cupbearer;
If from me he have wholesome beverage,
Account me not your servant.

Leontes.   This is all:
Do 't, and thou hast the one half of my heart;
Do 't not, thou split'st thine own.

350 *Camillo.*   I'll do 't, my lord.

Leontes. I will seem friendly, as thou hast advised me.
                         Exit.

Camillo. O miserable lady! But for me,
What case stand I in? I must be the poisoner
Of good Polixenes, and my ground to do 't
355   Is the obedience to a master—one
Who, in rebellion with himself, will have
All that are his so too. To do this deed,

327 **appoint** establish   333 **ripe** adequate, matured   334 **blench** swerve

Promotion follows; if I could find example
Of thousands that had struck anointed kings,
And flourished after, I'd not do 't; but since   360
Nor brass, nor stone, nor parchment bears not one,
Let villainy itself forswear 't.° I must
Forsake the court; to do 't, or no, is certain
To me a break-neck. Happy star reign now!
Here comes Bohemia.

                    Enter Polixenes.

Polixenes.   This is strange: methinks   365
  My favor here begins to warp. Not speak?
  Good day, Camillo.

Camillo.   Hail, most royal sir.

Polixenes. What is the news i' th' court?

Camillo.   None rare, my lord.

Polixenes. The King hath on him such a countenance,
  As he had lost some province, and a region   370
  Loved as he loves himself; even now I met him
  With customary compliment, when he,
  Wafting his eyes to th' contrary,° and falling
  A lip of much contempt, speed from me, and
  So leaves me to consider what is breeding   375
  That changes thus his manners.

Camillo. I dare not know, my lord.

Polixenes. How, dare not? Do not? Do you know, and
    dare not
  Be intelligent to me? 'Tis thereabouts;
  For to yourself, what you do know, you must,   380
  And cannot say you dare not.° Good Camillo,
  Your changed complexions are to me a mirror,
  Which shows me mine changed too: for I must be
  A party in this alteration, finding

358–62 **if I could example . . . forswear 't** if the records showed that king-killers prospered, I would not do it; but since they prove the contrary, villainy itself should forswear regicide   373 **Wafting his eyes to th' contrary** looking (contemptuously) away   378–81 **How, dare not? . . . you dare not** What do you mean, dare not? That you do not? Can it be that you know, and dare not tell me? That must be the explanation, since you can't say you don't dare tell yourself what you know

Myself thus altered with 't.

385 *Camillo.*   There is a sickness
Which puts some of us in distemper; but
I cannot name the disease; and it is caught
Of you, that yet are well.

Polixenes.   How caught of me?
Make me not sighted like the basilisk.°
I have looked on thousands, who have sped° the
390   better
By my regard, but killed none so. Camillo,
As you are certainly a gentleman, thereto
Clerklike experienced,° which no less adorns
Our gentry than our parents' noble names
395 In whose success° we are gentle:° I beseech you,
If you know aught which does behoove my knowledge
Thereof to be informed, imprison 't not
In ignorant concealment.

Camillo.   I may not answer.

Polixenes. A sickness caught of me, and yet I well?
400   I must be answered. Dost thou hear, Camillo,
I conjure° thee, by all the parts° of man,
Which honor does acknowledge, whereof the least
Is not this suit of mine, that thou declare
What incidency° thou dost guess of harm
405 Is creeping toward me; how far off, how near,
Which way to be prevented, if to be;
If not, how best to bear it.

Camillo.   Sir, I will tell you,
Since I am charged in honor, and by him
That I think honorable. Therefore mark my counsel,
410 Which must be ev'n as swiftly followed as
I mean to utter it; or both yourself and me,
Cry lost, and so good night.

Polixenes.   On, good Camillo.

Camillo. I am appointed him° to murder you.

389 **basilisk** a mythical serpent which killed by looking   390 **sped** prospered
393 **Clerklike experienced** with the experience of an educated man   395 **success** succession   395 **gentle** well born   401 **conjure** adjure   401 **parts** duties,
functions   404 **incidency** threat   413 **him** i.e., by Leontes

Polixenes. By whom, Camillo?

Camillo.   By the King.

Polixenes.   For what?

Camillo. He thinks, nay with all confidence he swears,   *415*
As he had seen 't, or been an instrument
To vice° you to 't, that you have touched his queen
Forbiddenly.

Polixenes.   Oh then my best blood turn
To an infected jelly, and my name
Be yoked with his, that did betray the Best!°   *420*
Turn then my freshest reputation to
A savor° that may strike the dullest nostril
Where I arrive, and my approach be shunned,
Nay, hated too, worse than the great'st infection
That e'er was heard, or read!

Camillo.   Swear his thought over°   *425*
By each particular star in heaven, and
By all their influences; you may as well
Forbid the sea for to obey the moon,
As or by oath remove or counsel shake
The fabric of his folly, whose foundation   *430*
Is piled upon his faith, and will continue
The standing of his body.°

Polixenes.   How should this grow?°

Camillo. I know not: but I am sure 'tis safer to
Avoid what's grown than question how 'tis born.
If therefore you dare trust my honesty,   *435*
That lies enclosèd in this trunk, which you
Shall bear along impawned,° away tonight.
Your followers I will whisper to the business,

417 **To vice** to force   420 **his, that did betray the Best** i.e., Judas   422 **savor** alluding to the idea that infection (e.g., of the plague) could be smelled (hence the use of flowers in posies as a prophylactic)   425 **Swear his thought over** deny his suspicion with oaths   429–32 **As or by oath ... of his body** i.e., you may as well attempt the obviously impossible as try to remove by your oaths or pull down by your advice the structure of his crazy delusion which has its foundations on settled belief, and will last as long as his life (stand up as long as he can)   432 **How should this grow?** How can this have grown up   437 **impawned** as a pledge of good faith (Camillo points to his body, which is the "trunk")

And will by twos and threes, at several posterns,°
440 Clear them o' th' city. For myself, I'll put
My fortunes to your service, which are here
By this discovery lost. Be not uncertain,
For by the honor of my parents, I
Have uttered truth; which if you seek to prove,°
445 I dare not stand by; nor shall you be safer,
Than one condemned by the King's own mouth, thereon
His execution sworn.°

Polixenes.   I do believe thee:
I saw his heart in 's face. Give me thy hand,
Be pilot to me, and thy places° shall
450 Still neighbor mine. My ships are ready, and
My people did expect my hence departure
Two days ago. This jealousy
Is for a precious creature; as she's rare,
Must it be great; and, as his person's mighty,
455 Must it be violent: and, as he does conceive,
He is dishonored by a man, which ever
Professed° to him, why his revenges must
In that be made more bitter. Fear o'ershades me;
Good expedition° be my friend, and comfort
460 The gracious Queen, part of his theme, but nothing
Of his ill-ta'en suspicion.° Come, Camillo,
I will respect thee as a father, if
Thou bear'st my life off hence; let us avoid.°

Camillo. It is in mine authority to command
465 The keys of all the posterns: please your Highness
To take the urgent hour. Come, sir, away.   *Exeunt.*

---

439 **posterns** gates   444 **prove** test   446–47 **mouth ... sworn** i.e., the King
having condemned him has sworn that the sentence will be death (Corrupt? See
list of emendations.)   449 **places** offices, functions, dignities   457 **Professed**
made professions (of friendship)   459 **expedition** speed   460–61 **part of his
theme ... suspicion** (obscure: Shakespeare's sense has perhaps not quite got
through. "May my speedy departure also help the Queen, who is involved in
Leontes' fantasy though she has no rightful place in his suspicions." But this
fails to explain why Polixenes thought his departure would help Hermione. Perhaps "expedition" is not the subject of "comfort"—then he is merely wishing
the Queen comfort in the troubles he is leaving her to, and the vagueness of the
expression matches the emptiness of the wish.)   463 **avoid** depart

ACT 2

Scene 1. [*Sicilia, the Court of Leontes.*]

Enter Hermione, Mamillius, Ladies.

Hermione. Take the boy to you; he so troubles me,
  'Tis past enduring.

First Lady.   Come, my gracious lord,
  Shall I be your playfellow?

Mamillius.   No, I'll none of you.

First Lady. Why, my sweet lord?

Mamillius. You'll kiss me hard, and speak to me, as if   5
  I were a baby still. I love you better.

Second Lady. And why so, my lord?

Mamillius.   Not for because
  Your brows are blacker; yet black brows, they say,
  Become some women best, so that there be not
  Too much hair there, but in a semicircle,   10
  Or a half-moon, made with a pen.

Second Lady.   Who taught'° this?

Mamillius. I learned it out of women's faces. Pray now,
  What color are your eyebrows?

First Lady.   Blue, my lord.

2.1.11 **taught'** taught you

23

Mamillius. Nay, that's a mock. I have seen a lady's nose
　　That has been blue, but not her eyebrows.

15　*First Lady.*　　　　　　　　　　　　　Hark ye,
　　The Queen, your mother, rounds apace; we shall
　　Present our services to a fine new prince
　　One of these days, and then you'd wanton° with us,
　　If we would have you.

Second Lady.　　　　　She is spread of late
20　Into a goodly bulk; good time encounter her!

Hermione. What wisdom stirs amongst you? Come, sir, now
　　I am for you again; pray you sit by us,
　　And tell 's a tale.

Mamillius.　　　　　Merry or sad shall 't be?

Hermione. As merry as you will.

25　*Mamillius.* A sad tale's best for winter; I have one
　　Of sprites and goblins.

Hermione.　　　　　　　Let's have that, good sir.
　　Come on, sit down; come on, and do your best,
　　To fright me with your sprites; you're powerful at it.

Mamillius. There was a man.

Hermione.　　　　　　Nay, come sit down; then on.

30　*Mamillius.* Dwelt by a churchyard—I will tell it softly,
　　Yond crickets° shall not hear it.

Hermione. Come on, then, and give 't me in mine ear.

[*Enter Leontes, Antigonus, and Lords.*]

Leontes. Was he met there? His train? Camillo with him?

Lord. Behind the tuft of pines I met them, never
35　Saw I men scour° so on their way. I eyed them
　　Even to their ships.

Leontes.　　　　　How blest am I

18 **wanton** play　31 **yond crickets** i.e., the chattering ladies　35 **scour** hurry

In my just censure,° in my true opinion!
Alack, for lesser knowledge! How accursed,
In being so blest! There may be in the cup
A spider° steeped, and one may drink, depart,　　　　40
And yet partake no venom, for his knowledge
Is not infected; but if one present
Th' abhorred ingredient to his eye, make known
How he hath drunk, he cracks his gorge, his sides,
With violent hefts.° I have drunk, and seen the
　　spider.　　　　45
Camillo was his help in this, his pander.
There is a plot against my life, my crown;
All's true that is mistrusted; that false villain,
Whom I employed, was pre-employed by him;
He has discovered° my design, and I　　　　50
Remain a pinched thing;° yea, a very trick
For them to play at will. How came the posterns
So easily open?

Lord. 　　　　　By his great authority;
Which often hath no less prevailed than so
On your command.

Leontes. 　　　　　I know 't too well.　　　　55
[*To Hermione*] Give me the boy. I am glad you did
　　not nurse him;
Though he does bear some signs of me, yet you
Have too much blood in him.

Hermione. 　　　　　What is this? Sport?

Leontes. Bear the boy hence, he shall not come about
　　her;

　　　　　　　　　[*Exit Mamillius and a Lady.*]
Away with him, and let her sport herself　　　　60
With that she's big with; for 'tis Polixenes
Has made thee swell thus.

Hermione. 　　　　　But I'd say he had not;

37 **censure** judgment　40 **spider** (spiders were thought of as venomous; there seems to have been a superstition that this was so only if one saw the spider)　45 **hefts** retchings　50 **discovered** revealed　51 **pinched thing** puppet, toy

And I'll be sworn you would believe my saying,
Howe'er you lean to th' nayward.°

Leontes.   You, my lords,
65 Look on her, mark her well; be but about
To say, "She is a goodly lady," and
The justice of your hearts will thereto add,
" 'Tis pity she's not honest, honorable";
Praise her but for this her without-door form,°
70 Which on my faith deserves high speech, and straight
The shrug, the hum or ha, these petty brands
That calumny doth use—oh, I am out!°
That mercy does, for calumny will sear
Virtue itself—these shrugs, these hum's and ha's,
75 When you have said she's goodly, come between,°
Ere you can say she's honest. But be 't known,
From him that has most cause to grieve it should be,
She's an adult'ress.

Hermione.   Should a villain say so,
The most replenished° villain in the world,
80 He were as much more villain; you, my lord,
Do but mistake.

Leontes.   You have mistook, my lady,
Polixenes for Leontes. O thou thing,
Which I'll not call a creature of thy place,°
Lest barbarism, making me the precedent,
85 Should a like language use to all degrees,°
And mannerly distinguishment leave out
Betwixt the prince and beggar. I have said
She's an adult'ress, I have said with whom.
More, she's a traitor, and Camillo is
90 A federary° with her, and one that knows
What she should shame to know herself
But with her most vile principal°—that she's
A bed-swerver,° even as bad as those

---

64 **nayward** negative   69 **without-door form** external appearance   72 **I am out** I have lost my place, got my speech wrong   75 **come between** pause, interrupt, break off   79 **replenished** complete, perfect   83 **place** rank   85 **degrees** social ranks   90 **federary** confederate, accomplice   92 **principal** partner (i.e., Polixenes)   93 **bed-swerver** adulteress

That vulgars give bold'st titles; ay, and privy
To this their late escape.

Hermione.   No, by my life,   95
Privy to none of this; how will this grieve you,
When you shall come to clearer knowledge, that
You thus have published° me! Gentle my lord,
You scarce can right me throughly then to say
You did mistake.

Leontes.   No; if I mistake   100
In those foundations which I build upon,
The center° is not big enough to bear
A schoolboy's top. Away with her to prison.
He who shall speak for her is afar off guilty,
But that he speaks.°

Hermione.   There's some ill planet reigns;   105
I must be patient, till the heavens look
With an aspect more favorable. Good my lords,
I am not prone to weeping, as our sex
Commonly are; the want of which vain dew
Perchance shall dry your pities. But I have   110
That honorable grief lodged here which burns
Worse than tears drown. Beseech you all, my lords,
With thoughts so qualified° as your charities
Shall best instruct you, measure me; and so
The King's will be performed!

Leontes.   Shall I be heard?   115

Hermione. Who is 't that goes with me? Beseech your
    Highness
My women may be with me, for you see
My plight requires it. Do not weep, good fools;
There is no cause; when you shall know your mis-
    tress
Has deserved prison, then abound in tears,   120
As I come out; this action I now go on

---

98 published publicly proclaimed or denounced   **102 center** (of the earth,
and so of the universe), i.e., "If I am mistaken, no foundation can be trusted"
105 But that he speaks i.e., in merely speaking he is found guilty as a remote
accomplice   **113 qualified** tempered, moderated

Is for my better grace.° Adieu, my lord.
I never wished to see you sorry; now
I trust I shall. My women come, you have leave.

125 *Leontes.* Go, do our bidding: Hence.

[*Exeunt Queen and Ladies.*]

Lord. Beseech your Highness, call the Queen again.

Antigonus. Be certain what you do, sir, lest your justice
Prove violence, in the which three great ones suffer,
Yourself, your queen, your son.

Lord.   For her, my lord,
130 I dare my life lay down, and will do 't, sir,
Please you t' accept it, that the Queen is spotless
I' th' eyes of heaven, and to you—I mean,
In this, which you accuse her.

Antigonus.   If it prove
She's otherwise, I'll keep my stables where
135 I lodge my wife;° I'll go in couples° with her;
Than when I feel and see her, no farther trust her;
For every inch of woman in the world,
Ay, every dram of woman's flesh is false,
If she be.

Leontes. Hold your peaces.

Lord.   Good my lord.

140 *Antigonus.* It is for you we speak, not for ourselves.
You are abused, and by some putter-on°
That will be damned for 't. Would I knew the villain,
I would land-damn° him! Be she honor-flawed,
I have three daughters: the eldest is eleven;
145 The second and the third, nine and some five:
If this prove true, they'll pay for 't. By mine honor,

121–22 **this action . . . grace** by contrast with one who goes to prison to be disgraced, I embark on this course to add to my honesty and credit   134–35 **I'll
keep my stables . . . wife** (obscure but certainly coarse. He will keep his stal-
lions locked up when his wife is near?)   135 **go in couples** be coupled by a
leash to her, for safety's sake (of course, he means that if the Queen is unchaste,
other women must be even more so)   141 **putter-on** plotter, one who instigates
143 **land-damn** severely beat (?)

2.1.   THE WINTER'S TALE   29

I'll geld 'em all; fourteen they shall not see
To bring false generations.° They are co-heirs,
And I had rather glib° myself than they
Should not produce fair issue.

Leontes.   Cease, no more!   150
You smell this business with a sense as cold
As is a dead man's nose; but I do see 't, and feel 't,
As you feel doing thus; and see withal
The instruments that feel.°

Antigonus.   If it be so,
We need no grave to bury honesty;   155
There's not a grain of it the face to sweeten
Of the whole dungy earth.

Leontes.   What? Lack I credit?°

Lord. I had rather you did lack than I, my lord,
Upon this ground; and more it would content me
To have her honor true than your suspicion,   160
Be blamed for 't how you might.

Leontes.   Why, what need we
Commune with you of this, but rather follow
Our forceful instigation? Our prerogative
Calls not your counsels, but our natural goodness
Imparts this;° which, if you, or stupefied,   165
Or seeming so, in skill,° cannot, or will not,
Relish a truth like us, inform yourselves,
We need no more of your advice. The matter,
The loss, the gain, the ord'ring on 't,
Is all properly ours.

Antigonus.   And I wish, my liege,   170
You had only in your silent judgment tried it,
Without more overture.

---

148 **false generations** illegitimate children   149 **glib** castrate   152–54 **but I
do see . . . that feel** (Leontes here strikes either Antigonus or himself. "But I
see it and feel it with immediate, vital force, as you do when you strike yourself
thus [or, when I strike you thus]—you feel it and see the hands that inflicted the
pain")   157 **Lack I credit?** am I not believed   163–65 **Our prerogative . . .
imparts this** i.e., I'm not obliged to seek your advice; it's out of the goodness
of my heart that I tell you this (Leontes, on his dignity, uses the royal "we")
166 **skill** reason

Leontes.   How could that be?
　　　Either thou art most ignorant by age,
　　　Or thou wert born a fool. Camillo's flight,
175　 Added to their familiarity—
　　　Which was as gross as ever touched conjecture,°
　　　That lacked sight only, naught for approbation°
　　　But only seeing, all other circumstances
　　　Made up to th' deed—doth push on this proceeding.
180　 Yet, for a greater confirmation—
　　　For in an act of this importance, 'twere
　　　Most piteous to be wild°—I have dispatched in post
　　　To sacred Delphos,° to Apollo's temple,
　　　Cleomenes and Dion, whom you know
185　 Of stuffed sufficiency.° Now, from the oracle
　　　They will bring all,° whose spiritual counsel had,
　　　Shall stop, or spur me. Have I done well?

Lord. Well done, my lord.

Leontes. Though I am satisfied, and need no more
190　 Than what I know, yet shall the oracle
　　　Give rest to th' minds of others—such as he,°
　　　Whose ignorant credulity will not
　　　Come up to th' truth. So have we thought it good
　　　From our free person she should be confined,
195　 Lest that the treachery of the two fled hence
　　　Be left her to perform.° Come, follow us,
　　　We are to speak in public: for this business
　　　Will raise° us all.

Antigonus.   [*Aside*] To laughter, as I take it,
　· If the good truth were known.   *Exeunt.*

---

176 **as ever touched conjecture** as ever conjecture reached to   177 **approbation** proof   182 **wild** rash   183 **Delphos** Delos (Shakespeare mistakenly thought the oracle of Apollo was there rather than at Delphi. In this error he follows his source, *Pandosto*)   185 **stuffed sufficiency** more than adequate dependability   186 **all** the whole truth   191 **such as he** i.e., Antigonus   195–96 **Lest that ... perform** (referring to the "plot against his life and crown" of which he accuses all three)   198 **raise** rouse

Scene 2. [*Sicilia, a prison.*]

Enter Paulina, a Gentleman, [and Attendants].

Paulina. The keeper of the prison, call to him;
Let him have knowledge who I am.

                              [*Exit Gentleman.*]
                              Good lady,
No court in Europe is too good for thee—
What dost thou then in prison?

        [*Enter Gentleman with the*] Jailer.
                              Now, good sir,
You know me, do you not?

Jailer.   For a worthy lady,   5
And one whom much I honor.

Paulina.   Pray you, then,
Conduct me to the Queen.

Jailer.   I may not, madam,
To the contrary I have express commandment.

Paulina. Here's ado, to lock up honesty and honor
        from
Th' access of gentle visitors! Is 't lawful, pray you,   10
To see her women? Any of them? Emilia?

Jailer. So please you, madam,
To put apart these your attendants, I
Shall bring Emilia forth.

Paulina.   I pray now call her.
Withdraw yourselves.

                    [*Exit Gentleman and Attendants.*]

Jailer.   And, madam,   15
I must be present at your conference.

Paulina. Well, be 't so, prithee.   [*Exit Jailer.*]
    Here's such ado to make no stain a stain,
    As passes coloring.°

        [*Enter Jailer, with*] *Emilia.*

                Dear gentlewoman,
20   How fares our gracious lady?

Emilia. As well as one so great and so forlorn
    May hold together. On her frights and griefs
    (Which° never tender lady hath borne greater)
    She is, something before her time, delivered.

Paulina. A boy?

25 *Emilia.*   A daughter, and a goodly babe,
    Lusty, and like to live; the Queen receives
    Much comfort in 't; says, "My poor prisoner,
    I am innocent as you."

Paulina.   I dare be sworn.
    These dangerous, unsafe lunes° i' th' King, beshrew
      them!
30   He must be told on 't, and he shall; the office
    Becomes a woman best. I'll take 't upon me.
    If I prove honey-mouthed, let my tongue blister,°
    And never to my red-looked anger be
    The trumpet° any more. Pray you, Emilia,
35   Commend my best obedience to the Queen;
    If she dares trust me with her little babe,
    I'll show 't the King, and undertake to be
    Her advocate to th' loud'st. We do not know
    How he may soften at the sight o' th' child;
40   The silence often of pure innocence
    Persuades, when speaking fails.

Emilia.   Most worthy madam,
    Your honor and your goodness is so evident,

2.2.19 **coloring** the art of dyeing (thus giving a specious appearance)
23 **Which** than which   29 **lunes** fits of lunacy   32 **tongue blister** (because lies
were supposed to blister the tongue)   33–34 **red-looked ... trumpet** (the figure is of an angry face as a herald dressed in red and preceded by a trumpet[er])

That your free undertaking cannot miss
A thriving issue: there is no lady living
So meet° for this great errand. Please your ladyship   45
To visit the next room, I'll presently°
Acquaint the Queen of your most noble offer,
Who but today hammered of° this design,
But durst not tempt° a minister of honor
Lest she should be denied.

Paulina.   Tell her, Emilia,   50
I'll use that tongue I have; if wit° flow from 't
As boldness from my bosom, let 't not be doubted
I shall do good.

Emilia.   Now be you blest for it!
I'll to the Queen. Please you come something nearer.

Jailer. Madam, if 't please the Queen to send the babe,   55
I know not what I shall incur to pass it,°
Having no warrant.

Paulina.   You need not fear it, sir:
This child was prisoner to the womb and is
By law and process of great Nature thence
Freed, and enfranchised; not a party to   60
The anger of the King, nor guilty of,
If any be, the trespass of the Queen.

Jailer. I do believe it.

Paulina. Do not you fear—upon mine honor, I
Will stand betwixt you and danger.   *Exeunt.*   65

___

45 **meet** fitting 46 **presently** immediately 48 **hammered of** deliberated upon 49 **tempt** make trial of 51 **wit** wisdom 56 **to pass it** (as a result of allowing it to pass)

Scene 3. [*Sicilia, the Court of Leontes.*]

Enter Leontes, Servants, Antigonus, and Lords.

Leontes. Nor night nor day no rest: it is but weakness
To bear the matter thus, mere weakness. If
The cause were not in being—part o' th' cause,°
She, th' adult'ress (for the harlot° king
5   Is quite beyond mine arm, out of the blank
And level° of my brain, plot-proof); but she,
I can hook to me—say that she were gone,
Given to the fire, a moiety° of my rest
Might come to me again. Who's there?

Servant.   My lord!

Leontes. How does the boy?

10   *First Attendant.* He took good rest tonight; 'tis hoped
His sickness is discharged.

Leontes.   To see his nobleness!
Conceiving the dishonor of his mother,
He straight declined, drooped, took it deeply,
Fastened, and fixed the shame on 't in himself;
15   Threw off his spirit, his appetite, his sleep,
And downright languished. Leave me solely; go,
See how he fares.   [*Exit Servant.*]
                      Fie, fie, no thought of him!°
The very thought of my revenges that way
Recoil upon me—in himself too mighty,
20   And in his parties, his alliance; let him be,

2.3.3 **th' cause** (Leontes interrupts himself, remembering that Polixenes is inaccessible, so that only part of the cause of his agony is within his power to destroy)   4 **harlot** lewd   5–6 **out of the blank/ And level** beyond my range ("blank" is the center of the target; "level" means "aim." The reference is to archery)   8 **moiety** half   17 **no thought of him** i.e., of Polixenes

Until a time may serve. For present vengeance
Take it on her. Camillo and Polixenes
Laugh at me, make their pastime at my sorrow;
They should not laugh if I could reach them, nor
Shall she within my power.

Enter Paulina [with the Baby].

Lord.   You must not enter.   25

Paulina. Nay, rather, good my lords, be second to° me.
  Fear you his tyrannous passion more, alas,
  Than the Queen's life? A gracious innocent soul,
  More free° than he is jealous.

Antigonus.   That's enough.

Servant. Madam, he hath not slept tonight, commanded   30
  None should come at him.

Paulina.   Not so hot, good sir;
  I come to bring him sleep. 'Tis such as you
  That creep like shadows by him, and do sigh
  At each his needless heavings—such as you
  Nourish the cause of his awaking. I   35
  Do come with words as medicinal as true,
  Honest as either, to purge him of that humor°
  That presses him from sleep.

Leontes.   What noise there, ho?

Paulina. No noise, my lord, but needful conference
  About some gossips° for your Highness.

Leontes.   How?   40
  Away with that audacious lady! Antigonus,
  I charged thee that she should not come about me;
  I knew she would.

Antigonus.   I told her so, my lord,
  On your displeasure's peril, and on mine,
  She should not visit you.

Leontes.   What? Canst not rule her?   45

26 **be second to** support   29 **free** innocent   37 **humor** illness   40 **gossips** godparents

Paulina. From all dishonesty he can: in this,
         Unless he take the course that you have done—
         Commit me for committing° honor, trust it,
         He shall not rule me.

Antigonus.   La you now, you hear,
50   When she will take the rein, I let her run;
         But she'll not stumble.°

Paulina.   Good my liege, I come—
         And I beseech you hear me, who profess
         Myself your loyal servant, your physician,
         Your most obedient counselor; yet that dares
55   Less appear so in comforting° your evils,
         Than such as most seem yours°—I say, I come
         From your good queen.

Leontes.   Good queen!

Paulina. Good queen, my lord, good queen, I say good
              queen,
         And would by combat° make her good, so were I
         A man, the worst° about you.

60 *Leontes.*   Force her hence.

Paulina. Let him that makes but trifles of his eyes
         First hand me. On mine own accord I'll off,
         But first I'll do my errand. The good queen
         (For she is good) hath brought you forth a daughter;
         Here 'tis; commends it to your blessing.
                                   [*She lays down the Baby.*]

65 *Leontes.*   Out!
         A mankind° witch! Hence with her, out o' door!

---

48 **Commit . . . committing** (the word is used in a punning sense, first meaning "send to prison," and secondly, "performing")   50–51 **rein . . . run . . .
stumble** (Antigonus, as usual, speaks of his wife as if she were a
horse)   55 **comforting** abetting, countenancing   56 **as most seem yours** as
are nearest to you   59 **by combat** in a trial by combat (which would, in the
code of chivalry, vindicate a lady's honor)   60 **the worst** the lowest in degree   66 **mankind** male, ferocious, violent

A most intelligencing° bawd!

Paulina.   Not so;
I am as ignorant in that as you
In so entitling me; and no less honest
Than you are mad; which is enough, I'll warrant,   70
As this world goes, to pass for honest.

Leontes.   Traitors!
Will you not push her out? [*To Antigonus*] Give her
  the bastard,
Thou dotard, thou art woman-tired,° unroosted
By thy Dame Partlet° here. Take up the bastard,
Take 't up, I say; give 't to thy crone.

Paulina.   Forever   75
Unvenerable be thy hands, if thou
Tak'st up the Princess, by that forcèd baseness°
Which he has put upon 't!

Leontes.   He dreads his wife.

Paulina. So I would you did; then 'twere past all doubt
  You'd call your children yours.

Leontes.   A nest of traitors.   80

Antigonus. I am none, by this good light.

Paulina.   Nor I: nor any
But one that's here, and that's himself; for he, .
The sacred honor of himself, his queen's,
His hopeful son's, his babe's, betrays to slander,
Whose sting is sharper than the sword's; and will not   85
(For as the case now stands, it is a curse
He cannot be compelled to 't) once remove
The root of his opinion, which is rotten
As ever oak or stone was sound.

Leontes.   A callat°
Of boundless tongue, who late hath beat her husband,   90

---

67 **intelligencing** i.e., acting as a pander 73 **woman-tired** henpecked 74 **Dame Partlet** (traditionally the name of the hen; compare Reynard the fox, etc.) 77 **forcèd baseness** falsely base name (bastard) 89 **callat** scold

And now baits° me! This brat is none of mine;
It is the issue of Polixenes.
Hence with it, and together with the dam,
Commit them to the fire.

Paulina.   It is yours:
95   And might we lay th' old proverb° to your charge,
So like you, 'tis the worse. Behold, my lords,
Although the print be little, the whole matter
And copy° of the father: eye, nose, lip,
The trick of 's frown, his forehead, nay, the valley,
The pretty dimples of his chin and cheek; his
100   smiles;
The very mold and frame of hand, nail, finger.
And thou, good goddess Nature, which hast made it
So like to him that got° it, if thou hast
The ordering of the mind too, 'mongst all colors
105   No yellow° in 't, lest she suspect, as he does,
Her children not her husband's.

Leontes.   A gross hag!
And lozel,° thou art worthy to be hanged,
That wilt not stay her tongue.

Antigonus.   Hang all the husbands
That cannot do that feat, you'll leave yourself
Hardly one subject.

110 *Leontes.*   Once more, take her hence.

Paulina. A most unworthy and unnatural lord
Can do no more.

Leontes.   I'll ha' thee burned.

Paulina.   I care not;
It is an heretic that makes the fire,
Not she which burns in 't. I'll not call you tyrant;
115   But this most cruel usage of your queen
(Not able to produce more accusation

90–91 **beat . . . baits** (pronounced alike)   95 **th' old proverb** i.e., "They are
so like that they are the worse for it"   97–98 **print . . . matter . . . copy** (the
figure is derived from printing)   103 **got** begot   105 **yellow** (the color of
jealousy)   107 **lozel** worthless fellow

Than your own weak-hinged° fancy) something
  savors
Of tyranny, and will ignoble make you,
Yea, scandalous to the world.

Leontes.   On your allegiance,°
  Out of the chamber with her! Were I a tyrant,°   *120*
  Where were her life? She durst not call me so,
  If she did know me one. Away with her.

Paulina. I pray you do not push me, I'll be gone.
  Look to your babe, my lord, 'tis yours: Jove send her
  A better guiding spirit. What needs these hands?   *125*
  You, that are thus so tender o'er his follies,
  Will never do him good, not one of you.
  So, so; farewell, we are gone.   *Exit.*

Leontes. Thou, traitor, hast set on thy wife to this.
  My child? Away with 't! Even thou, that hast   *130*
  A heart so tender o'er it, take it hence,
  And see it instantly consumed with fire.
  Even thou, and none but thou. Take it up straight;
  Within this hour bring me word 'tis done,
  And by good testimony, or I'll seize° thy life,   *135*
  With what thou else call'st thine; if thou refuse,
  And wilt encounter with my wrath, say so;
  The bastard brains with these my proper° hands
  Shall I dash out. Go, take it to the fire,
  For thou sett'st on thy wife.

Antigonus.   I did not, sir;   *140*
  These lords, my noble fellows, if they please,
  Can clear me in 't.

Lords.   We can: my royal liege,
  He is not guilty of her coming hither.

Leontes. You're liars all.

---

117 **weak-hinged** ill-supported (a door hangs on its hinges)   119 **On your allegiance** (the ultimate command; to disobey it is treason)   120 **tyrant**
(Paulina avoided calling him tyrant, but in coming close to so doing reminded
him that this interpretation might all too easily be put upon his actions)
135 **seize** confiscate   138 **proper** own

145 *Lord.* Beseech your Highness, give us better credit.
  We have always truly served you, and beseech
  So to esteem of us; and on our knees we beg,
  As recompense of our dear services
  Past, and to come, that you do change this purpose,
150   Which being so horrible, so bloody, must
  Lead on to some foul issue. We all kneel.

  Leontes. I am a feather for each wind that blows.
  Shall I live on to see this bastard kneel
  And call me father? Better burn it now
155   Than curse it then. But be it; let it live.
  It shall not neither. You, sir, come you hither:
  You that have been so tenderly officious
  With Lady Margery,° your midwife there,
  To save this bastard's life—for 'tis a bastard,
  So sure as this beard's gray°—what will you adven-
160   ture,
  To save this brat's life?

  Antigonus.   Anything, my lord,
  That my ability may undergo,
  And nobleness impose—at least thus much:
  I'll pawn° the little blood which I have left,
165   To save the innocent—anything possible.

  Leontes. It shall be possible. Swear by this sword°
  Thou wilt perform my bidding.

  Antigonus.   I will, my lord.

  Leontes. Mark, and perform it: seest thou? For the
  fail°
  Of any point in 't, shall not only be
170   Death to thyself, but to thy lewd-tongued wife,
  Whom for this time we pardon. We enjoin thee,
  As thou art liegeman to us, that thou carry
  This female bastard hence, and that thou bear it
  To some remote and desert place, quite out

---

158 **Lady Margery** (another facetious name of the hen)   160 **this beard's gray** (Leontes here, presumably, refers to—perhaps touches—the beard of Antigonus)   164 **pawn** pledge   166 **by this sword** by the cross on the handle, or that formed by the hilt and the blade   168 **fail** failure

Of our dominions; and that there thou leave it,   175
Without more mercy, to its own protection
And favor of the climate. As by strange fortune
It came to us, I do in justice charge thee,
On thy soul's peril, and thy body's torture,
That thou commend it strangely° to some place,   180
Where chance may nurse or end it. Take it up.

Antigonus. I swear to do this, though a present death
Had been more merciful. Come on, poor babe,
Some powerful spirit instruct the kites and ravens
To be thy nurses! Wolves and bears, they say,   185
Casting their savageness aside, have done
Like offices of pity. Sir, be prosperous
In more than this deed does require!° And blessing
Against this cruelty fight on thy side,
Poor thing, condemned to loss. *Exit* [*with the Baby*].

Leontes.   No, I'll not rear   190
Another's issue.

                    Enter a Servant.

Servant.   Please your Highness, posts
From those you sent to th' oracle are come
An hour since: Cleomenes and Dion,
Being well arrived from Delphos, are both landed,
Hasting to th' court.

Lord.   So please you, sir, their speed   195
Hath been beyond accompt.°

Leontes.   Twenty-three days
They have been absent; 'tis good speed; foretells
The great Apollo suddenly will have
The truth of this appear. Prepare you, lords,
Summon a session,° that we may arraign   200
Our most disloyal lady; for as she hath
Been publicly accused, so shall she have
A just and open trial. While she lives,
My heart will be a burden to me. Leave me,
And think upon my bidding.   *Exeunt.*   205

180 **strangely** as a stranger   188 **require** deserve   196 **beyond accompt** un-
precedented   200 **session** judicial trial or investigation

ACT 3

Scene 1. [*Sicilia. On a high road.*]

Enter Cleomenes and Dion.

Cleomenes. The climate's delicate, the air most sweet,
    Fertile the isle,° the temple much surpassing
    The common praise it bears.

Dion.   I shall report,
    For most it caught me, the celestial habits°
5 (Methinks I so should term them) and the reverence
    Of the grave wearers. O, the sacrifice,
    How ceremonious, solemn, and unearthly
    It was i' th' off'ring!

Cleomenes.   But of all, the burst
    And the ear-deaf'ning voice o' th' oracle,
10 Kin to Jove's thunder, so surprised my sense,
    That I was nothing.

Dion.   If th' event° o' th' journey
    Prove as successful to the Queen (O be 't so!)
    As it hath been to us rare, pleasant, speedy,
    The time is worth the use on 't.

Cleomenes.   Great Apollo
15 Turn all to th' best; these proclamations,

3.1.2 **the isle** i.e., Delos (as in 2.1.183; again by mistake for Delphi)   4 **celestial habits** heavenly clothing   11 **event** outcome

42

So forcing faults upon Hermione,
I little like.

Dion.   The violent carriage° of it
Will clear or end the business when the oracle,
Thus by Apollo's great divine° sealed up,
Shall the contents discover, something rare   20
Even then will rush to knowledge. Go; fresh horses,
And gracious be the issue!   _Exeunt._

Scene 2. [_Sicilia, a court of justice._]

Enter Leontes, Lords, Officers.

Leontes. This session, to our great grief we pronounce,
Even pushes 'gainst our heart. The party tried,
The daughter of a king, our wife, and one
Of us too much beloved. Let us be cleared
Of being tyrannous, since we so openly   5
Proceed in justice, which shall have due course,
Even to the guilt or the purgation.°
Produce the prisoner.

Officer. It is his Highness' pleasure that the Queen
Appear in person here in court.

[_Enter_] _Hermione, as to her trial,_° [_Paulina and_]
Ladies.

                    Silence.°   10

Leontes. Read the indictment.

Officer. "Hermione, Queen to the worthy Leontes, King
of Sicilia, thou art here accused and arraigned of high

---

17 **carriage** management   19 **great divine** chief priest   3.2.7 **purgation**
acquittal   10 s.d. **as to her trial** (this direction occurs in the Folio at the head
of the scene)   10 **Silence** (italic in Folio, as if a stage direction. But presumably the Officer calls out the word)

treason, in committing adultery with Polixenes, King
15 of Bohemia, and conspiring with Camillo to take away
the life of our sovereign lord the King, thy royal husband; the pretense° whereof being by circumstances
partly laid open, thou, Hermione, contrary to the faith
and allegiance of a true subject, didst counsel and aid
20 them, for their better safety, to fly away by night."

Hermione. Since what I am to say must be but that
Which contradicts my accusation, and
The testimony on my part no other
But what comes from myself, it shall·scarce boot°
me
25 To say, "Not guilty"; mine integrity
Being counted falsehood, shall, as I express it,
Be so received. But thus: if powers divine
Behold our human actions—as they do—
I doubt not then, but Innocence shall make
30 False Accusation blush, and Tyranny
Tremble at Patience. You, my lord, best know—
Who least will seem to do so—my past life
Hath been as continent, as chaste, as true,
As I am now unhappy; which is more
35 Than history can pattern,° though devised
And played to take° spectators. For behold me,
A fellow of the royal bed, which owe°
A moiety of the throne, a great king's daughter,
The mother to a hopeful prince, here standing
40 To prate and talk for life and honor, 'fore
Who please to come and hear. For life, I prize it
As I weigh grief, which I would spare; for honor,
'Tis a derivative from me to·mine,°
And only that I stand for. I appeal
45 To your own conscience, sir, before Polixenes
Came to your court, how I was in your grace,
How merited to be so; since he came,
With what encounter so uncurrent, I

17 **pretense** design   24 **boot** assist   35 **can pattern** can offer parallels
36 **take** move   37 **owe** own   42 **'Tis . . . mine** i.e., it is my son's inheritance

Have strained t' appear thus;° if one jot beyond
The bound of honor, or in act or will   50
That way inclining,° hardened be the hearts
Of all that hear me, and my near'st of kin
Cry fie upon my grave!

Leontes.   I ne'er heard yet
That any of these bolder vices wanted
Less impudence to gainsay what they did,   55
Than to perform it first.°

Hermione.   That's true enough,
Though 'tis a saying, sir, not due to me.

Leontes. You will not own it.

Hermione.   More than mistress of
Which comes to me in name of fault, I must not
At all acknowledge.° For Polixenes,   60
With whom I am accused, I do confess
I loved him, as in honor he required;°
With such a kind of love, as might become
A lady like me; with a love, even such,
So, and no other, as yourself commanded;   65
Which not to have done, I think had been in me
Both disobedience and ingratitude
To you, and toward your friend, whose love had
    spoke,
Even since it could speak, from an infant, freely,
That it was yours. Now, for conspiracy,   70
I know not how it tastes, though it be dished°
For me to try how; all I know of it,
Is that Camillo was an honest man;
And why he left your court, the gods themselves,
Wotting° no more than I, are ignorant.   75

48–49 With what . . . appear thus by what outrageous conduct I have acted so
unlike myself as to bring upon myself the ordeal of this appearance in
court   **50–51 or in act . . . inclining** either in performance or intention
approaching the bounds of honor   **55–56 Less impudence . . . first** (the point
is that if one is bold enough to commit the crime one will be bold enough
to deny it; but the expression is not very clear)   **58–60 More than mistress . . .
acknowledge** I must refuse to acknowledge as my own, faults which I do not in
fact possess   **62 required** was entitled to   **71 dished** served (as of food)
75 Wotting if they know

Leontes. You knew of his departure, as you know
　　What you have underta'en to do in 's absence.

Hermione.   Sir,
　　You speak a language that I understand not.
　　My life stands in the level° of your dreams,
　　Which I'll lay down.

80 *Leontes.*   Your actions are my dreams.
　　You had a bastard by Polixenes,
　　And I but dreamed it. As you were past all shame—
　　Those of your fact° are so—so past all truth;
　　Which to deny concerns more than avails;° for as
85 Thy brat hath been cast out, like to itself,°
　　No father owning it (which is indeed
　　More criminal in thee than it) so thou
　　Shalt feel our justice; in whose easiest passage
　　Look for no less than death.

Hermione.   Sir, spare your threats:
90 The bug° which you would fright me with, I seek.
　　To me can life be no commodity.°
　　The crown and comfort of my life, your favor,
　　I do give° lost, for I do feel it gone,
　　But know not how it went. My second joy,
95 And first fruits of my body, from his presence
　　I am barred, like one infectious. My third comfort,
　　Starred° most unluckily, is from my breast,
　　The innocent milk in its most innocent mouth,
　　Haled out to murder. Myself on every post°
100 Proclaimed a strumpet; with immodest hatred
　　The childbed privilege denied, which 'longs°
　　To women of all fashion.° Lastly, hurried

---

79 **level** range (archery)　83 **Those of your fact** those guilty of your crime
84 **concerns more than avails** is more trouble to you than it's worth　85 **like
to itself** i.e., appropriately, since it has no father　90 **bug** bogey, bugbear
91 **commodity** advantage, asset　93 **give** reckon as　97 **starred** fated　99 **post**
(on which public notices and advertisements were placed. In Greene's novel
the King issues a proclamation concerning his wife's guilt, which is "blazed
through the country")　101 **longs** belongs　102 **fashion** rank

Here to this place, i' th' open air, before
I have got strength of limit.° Now, my liege,
Tell me, what blessings I have here alive,   *105*
That I should fear to die? Therefore proceed.
But yet hear this—mistake me not: for life,
I prize it not a straw, but for mine honor,
Which I would free—if I shall be condemned
Upon surmises, all proofs sleeping else   *110*
But what your jealousies awake, I tell you
'Tis rigor, and not law.° Your honors all,
I do refer me to the oracle:
Apollo be my judge!

Lord.   This your request
Is altogether just; therefore bring forth,   *115*
And in Apollo's name, his oracle. [*Exeunt Officers.*]

Hermione. The Emperor of Russia° was my father.
Oh that he were alive, and here beholding
His daughter's trial! That he did but see
The flatness° of my misery; yet with eyes   *120*
Of pity, not revenge!

    [*Enter Officers, with*] *Cleomenes* [*and*] *Dion.*

Officer. You here shall swear upon this sword of
    justice,
That you, Cleomenes and Dion, have
Been both at Delphos, and from thence have brought
This sealed-up oracle, by the hand delivered   *125*
Of great Apollo's priest; and that since then
You have not dared to break the holy seal,
Nor read the secrets in 't.

Cleomenes, Dion.   All this we swear.

Leontes. Break up the seals and read.

Officer. "Hermione is chaste, Polixenes blameless, Ca-   *130*
    millo a true subject, Leontes a jealous tyrant, his
    innocent babe truly begotten, and the King shall live
    without an heir, if that which is lost be not found."

104 **strength of limit** strength to go out   112 **rigor, and not law** tyranny, not
justice   117 **Emperor of Russia** (in *Pandosto* it is the wife of Polixenes who
is daughter of this emperor)   120 **flatness** completeness

Lords. Now blessèd be the great Apollo!

Hermione.   Praised!

Leontes. Hast thou read truth?

135 *Officer.*   Ay, my lord, even so
    As it is here set down.

Leontes. There is no truth at all i' th' oracle.
    The sessions shall proceed; this is mere falsehood.

          [*Enter a Servant.*]

Servant. My lord, the King, the King!

Leontes.   What is the business?

140 *Servant.* O sir, I shall be hated to report it.
    The Prince, your son, with mere conceit° and fear
    Of the Queen's speed,° is gone.

Leontes.   How? Gone?

Servant.   Is dead.

Leontes. Apollo's angry, and the heavens themselves
    Do strike at my injustice. [*Hermione faints.*] How
    now there!

Paulina. This news is mortal° to the Queen—look
145   down
    And see what death is doing.

Leontes.   Take her hence;
    Her heart is but o'ercharged, she will recover.
    I have too much believed mine own suspicion.
    Beseech you tenderly apply to her
    Some remedies for life.

          [*Exeunt Paulina and Ladies, with Hermione.*]

150   Apollo, pardon
    My great profaneness 'gainst thine oracle.
    I'll reconcile me to Polixenes,
    New woo my queen, recall the good Camillo—

141 **conceit** concept, thought   142 **speed** fortune, success   145 **mortal** deadly

Whom I proclaim a man of truth, of mercy.
For, being transported by my jealousies   155
To bloody thoughts and to revenge, I chose
Camillo for the minister to poison
My friend Polixenes; which had been done,
But that the good mind of Camillo tardied
My swift command, though I with death and with   160
Reward did threaten and encourage him,
Not doing it and being done.° He, most humane,
And filled with honor, to my kingly guest
Unclasped my practice,° quit his fortunes here—
Which you knew great—and to the hazard°   165
Of all incertainties himself commended,
No richer than his honor. How he glisters
Through my rust!° And how his piety
Does my deeds make the blacker!

[*Enter Paulina.*]

Paulina.   Woe the while!
O cut my lace,° lest my heart, cracking it,   170
Break too!

Lord. What fit is this, good lady?

Paulina. What studied torments, tyrant, hast for me?
What wheels, racks, fires? What flaying, boiling
In leads or oils? What old or newer torture   175
Must I receive, whose every word deserves
To taste of thy most worst. Thy tyranny,
Together working with thy jealousies,
Fancies too weak for boys, too green and idle
For girls of nine—O, think what they have done,   180
And then run mad indeed, stark mad; for all

160–62 **though I ... being done** though I threatened him with death for not
doing it, and promised him rewards for doing it   164 **Unclasped my practice**
revealed my plot   165 **Which ... hazard** (the line apparently lacks a foot,
which the Second Folio—with the approval of some editors—supplies by in-
serting the word "certain" before "hazard")   168 **Through my rust** (again, to
mend the meter, F2 reads "through my dark rust." Some editors read "Thorough," which is interchangeable with "Through")   170 **cut my lace** (to give
her more breath)

Thy bygone fooleries were but spices° of it.
That thou betrayedst Polixenes, 'twas nothing;
That did but show thee, of a fool,° inconstant,
185 And damnable ingrateful. Nor was 't much
Thou wouldst have poisoned good Camillo's honor,
To have him kill a king—poor trespasses,
More monstrous standing by;° whereof I reckon
The casting forth to crows thy baby daughter
190 To be or none, or little; though a devil
Would have shed water out of fire,° ere done 't;
Nor is 't directly laid to thee the death
Of the young Prince, whose honorable thoughts,
Thoughts high for one so tender, cleft the heart
195 That could conceive a gross and foolish sire
Blemished his gracious dam. This is not, no,
Laid to thy answer; but the last—O lords,
When I have said,° cry "woe": the Queen, the Queen,
The sweet'st, dear'st creature's dead; and vengeance for 't
Not dropped down yet.

200 *Lords.*   The higher pow'rs forbid!

Paulina. I say she's dead; I'll swear 't. If word nor oath
Prevail not, go and see; if you can bring
Tincture or luster in her lip, her eye,
Heat outwardly or breath within, I'll serve you
205 As I would do the gods. But, O thou tyrant,
Do not repent these things, for they are heavier
Than all thy woes can stir;° therefore betake thee
To nothing but despair. A thousand knees,
Ten thousand years together, naked, fasting,
210 Upon a barren mountain, and still winter°
In storm perpetual, could not move the gods
To look that way thou wert.

Leontes.   Go on, go on;

---

182 **spices** samples   184 **of a fool** for a fool   188 **standing by** i.e., and so available for comparison   191 **shed water out of fire** wept out of burning eyes   198 **said** said it   207 **all thy woes can stir** all thy penitence can remove   218 **still winter** forever winter

Thou canst not speak too much, I have deserved
All tongues to talk their bitt'rest.

Lord.   Say no more;
Howe'er the business goes, you have made fault   215
I' th' boldness of your speech.

Paulina.   I am sorry for 't;
All faults I make, when I shall come to know them,
I do repent. Alas, I have showed too much
The rashness of a woman; he is touched
To th' noble heart. What's gone and what's past
   help   220
Should be past grief; do not receive affliction
At my petition;° I beseech you, rather
Let me be punished that have minded you
Of what you should forget. Now, good my liege,
Sir, royal sir, forgive a foolish woman.   225
The love I bore your queen—lo, fool again!
I'll speak of her no more, nor of your children;
I'll not remember° you of my own lord,
Who is lost too. Take your patience to you,
And I'll say nothing.

Leontes.   Thou didst speak but well,°   230
When most the truth° which I receive much better
Than to be pitied of thee. Prithee bring me
To the dead bodies of my queen and son.
One grave shall be for both; upon them shall
The causes of their death appear, unto   235
Our shame perpetual. Once a day I'll visit
The chapel where they lie, and tears shed there
Shall be my recreation.° So long as nature
Will bear up with this exercise, so long
I daily vow to use it. Come, and lead me   240
To these sorrows.   *Exeunt.*

221–22 **do not receive ... petition** I would not have you suffer because I prayed that you should   228 **remember** remind   230–31 **Thou didst ... the truth** You spoke well only when most telling the truth   238 **recreation** diversion (to do so will be his only pastime)

Scene 3. [*Bohemia,° the seacoast.*]

Enter Antigonus [and] a Mariner, [with a] Babe.

Antigonus. Thou art perfect° then our ship hath touched
    upon
The deserts of Bohemia?

Mariner.   Ay, my lord, and fear
We have landed in ill time; the skies look grimly,
And threaten present blusters. In my conscience,°
5   The heavens with that we have in hand are angry
And frown upon 's.

Antigonus. Their sacred wills be done! Go get aboard,
Look to thy bark, I'll not be long before
I call upon thee.

Mariner.   Make your best haste, and go not
10   Too far i' th' land; 'tis like to be loud weather;
Besides, this place is famous for the creatures
Of prey that keep° upon 't.

Antigonus.   Go thou away,
I'll follow instantly.

Mariner.   I am glad at heart
To be so rid o' th' business.   *Exit.*

Antigonus.   Come, poor babe;
15   I have heard, but not believed, the spirits o' th' dead
May walk again; if such thing be,° thy mother
Appeared to me last night; for ne'er was dream

3.3.s.d. **Bohemia** (substituted for the Sicily of *Pandosto.* Bohemia, as is noto-
rious, had no seacoast) 1 **perfect** certain 4 **conscience** knowledge, awareness (but with something of the modern meaning also) 12 **keep** live 16 **if
such thing be** (Antigonus takes the skeptical Protestant view as a rule, but is
convinced of the reality of the vision. Possibly Shakespeare, when he wrote
this scene, had not yet had the idea of reanimating Hermione)

So like awaking. To me comes a creature,
Sometimes her head on one side, some another;
I never saw a vessel of like sorrow   20
So filled, and so becoming.° In pure white robes,
Like very sanctity,° she did approach
My cabin° where I lay; thrice bowed before me,
And, gasping to begin some speech, her eyes
Became two spouts; the fury spent, anon   25
Did this break from her: "Good Antigonus,
Since fate, against thy better disposition,
Hath made thy person for the thrower-out
Of my poor babe, according to thine oath,
Places remote enough are in Bohemia,   30
There weep, and leave it crying; and for the babe
Is counted lost forever, Perdita°
I prithee call 't. For this ungentle business
Put on thee by my lord, thou ne'er shalt see
Thy wife Paulina more." And so, with shrieks,   35
She melted into air. Affrighted much,
I did in time collect myself, and thought
This was so,° and no slumber. Dreams are toys;°
Yet for this once, yea superstitiously,°
I will be squared° by this. I do believe   40
Hermione hath suffered death, and that
Apollo would (this being indeed the issue
Of King Polixenes) it should here be laid
Either for life, or death, upon the earth
Of its right father. Blossom, speed thee well!   45

                          [*He lays down the Baby.*]

There lie, and there thy character:° there these,

                          [*Lays down a bundle.*]

Which may, if Fortune please, both breed thee,°
   pretty,

21 **so filled and so becoming** so filled with sorrow, and so beautiful in
sorrow   22 **very sanctity** sanctity itself   23 **cabin** berth   32 **Perdita** (meaning "the lost girl")   38 **This was so** this was real   38 **toys** trifles   39 **superstitiously** (again the Protestant view of ghosts)   40 **squared** regulated,
ordered   46 **character** description (by which Perdita is later to be recognized)   47 **breed thee** raise you, pay for your upbringing

And still rest thine.° The storm begins; poor wretch,
That for thy mother's fault art thus exposed
50   To loss, and what may follow! Weep I cannot,°
But my heart bleeds; and most accursed am I
To be by oath enjoined to this. Farewell,
The day frowns more and more; thou 'rt like to have
A lullaby too rough; I never saw
55   The heavens so dim by day. A savage clamor!°
Well may I get aboard! This is the chase;°
I am gone forever.   *Exit, pursued by a bear.*

[Enter] Shepherd.

Shepherd. I would there were no age between ten and
three-and-twenty, or that youth would sleep out the
60   rest; for there is nothing in the between but getting
wenches with child, wronging the ancientry, stealing,
fighting. Hark you now! Would any but these boiled°
brains of nineteen and two-and-twenty hunt this
weather? They have scared away two of my
65   best sheep, which I fear the wolf will sooner find
than the master; if anywhere I have them, 'tis by the
seaside, browsing of ivy.° Good luck, an 't be thy
will, what have we here? Mercy on 's, a barne!° A
very pretty barne; a boy or a child,° I wonder?
70   A pretty one, a very pretty one; sure, some scape;°
though I am not bookish, yet I can read waiting-
gentlewoman in the scape. This has been some stair-
work, some trunk-work,° some behind-door-work;
they were warmer that got this than the poor thing
75   is here. I'll take it up for pity; yet I'll tarry till my
son come; he hallowed but even now. Whoa-ho
hoa!

---

48 **And still rest thine** there will be something over   50 **Weep I cannot**
(though the ghost had told him to)   55 **savage clamor** the noise of the
hunters   56 **chase** the bear   63 **boiled** seething, hot   67 **browsing of ivy**
("whereon they do greatly feed," according to *Pandosto*)   68 **barne** child
(compare mod. Scots "bairn")   69 **a boy or a child** a boy or a girl ("child" for
"girl" is a dialect form and presumably was so in 1610)   70 **scape** sexual mis-
adventure   73 **trunk-work** secret or clandestine action

Enter Clown.

Clown. Hilloa, loa!

Shepherd. What? Art so near? If thou 'lt see a thing to
talk on, when thou art dead and rotten, come hither.   80
What ail'st thou, man?

Clown. I have seen two such sights, by sea and by land!
But I am not to say it is a sea, for it is now the sky;
betwixt the firmament and it, you cannot thrust a
bodkin's point.   85

Shepherd. Why, boy, how is it?

Clown. I would you did but see how it chafes, how
it rages, how it takes up° the shore, but that's not
to the point. O, the most piteous cry of the poor
souls! Sometimes to see 'em, and not to see 'em;   90
now the ship boring the moon with her mainmast,
and anon swallowed with yeast and froth, as you'd
thrust a cork into a hogshead. And then for the
land-service,° to see how the bear tore out his
shoulder bone, how he cried to me for help, and   95
said his name was Antigonus, a nobleman! But to
make an end of the ship, to see how the sea flap-
dragoned° it; but first, how the poor souls roared,
and the sea mocked them; and how the poor
gentleman roared, and the bear mocked him, both   100
roaring louder than the sea or weather.

Shepherd. Name of mercy, when was this, boy?

Clown. Now, now; I have not winked since I saw these
sights; the men are not yet cold under water, nor
the bear half dined on the gentleman; he's at it now.   105

Shepherd: Would I had been by, to have helped the
old man!

Clown. I would you had been by the ship's side, to have

---

88 **takes up** rebukes   94 **land-service** i.e., the soldier who serves on land
(Antigonus) as opposed to the seamen aboard the ship (perhaps with a pun on
"service" meaning "dish"—Antigonus being food for the bear)   97–98 **flap-
dragoned** swallowed down (as drinkers swallowed flapdragons [raisins, etc.]
out of burning brandy)

helped her; there your charity would have lacked
110 footing.°

Shepherd. Heavy matters, heavy matters! But look
thee here, boy. Now bless thyself; thou met'st with
things dying, I with things new born. Here's a sight
for thee; look thee, a bearing-cloth° for a squire's
115 child; look thee here, take up, take up, boy; open
it; so, let's see; it was told me I should be rich by the
fairies. This is some changeling;° open 't; what's
within, boy?

Clown. You're a made° old man; if the sins of your
120 youth are forgiven you, you're well to live. Gold,
all gold!

Shepherd. This is fairy gold, boy, and 'twill prove so;
up with 't, keep it close;° home, home, the next°
way! We are lucky, boy, and to be so still° requires
125 nothing but secrecy. Let my sheep go; come, good
boy, the next way home.

Clown. Go you the next way with your findings, I'll go
see if the bear be gone from the gentleman, and
how much he hath eaten. They are never curst° but
130 when they are hungry. If there be any of him left,
I'll bury it.

Shepherd. That's a good deed. If thou mayest discern by
that which is left of him what he is, fetch me to th'
sight of him.

135 *Clown.* Marry° will I; and you shall help to put him i'
th' ground.

Shepherd. 'Tis a lucky day, boy, and we'll do good
deeds on 't.

Exeunt.

109-10 **charity ... footing** (alluding to the establishment of charitable foundations) 114 **bearing-cloth** christening robe 117 **changeling** (usually the
inferior child left by the fairies; here the child they stole, found with their gold,
which must be kept secret) 119 **made** (Folio reads "mad," but this emendation of Theobald is supported by the parallel passage in *Pandosto*) 123 **close**
secret 123 **next** nearest 124 **still** always 129 **curst** vicious 135 **Marry** indeed (from "By Mary")

ACT 4

Scene 1.

Enter Time, the Chorus.

Time. I that please some, try° all, both joy and terror
  Of good and bad; that makes and unfolds error,
  Now take upon me, in the name of Time,
  To use my wings. Impute it not a crime
  To me, or my swift passage, that I slide   5
  O'er sixteen years, and leave the growth untried°
  Of that wide gap, since it is in my pow'r
  To o'erthrow law, and in one self-born hour
  To plant, and o'erwhelm custom.° Let me pass;°
  The same I am, ere ancient'st order was   10
  Or what is now received. I witness to
  The times that brought them in; so shall I do
  To th' freshest things now reigning, and make stale
  The glistering of this present, as my tale
  Now seems to it.° Your patience this allowing,   15
  I turn my glass, and give my scene such growing

4.1.1 **try** test   6 **growth untried** (Time asks to be excused from detailed accounts of the interim period and its developments, for instance Perdita's childhood)   8–9 **law ... custom** (note the distinction: Time "plants" Custom but not Law. Custom lacks the authority of Law, and relates to erroneous Opinion; hence the contemporary use of the word in attacks on such ceremonies of the Roman Church as seemed to Protestants without Scriptural authority)   9 **Let me pass** ... (not clear in detail, but the sense is: Let me pass over that gap; I alone remain unchanged from the beginning—and have passed over that far greater gap)   14–15 **as my tale ... to it** as my tale seems stale compared with the play it interrupts

As you had slept between. Leontes leaving—
Th' effects of his fond° jealousies so grieving,
That he shuts up himself—imagine me,
20 Gentle spectators, that I now may be
In fair Bohemia; and remember well,
I mentioned° a son o' th' King's, which Florizel
I now name to you; and with speed so pace
To speak of Perdita, now grown in grace
25 Equal with wond'ring.° What of her ensues
I list not° prophesy; but let Time's news
Be known when 'tis brought forth. A shepherd's daughter,
And what to her adheres,° which follows after,°
Is th' argument° of Time. Of this allow,
30 If ever you have spent time worse, ere now;
If never, yet that Time himself doth say,
He wishes earnestly you never may.   *Exit.*

Scene 2. [*Bohemia, the Court of Polixenes.*]

Enter Polixenes and Camillo.

Polixenes. I pray thee, good Camillo, be no more importunate. 'Tis a sickness denying thee anything, a death to grant this.

Camillo. It is fifteen years since I saw my country;
5   though I have, for the most part, been aired abroad, I desire to lay my bones there. Besides, the penitent King, my master, hath sent for me, to whose feeling sorrows I might be some allay, or I

18 **fond** foolish   22 **mentioned** (unless the whole play is thought of as Time's report, this is not so; various emendations have been suggested, of which the best is "A mentioned son ...")   25 **Equal with wond'ring** to a degree demanding admiration   26 **I list not** I do not care to   28 **adheres** belongs   28 **after** (at this period an acceptable rhyme for "daughter")   29 **argument** story

o'erween to° think so, which is another spur to my
departure.   10

Polixenes. As thou lov'st me, Camillo, wipe not out the
rest of thy services by leaving me now. The need I
have of thee, thine own goodness hath made. Better
not to have had thee, than thus to want° thee; thou,
having made me businesses, which none, without   15
thee, can sufficiently manage, must either stay to
execute them thyself, or take away with thee the
very services thou hast done; which if I have not
enough considered—as too much I cannot—to be
more thankful to thee shall be my study, and my   20
profit therein the heaping friendships.° Of that fatal
country Sicilia, prithee speak no more, whose very
naming punishes me with the remembrance of that
penitent (as thou call'st him) and reconciled king,
my brother, whose loss of his most precious queen   25
and children are even now to be afresh lamented.
Say to me, when saw'st thou the Prince Florizel, my
son? Kings are no less unhappy, their issue not
being gracious, than they are in losing them when
they have approved their virtues.°   30

Camillo. Sir, it is three days since I saw the Prince.
What his happier affairs may be are to me unknown;
but I have missingly° noted, he is of late much
retired from court, and is less frequent to his
princely exercises° than formerly he hath appeared.   35

Polixenes. I have considered so much, Camillo, and
with some care, so far that I have eyes under my
service, which look upon his removedness;° from
whom I have this intelligence,° that he is seldom
from the house of a most homely shepherd—a man,   40
they say, that from very nothing, and beyond the

4.2.9 **o'erween** am boastful enough to   14 **want** be without   21 **friendships**
friendly offices   28–30 **Kings . . . virtues** it is as hard for kings to bear the disobedience and ill conduct of their children as to lose them when convinced of
their virtues   33 **missingly** (because he noted not the Prince, but his absence)
35 **exercises** military and sporting activities   37–38 **so far that . . . removedness** to the extent that I'm having him watched in the place where he is hiding
himself   39 **intelligence** report

imagination of his neighbors, is grown into an unspeakable estate.

Camillo. I have heard, sir, of such a man, who hath
45   a daughter of most rare note; the report of her is
extended more than can be thought to begin from
such a cottage.

Polixenes. That's likewise part of my intelligence; but, I
fear, the angle° that plucks our son thither. Thou
50   shalt accompany us to the place, where we will, not
appearing what we are, have some question° with
the shepherd; from whose simplicity I think it not
uneasy to get the cause of my son's resort thither.
Prithee be my present partner in this business, and
55   lay aside the thoughts of Sicilia.

Camillo. I willingly obey your command.

Polixenes. My best Camillo! We must disguise ourselves.

                              Exit [*Polixenes with Camillo*].

Scene 3. [*A road near the Shepherd's cottage.*]

Enter Autolycus, singing.

When daffodils begin to peer,
  With heigh the doxy° over the dale,
Why, then comes in the sweet o' the year,
  For the red blood reigns in the winter's pale.°

5   The white sheet bleaching on the hedge,
  With heigh the sweet birds, O how they sing!

---

49 **angle** fishhook   51 **question** talk   4.3.2 **doxy** beggar's mistress   4 **pale**
(1) enclosure (2) paleness

Doth set my pugging° tooth an edge,
For a quart of ale is a dish for a king.

The lark, that tirra-lirra chants,
With heigh, with heigh, the thrush and the jay!   10
Are summer songs for me and my aunts°
While we lie tumbling in the hay.

I have served Prince Florizel, and in my time wore
three-pile,° but now I am out of service.

But shall I go mourn for that, my dear?   15
    The pale moon shines by night;
And when I wander here and there
    I then do most go right.
If tinkers may have leave to live,
    And bear the sow-skin budget,°   20
Then my account I well may give,
    And in the stocks avouch° it.

My traffic is sheets; when the kite builds, look to
lesser linen.° My father named me Autolycus,° who
being, as I am, littered under Mercury,° was like-   25
wise a snapper-up of unconsidered trifles. With die
and drab,° I purchased this caparison, and my
revenue is the silly cheat.° Gallows and knock°
are too powerful on the highway. Beating and hanging are terrors to me; for the life to come, I sleep   30
out the thought of it. A prize, a prize.

---

7 **pugging** thieving (to "pug" means to "pull off"; perhaps Autolycus is thinking of his sheet-stealing; he is all set to begin snatching them off the hedges)
11 **aunts** whores   14 **three-pile** the best velvet   20 **sow-skin budget** pigskin
toolbag   22 **avouch** corroborate   23–24 **when the kite ... linen** (this is a
warning. The kite will use bits of household linen for its nest; Autolycus will
snatch your sheets)   24 **Autolycus** (son of Chione by Mercury, grandfather of
Ulysses; Homer says he excelled in thieving, and Ovid that "in theft and filch-
ing" he "had no peers")   25 **under Mercury** under the influence of the star
Mercury (Mercury was the patron of thieves)   26–27 **die and drab** (dice and
whores are responsible for my having no clothes but these)   28 **silly cheat**
simple (petty) theft   28 **knock** beating (the risks of highway robbery, death,
or combat on the road seem too great)

Enter Clown.

Clown. Let me see, every 'leven wether tods,° every tod
        yields pound and odd shilling; fifteen hundred shorn,
        what comes the wool to?

35 Autolycus. [*Aside*] If the springe° hold, the cock's°
        mine.

Clown. I cannot do 't without counters. Let me see,
        what am I to buy for our sheep-shearing feast?
        Three pound of sugar, five pound of currants, rice—
40   what will this sister of mine do with rice? But my
        father hath made her mistress of the feast, and she lays
        it on. She hath made me four-and-twenty nosegays
        for the shearers (three-man song-men° all, and very
        good ones), but they are most of them means°
45   and basses; but one Puritan amongst them, and he
        sings psalms to hornpipes.° I must have saffron to
        color the warden pies;° mace;° dates, none, that's
        out of my note; nutmegs, seven; a race or two of gin-
        ger, but that I may beg; four pound of prunes,
50   and as many of raisins o' th' sun.°

Autolycus. Oh, that ever I was born!

Clown. I' th' name of me!

Autolycus. Oh help me, help me; pluck but off these
        rags; and then, death, death!

55 Clown. Alack, poor soul, thou hast need of more rags to
        lay on thee, rather than have these off.

Autolycus. Oh sir, the loathsomeness of them offends
        me more than the stripes I have received, which are
        mighty ones and millions.

60 Clown. Alas, poor man, a million of beating may come
        to a great matter.

---

32 **every 'leven wether tods** every eleven sheep yield a tod (28 lbs.) of wool
35 **springe** snare   35 **cock's** woodcock's   43 **three-man song-men** singers
of lively catches for three voices   44 **means** tenors   46 **psalms to hornpipes**
i.e., he is an unusually cheerful Puritan   47 **warden pies** pies made of warden
pears   47 **mace** spice made of nutmeg   50 **o' th' sun** sun-dried

Autolycus. I am robbed, sir, and beaten; my money
and apparel ta'en from me, and these detestable
things put upon me.

Clown. What, by a horseman or a footman?°   65

Autolycus. A footman, sweet sir, a footman.

Clown. Indeed, he should be a footman, by the garments he has left with thee; if this be a horseman's
coat, it hath seen very hot service. Lend me thy
hand, I'll help thee. Come, lend me thy hand.   70

[*Helps him up.*]

Autolycus. Oh good sir, tenderly, oh!

Clown. Alas, poor soul!

Autolycus. Oh good sir, softly, good sir; I fear, sir,
my shoulder blade is out.

Clown. How now? Canst stand?   75

Autolycus. Softly, dear sir; good sir, softly; you ha'
done me a charitable office.

[*Picks his pocket.*]

Clown. Dost lack any money? I have a little money
for thee.

Autolycus. No, good sweet sir; no, I beseech you, sir;   80
I have a kinsman not past three-quarters of a mile
hence, unto whom I was going. I shall there have
money, or anything I want; offer me no money, I
pray you; that kills my heart.

Clown. What manner of fellow was he that robbed   85
you?

Autolycus. A fellow, sir, that I have known to go about
with troll-my-dames;° I knew him once a servant
of the Prince. I cannot tell, good sir, for which of
his virtues it was, but he was certainly whipped out   90
of the court.

Clown. His vices,° you would say; there's no virtue

---

65 **footman** foot soldier   88 **troll-my-dames** a game played by women,
rather like bagatelle   92 **vices** (the Clown fails to see Autolycus' little joke)

whipped out of the court; they cherish it to make it
stay there; and yet it will no more but abide.°

95 *Autolycus.* Vices, I would say, sir. I know this man
well; he hath been since an ape-bearer;° then a
process-server,° a bailiff: then he compassed a mo-
tion° of the Prodigal Son,° and married a tinker's
wife within a mile where my land and living° lies;
100 and, having flown over many knavish professions,
he settled only in rogue. Some call him Autolycus.

Clown. Out upon him! Prig,° for my life, prig! He
haunts wakes, fairs, and bear-baitings.

105 *Autolycus.* Very true, sir; he, sir, he; that's the rogue
that put me into this apparel.

Clown. Not a more cowardly rogue in all Bohemia; if
you had but looked big, and spit at him, he'd have
run.

110 *Autolycus.* I must confess to you, sir, I am no fighter; I
am false of heart that way, and that he knew, I warrant him.

Clown. How do you now?

Autolycus. Sweet sir, much better than I was. I can
115 stand and walk. I will even take my leave of you,
and pace softly towards my kinsman's.

Clown. Shall I bring thee on the way?

Autolycus. No, good-faced sir, no, sweet sir.

Clown. Then fare thee well; I must go buy spices for
120 our sheep-shearing.   *Exit.*

Autolycus. Prosper you, sweet sir! Your purse is not hot
enough to purchase your spice. I'll be with you at
your sheep-shearing too; if I make not this cheat

---

94 **abide** make a brief stay   96 **ape-bearer** one who carries a monkey about
for exhibition   97 **process-server** server of writs, bailiff   97–98 **compassed
a motion** got possession of a puppet show   98 **Prodigal Son** (a favorite
theme for representation)   99 **land and living** (Autolycus refers grandly to
his estates)   103 **Prig** thief

bring out another, and the shearers prove sheep, let
me be unrolled,° and my name put in the book of   125
virtue!

Song.

Jog on, jog on, the footpath way,
    And merrily hent° the stile-a;
A merry heart goes all the day,
    Your sad tires in a mile-a.   130

                                                   Exit.

Scene 4. [*Bohemia, the Shepherd's cottage.*]

Enter Florizel [and] Perdita.

Florizel. These your unusual weeds° to each part of
        you
Do give a life; no shepherdess, but Flora,°
Peering in April's front.° This your sheep-shearing
Is as a meeting of the petty gods,
And you the Queen on 't.

Perdita.   Sir, my gracious lord,   5
To chide at your extremes° it not becomes me—
Oh pardon, that I name them! Your high self,
The gracious mark° o' th' land, you have obscured
With a swain's wearing; and me, poor lowly maid,
Most goddesslike pranked up. But that our feasts   10
In every mess have folly, and the feeders
Digest it with a custom,° I should blush

125 **unrolled** struck off the honorable list of vagabonds   128 **hent** take hold
of (to leap over)   4.4.1 **unusual weeds** unaccustomed garments (Perdita is
dressed to be mistress of the feast)   2 **Flora** (Perdita's costume may have resembled that of the Roman goddess)   3 **Peering in April's front** i.e., Flora in
April, when the flowers peep out rather than boldly appear   6 **extremes** exag-
gerations   8 **mark** the object of everyone's attention   10–12 **our feasts . . .
custom** our feasts, at every social level, admit licensed folly, which the guests
tolerate, calling it a custom

To see you so attired; swoon, I think,
To show myself a glass.

Florizel.   I bless the time
15 When my good falcon made her flight across
Thy father's ground.

Perdita.   Now Jove afford you cause!
To me the difference° forges dread; your greatness
Hath not been used to fear. Even now I tremble
To think your father by some accident
20 Should pass this way, as you did: oh, the fates!
How would he look to see his work, so noble,
Vilely bound up?° What would he say? Or how
Should I, in these my borrowed flaunts,° behold
The sternness of his presence?

Florizel.   Apprehend
25 Nothing but jollity. The gods themselves,
Humbling their deities to love, have taken
The shapes of beasts upon them. Jupiter
Became a bull, and bellowed; the green Neptune
A ram, and bleated; and the fire-robed god,
30 Golden Apollo, a poor humble swain,°
As I seem now. Their transformations
Were never for a piece° of beauty rarer,
Nor in a way° so chaste, since my desires
Run not before mine honor, nor my lusts
Burn hotter than my faith.

35 *Perdita.*   Oh, but sir,
Your resolution cannot hold when 'tis
Opposed, as it must be, by th' power of the King.
One of these two must be necessities,
Which then will speak, that you must change this
   purpose,
Or I my life.°

---

17 **difference** i.e., in our ranks   22 **Vilely bound up** (the analogy is with a good
book shabbily bound)   23 **flaunts** finery   27-30 **Jupiter ... swain** (Jupiter
took the shape of a bull to carry off Europa; Neptune became a ram to woo Theo-
phane; Apollo served as a shepherd to help Admetus win Alcestis)   32 **piece**
work of art   33 **in a way** (he refers to the chastity of his intentions, not to Perdita
herself)   38-40 **One of these two ... I my life** i.e., the time will come when
Florizel will have to give up his plans, or Perdita will lose her life

Florizel.   Thou dearest Perdita,   40
     With these forced° thoughts, I prithee, darken not
     The mirth o' th' feast: or I'll be thine, my fair,
     Or° not my father's. For I cannot be
     Mine own, nor anything to any, if
     I be not thine. To this I am most constant,   45
     Though destiny say no. Be merry, gentle;
     Strangle such thoughts as these, with anything
     That you behold the while. Your guests are coming;
     Lift up your countenance, as it were the day
     Of celebration of that nuptial, which   50
     We two have sworn shall come.

Perdita.   O Lady Fortune,
     Stand you auspicious!

Florizel.   See, your guests approach.
     Address yourself to entertain them sprightly,
     And let's be red with mirth.

     [*Enter*] *Shepherd, Clown, Polixenes, Camillo*
     [*disguised*], *Mopsa, Dorcas, Servants.*

Shepherd. Fie, daughter! When my old wife lived, upon   55
     This day, she was both pantler,° butler, cook;
     Both dame and servant; welcomed all, served all;
     Would sing her song, and dance her turn; now here
     At upper end o' th' table, now i' th' middle;
     On his shoulder,° and his; her face o' fire   60
     With labor and the thing she took to quench it,
     She would to each one sip. You are retired,°
     As if you were a feasted one, and not
     The hostess of the meeting. Pray you bid
     These unknown friends to 's welcome, for it is   65
     A way to make us better friends, more known.
     Come, quench your blushes, and present yourself
     That which you are, mistress o' th' feast. Come on,
     And bid us welcome to your sheep-shearing,
     As your good flock shall prosper.

Perdita.   [*To Polixenes*] Sir,
     welcome.   70

---

41 **forced** strained, unduly fearful   42–43 **or ... Or** either ... or   56 **pantler** keeper of the pantry   60 **on his shoulder** at his shoulder   62 **retired** withdrawn

It is my father's will I should take on me
The hostess-ship o' th' day. [*To Camillo*] You're
     welcome, sir.
Give me those flow'rs there, Dorcas. Reverend sirs,
For you there's rosemary and rue; these keep
75   Seeming and savor° all the winter long.
Grace and remembrance° be to you both,
And welcome to our shearing!

Polixenes.   Shepherdess—
A fair one are you—well you fit our ages
With flow'rs of winter.

Perdita.   Sir, the year growing ancient,
80   Not yet on summer's death, nor on the birth
Of trembling winter, the fairest flow'rs o' th' season
Are our carnations, and streaked gillyvors,°
Which some call Nature's bastards;° of that kind
Our rustic garden's barren; and I care not
To get slips of them.

85   *Polixenes.*   Wherefore, gentle maiden,
Do you neglect them?

Perdita.   For I have heard it said,
There is an art, which in their piedness shares
With great creating Nature.

Polixenes.   Say there be;
Yet Nature is made better by no mean
90   But Nature makes that mean; so over that art,
Which you say adds to Nature, is an art,
That Nature makes. You see, sweet maid, we marry
A gentler scion to the wildest stock,
And make conceive a bark of baser kind
95   By bud of nobler race. This is an art

---

75 **Seeming and savor** color and scent   76 **Grace and remembrance** (rue is for grace and repentance; rosemary for remembrance, because the fragrance lasted indefinitely)   82 **gillyvors** pinks (sometimes in modern regional usage, "wallflowers"; but here Perdita means carnations, pinks, sweet william—the blooms have streaks of color, and for this reason were associated with loose women. The whole debate on the gillyvors is discussed in the Introduction)   83 **Nature's bastards** (see Introduction)

Which does mend Nature, change it rather; but
The art itself is Nature.°

Perdita.   So it is.

Polixenes. Then make your garden rich in gillyvors,
And do not call them bastards.

Perdita.   I'll not put
The dibble° in earth, to set one slip of them;   100
No more than were I painted, I would wish
This youth should say 'twere well, and only therefore
Desire to breed by me. Here's flow'rs for you:
Hot lavender,° mints, savory, marjoram,
The marigold that goes to bed wi' th' sun,   105
And with him rises, weeping; these are flow'rs
Of middle summer, and I think they are given
To men of middle age. You're very welcome.

Camillo. I should leave grazing, were I of your flock,
And only live by gazing.

Perdita.   Out, alas!   110
You'd be so lean that blasts of January
Would blow you through and through. [*To Florizel*]
Now, my fair'st friend,
I would I had some flow'rs o' th' spring, that might
Become your time of day—[*to Shepherdesses*] and
yours, and yours,
That wear upon your virgin branches yet   115
Your maidenheads growing. O Proserpina,
For the flow'rs now, that, frighted, thou let'st fall
From Dis's wagon!° Daffodils,
That come before the swallow dares, and take°
The winds of March with beauty; violets, dim,   120
But sweeter than the lids of Juno's eyes,

89–97 **Yet Nature is made … itself is Nature** (see Introduction)   100 **dib-ble** tool for making holes to plant seeds or cuttings   104 **Hot lavender** (the epithet has not been satisfactorily explained)   116–18 **Proserpina … Dis's wagon** (the God of the Underworld bore off Proserpina as she gathered flow-ers with her mother, Ceres, in the Vale of Enna. Ovid's account [*Metamor-phoses* V.398–99] mentions that she dropped the flowers she had picked)   119 **take** charm, captivate

Or Cytherea's° breath; pale primroses,
That die unmarried° ere they can behold
Bright Phoebus in his strength (a malady
125 Most incident to maids); bold oxlips, and
The crown imperial; lilies of all kinds,
The flower-de-luce being one. O, these I lack
To make you garlands of, and my sweet friend,
To strew him o'er and o'er!

Florizel.   What, like a corse?°

130 *Perdita.* No, like a bank for Love to lie and play on;
Not like a corse; or if, not to be buried,
But quick° and in mine arms. Come, take your
        flow'rs;
Methinks I play as I have seen them do
In Whitsun pastorals;° sure this robe of mine
Does change my disposition.

135 *Florizel.*   What you do
Still betters what is done. When you speak, sweet,
I'd have you do it ever; when you sing,
I'd have you buy and sell so; so give alms,
Pray so; and for the ord'ring your affairs,
140 To sing them too. When you do dance, I wish you
A wave o' th' sea, that you might ever do
Nothing but that—move still, still so,
And own no other function. Each your doing,
So singular in each particular,
145 Crowns what you are doing in the present deeds,
That all your acts are queens.°

Perdita.   O Doricles,°
Your praises are too large; but that your youth
And the true blood which peeps° fairly through 't,

---

122 **Cytherea's** Venus'   128 **die unmarried** (because it grows in shade, and
in spring, Milton has "the rathe primrose that forsaken dies")   129 **corse**
corpse   132 **quick** alive   134 **Whitsun pastorals** (Whitsun was the season
for games related to old spring festivals, and Perdita refers probably to the
King and Queen in these games—identified with Robin Hood and Marian)
143–46 **Each your doing ... queens** "Your manner in each act crowns the
act" (Dr. Johnson)   146 **Doricles** (Florizel's pseudonym)   148 **peeps** shows

Do plainly give you out an unstained shepherd,
With wisdom I might fear, my Doricles,   150
You wooed me the false way.°

Florizel.   I think you have
As little skill° to fear, as I have purpose
To put you to 't. But come, our dance, I pray;
Your hand, my Perdita; so turtles° pair
That never mean to part.

Perdita.   I'll swear for 'em.   155

Polixenes. This is the prettiest low-born lass that ever
Ran on the greensward; nothing she does or seems
But smacks of something greater than herself,
Too noble for this place.

Camillo.   He tells her something
That makes her blood look out;° good sooth° she
is   160
The queen of curds and cream.°

Clown.   Come on, strike up.

Dorcas. Mopsa must be your mistress; marry, garlic
To mend her kissing with!°

Mopsa.   Now, in good time!°

Clown. Not a word, a word, we stand upon our manners.
Come, strike up.   165

Here a dance of Shepherds and Shepherdesses.

Polixenes. Pray, good shepherd, what fair swain is this,
Which dances with your daughter?

Shepherd. They call him Doricles, and boasts himself
To have a worthy feeding;° but I have it

---

151 **the false way** i.e., by flattery 152 **skill** reason 154 **turtles** doves
160 **blood look out** blush 160 **good sooth** in truth 161 **queen of curds
and cream** (J. D. Wilson argues that Camillo is calling Perdita a "white-pot
queen"—the name given in some May games to the queen, by association with
a dish called "white-pot," made of custard, cream, spices, apples, etc.)
162–63 **garlic . . . kissing with** use garlic to overcome her bad breath 163 **in
good time** (expression of indignation) 169 **feeding** landed property

170 Upon his own report, and I believe it:
He looks like sooth. He says he loves my daughter;
I think so too; for never gazed the moon
Upon the water, as he'll stand and read,
As 'twere, my daughter's eyes; and, to be plain,
175 I think there is not half a kiss to choose
Who loves another° best.

Polixenes.   She dances featly.°

Shepherd. So she does anything, though I report it
That should be silent. If young Doricles
Do light upon her, she shall bring him that
180 Which he not dreams of.

Enter Servant.

Servant. O master, if you did but hear the peddler at
the door, you would never dance again after a
tabor° and pipe; no, the bagpipe could not move
you. He sings several tunes faster than you'll tell°
185 money; he utters them as he had eaten ballads,°
and all men's ears grew to his tunes.

Clown. He could never come better; he shall come in;
I love a ballad but even too well, if it be doleful
matter merrily set down; or a very pleasant thing
190 indeed, and sung lamentably.

Servant. He hath songs for man or woman of all sizes;
no milliner can so fit his customers with gloves. He
has the prettiest love songs for maids, so without
bawdry, which is strange; with such delicate bur-
195 dens° of dildos and fadings:° "Jump her, and thump
her";° and where some stretch-mouthed rascal
would, as it were, mean mischief, and break a foul
gap° into the matter, he makes the maid to answer,

---

176 **another** the other   176 **featly** nimbly   183 **tabor** little drum   184 **tell**
count 185 **ballads** broadsheet words and music, to familiar tunes and on topical subjects   194–95 **burdens** refrains   195 **dildos and fadings** (dildos, often mentioned in ballad refrains, are phalli; fadings are indecent refrains)
195–96 **Jump her and thump her** (familiar ballad refrains)   197–98 **foul
gap** i.e., a break in the song for obscene patter

"Whoop, do me no harm, good man";° puts him off,
slights him, with "Whoop, do me no harm, good
man." 200

Polixenes. This is a brave fellow.

Clown. Believe me, thou talkest of an admirable
conceited° fellow. Has he any unbraided° wares?

Servant. He hath ribbons of all the colors i' th' rain- 205
bow; points,° more than all the lawyers in Bohemia
can learnedly handle, though they come to him
by th' gross;° inkles,° caddisses,° cambrics, lawns.
Why, he sings 'em over, as they were gods or
goddesses; you would think a smock were a she- 210
angel, he so chants to the sleevehand,° and the
work about the square° on 't.

Clown. Prithee bring him in, and let him approach
singing.

Perdita. Forewarn him that he use no scurrilous words 215
in 's tunes.

[*Exit Servant.*]

Clown. You have of these peddlers° that have more in
them than you'd think, sister.

Perdita. Ay, good brother, or go about to° think.

Enter Autolycus, singing.

Lawn as white as driven snow, 220
Cypress° black as e'er was crow,
Gloves as sweet as damask roses,°
Masks for faces, and for noses;°

---

199 **Whoop . . . good man** (an extant ballad, coarse in character, has this refrain.
The joke in this speech lies in the servant's praising Autolycus for the decency
of his songs, and simultaneously betraying the fact of their indecency)
204 **conceited** witty   204 **unbraided** new ("braided wares" are shop-soiled)
206 **points** tagged laces, by which clothes were held up (with a pun on the sense
of "arguments")   208 **gross** twelve dozen points (also with reference to clerkly
"engrossing," the lawyer's fair copying)   208 **inkles** linen tapes   208 **caddisses** worsted tapes for garters   211 **sleevehand** cuff   212 **square** embroidered yoke   217 **You have of these peddlers** there are peddlers   219 **go
about to** intend to   221 **Cypress** crape   222 **Gloves . . . roses** (it was the fashion to perfume gloves)   223 **Masks . . . noses** (to protect ladies' faces or noses
from the sun)

Bugle-bracelet,° necklace-amber,
225   Perfume for a lady's chamber;
Golden quoifs° and stomachers
For my lads to give their dears;
Pins and poking-sticks° of steel;
What maids lack from head to heel!
230   Come buy of me, come, come buy, come buy,
Buy lads, or else your lasses cry; come buy!

Clown. If I were not in love with Mopsa, thou shouldst
take no money of me; but being enthralled as I
am, it will also be the bondage° of certain ribbons
235   and gloves.

Mopsa. I was promised them against° the feast, but they
come not too late now.

Dorcas. He hath promised you more than that, or there
be liars.

240   *Mopsa.* He hath paid you all he promised you; may·be
he has paid you more, which will shame you to give
him again.°

Clown. Is there no manners left among maids? Will
they wear their plackets° where they should bear
245   their faces? Is there not milking-time, when you are
going to bed, or kiln-hole,° to whistle of these secrets, but you must be tittle-tattling before all our
guests? 'Tis well they are whis'pring. Clammer°
your tongues, and not a word more.

---

224 **Bugle-bracelet** bracelet of beads   226 **quoifs** head scarves   228 **poking-sticks** metal rods used in ironing starched ruffs   234 **bondage** i.e., he is a pris-oner of Mopsa, and will take the fairings into captivity with him   236 **against** before   241–42 **paid you more . . . give him again** (this girlish insult means: "Perhaps he has made you pregnant")   244 **plackets** petticoats, or slits in petti-coats (often used indecently. Here the Clown merely means that they should not as it were wash their dirty linen in public)   246 **kiln-hole** the place containing the fire for malt making (convenient for confidential talk)   248 **Clammer** si-lence (technical term in bellringing)

Mopsa. I have done. Come, you promised me a 250
tawdry-lace,° and a pair of sweet gloves.

Clown. Have I not told thee how I was cozened by the
way, and lost all my money?

Autolycus. And indeed, sir, there are cozeners abroad;
therefore it behooves men to be wary.   255

Clown. Fear not thou, man; thou shalt lose nothing
here.

Autolycus. I hope so, sir, for I have about me many
parcels of charge.°

Clown. What hast here? Ballads?   260

Mopsa. Pray now, buy some. I love a ballad in print,
a-life,° for then we are sure they are true.

Autolycus. Here's one to a very doleful tune, how a
usurer's wife was brought to bed of twenty money-
bags at a burden, and how she longed to eat adders' 265
heads and toads carbonadoed.°

Mopsa. Is it true, think you?

Autolycus. Very true, and but a month old.

Dorcas. Bless me from marrying a usurer!

Autolycus. Here's the midwife's name to 't: one Mis- 270
tress Taleporter, and five or six honest wives that
were present. Why should I carry lies abroad?

Mopsa. Pray you now, buy it.

Clown. Come on, lay it by, and let's first see moe°
ballads; we'll buy the other things anon.   275

Autolycus. Here's another ballad, of a fish° that appeared upon the coast on Wednesday the fourscore of April, forty thousand fathom above water,
and sung this ballad against the hard hearts of

---

251 **tawdry-lace** silk worn around the neck (called after St. Audrey
[Ethelreda], who was punished for youthful ostentation—especially fine neck-
laces—by a tumor in the throat)   259 **parcels of charge** goods of
value   262 **a-life** dearly   266 **carbonadoed** cut up and broiled   274 **moe**
more   276 **of a fish** (records of very similar ballads survive)

280   maids; it was thought she was a woman, and was
turned into a cold fish for she would not exchange
flesh with one that loved her. The ballad is very
pitiful, and as true.

Dorcas. Is it true too, think you?

285 *Autolycus.* Five justices' hands at it, and witnesses more
than my pack will hold.

Clown. Lay it by too; another.

Autolycus. This is a merry ballad, but a very pretty
one.

290 *Mopsa.* Let's have some merry ones.

    Autolycus. Why, this is a passing merry one, and goes to
the tune of "Two Maids Wooing a Man." There's
scarce a maid westward but she sings it; 'tis in
request, I can tell you.

295 *Mopsa.* We can both sing it. If thou 'lt bear a part, thou
shalt hear; 'tis in three parts.

Dorcas. We had the tune on 't, a month ago.

Autolycus. I can bear my part, you must know 'tis my
occupation. Have at it with you.

Song.

300 *Autolycus.*	Get you hence, for I must go
	Where it fits not you to know.
Dorcas.	Whither?
Mopsa.	O whither?
Dorcas.	Whither?
305 *Mopsa.*	It becomes thy oath full well,
	Thou to me thy secrets tell.
Dorcas.	Me too; let me go thither.
Mopsa.	Or thou go'st to th' grange or mill,
Dorcas.	If to either thou dost ill.
310 *Autolycus.*	Neither.
Dorcas.	What, neither?

Autolycus. Neither.

Dorcas. Thou hast sworn my love to be.

Mopsa. Thou hast sworn it more to me.
    Then whither goest? Say, whither? 315

Clown. We'll have this song out anon by ourselves;
my father and the gentlemen are in sad° talk, and
we'll not trouble them. Come bring away thy pack
after me; wenches, I'll buy for you both. Peddler,
let's have the first choice; follow me, girls. 320

       [*Exeunt Clown, Dorcas, and Mopsa.*]

Autolycus. And you shall pay well for 'em.

            Song.

Will you buy any tape, or lace for your cape,
   My dainty duck, my dear-a?
Any silk, any thread, any toys for your head,
   Of the new'st, and fin'st fin'st wear-a? 325
Come to the peddler, money's a meddler,
   That doth utter° all men's ware-a.

                          Exit.

         Enter Servant.

Servant. Master, there is three carters, three shepherds,
three neatherds,° three swineherds that have
made themselves all men of hair;° they call them- 330
selves saltiers,° and they have a dance, which the
wenches say is a gallimaufry° of gambols, because
they are not in 't; but they themselves are o' th'
mind, if it be not too rough for some that know
little but bowling,° it will please plentifully. 335

Shepherd. Away! We'll none on 't; here has been too
much homely foolery already. I know, sir, we weary
you.

Polixenes. You weary those that refresh us; pray let's
see these four threes of herdsmen.

317 **sad** serious 327 **utter** put forth 329 **neatherds** cowherds 330 **men of hair** hairy men, satyrs (or the wild men of medieval art and entertainment) 331 **saltiers**, satyrs (or perhaps leapers, vaulters, from Fr. *saultier*, "vaulter") 332 **gallimaufry** hodgepodge 335 **bowling** (here, a gentle activity, contrasted with the acrobatic dance)

340 *Servant.* One three of them, by their own report, sir,
    hath danced before the King;° and not the worst
    of the three but jumps twelve foot and a half by
    th' squier.°

    Shepherd. Leave your prating; since these good men
345 are pleased, let them come in; but quickly now.

    Servant. Why, they stay at door, sir.   [*Exit.*]

          Here a dance of twelve Satyrs.

    Polixenes [*To Shepherd*] O father, you'll know more of
          that hereafter.

          [*To Camillo*] Is it not too far gone? 'Tis time to part
          them.

          He's simple and tells much. How now, fair shep-
          herd!

350   Your heart is full of something that does take
          Your mind from feasting. Sooth, when I was young,
          And handed° love as you do, I was wont
          To load my she with knacks; I would have ransacked
          The peddler's silken treasury, and have poured it
355   To her acceptance: you have let him go,
          And nothing marted with° him. If your lass
          Interpretation should abuse,° and call this
          Your lack of love or bounty, you were straited°
          For a reply, at least if you make a care
          Of happy holding her.

360 *Florizel.*   Old sir, I know
          She prizes not such trifles as these are;
          The gifts she looks from me are packed and locked
          Up in my heart, which I have given already,
          But not delivered.° O, hear me breathe my life
365   Before this ancient sir, who, it should seem,
          Hath sometime loved: I take thy hand, this hand
          As soft as dove's down, and as white as it,

---

341 **before the King** (the performers of this dance had certainly done so, perhaps in this very dance)   343 **squier** rule   352 **handed** dealt with   356 **marted**
with bought of   357 **Interpretation should abuse** choose to misunderstand
358 **straited** in difficulties   363–64 **given … delivered** the deal is settled, but
the goods not yet handed over

Or Ethiopian's tooth, or the fanned snow that's
  bolted°
By th' northern blasts twice o'er——

Polixenes.   What follows
  this?
How prettily th' young swain seems to wash   *370*
The hand was fair° before! I have put you out;
But to your protestation: let me hear
What you profess.

Florizel.   Do, and be witness to 't.

Polixenes. And this my neighbor too?

Florizel.   And he, and more
Than he, and men; the earth, the heavens, and all: *375*
That were I crowned the most imperial monarch,
Thereof most worthy; were I the fairest youth
That ever made eye swerve; had force and knowl-
  edge
More than was ever man's, I would not prize them
Without her love; for her, employ them all,   *380*
Commend them, and condemn them to her service,
Or to their own perdition.°

Polixenes.   Fairly offered.

Camillo. This shows a sound affection.

Shepherd.   But, my daughter,
Say you the like to him?

Perdita.   I cannot speak
So well, nothing so well; no, nor mean better.   *385*
By th' pattern of mine own thoughts I cut out
The purity of his.

Shepherd.   Take hands, a bargain;
And friends unknown, you shall bear witness to 't:
I give my daughter to him, and will make
Her portion equal his.

Florizel.   O, that must be   *390*

---

368 **bolted** sifted   371 **was fair** that was fair   381–82 **Commend . . . perdition** commend them to her service, or condemn them to their own perdition

I' th' virtue of your daughter. One being dead,
I shall have more than you can dream of yet,
Enough then for your wonder.° But come on,
Contract us 'fore these witnesses.

Shepherd.   Come, your hand;
And, daughter, yours.

395 *Polixenes.*   Soft, swain, awhile, beseech you,
Have you a father?

Florizel.   I have; but what of him?

Polixenes. Knows he of this?

Florizel.   He neither does, nor shall.

Polixenes. Methinks a father
Is at the nuptial of his son a guest
400 That best becomes the table. Pray you once more,
Is not your father grown incapable
Of reasonable affairs? Is he not stupid
With age and alt'ring rheums?° Can he speak, hear?
Know man from man? Dispute his own estate?
405 Lies he not bed-rid? And again does nothing
But what he did being childish?

Florizel.   No, good sir;
He has his health, and ampler strength indeed
Than most have of his age.

Polixenes.   By my white beard,
You offer him, if this be so, a wrong
410 Something unfilial. Reason my son°
Should choose himself a wife, but as good reason
The father, all whose joy is nothing else
But fair posterity, should hold some counsel
In such a business.

Florizel.   I yield all this;
415 But for some other reasons, my grave sir,
Which 'tis not fit you know, I not acquaint

392-93 **I shall have more ... your wonder** I shall have more than you can at
this time dream of, and enough to amaze you when you know of it   403 **alt'ring
rheums** i.e., rheumatic afflictions which disturb his judgment   410 **Reason my
son** there is reason that my son

My father of this business.

Polixenes.   Let him know 't.

Florizel. He shall not.

Polixenes.   Prithee, let him.

Florizel.   No, he must not.

Shepherd. Let him, my son; he shall not need to grieve
    At knowing of thy choice.

Florizel.   Come, come, he must not.   420
    Mark our contract.°

Polixenes. [*Discovering himself*] Mark your divorce,
        young sir,
    Whom son I dare not call; thou art too base
    To be acknowledged. Thou, a scepter's heir,
    That thus affect'st° a sheep-hook! Thou, old traitor,
    I am sorry that by hanging thee, I can   425
    But shorten thy life one week. And thou, fresh piece
    Of excellent witchcraft, who of force must know
    The royal fool thou cop'st with——

Shepherd.   O my heart!

Polixenes. I'll have thy beauty scratched with briers and
        made
    More homely than thy state. For thee, fond boy,   430
    If I may ever know thou dost but sigh
    That thou no more shalt see this knack—as never
    I mean thou shalt—we'll bar thee from succession;
    Not hold thee of our blood, no not our kin,
    Farre than Deucalion off.° Mark thou my words.   435
    Follow us to the court. Thou, churl, for this time,
    Though full of our displeasure, yet we free thee
    From the dead blow of it. And you, enchantment,

---

421 **contract** (J. D. Wilson in the New Cambridge edition points out that "we have here a description, all but the final solemn words, of one of those betrothal ceremonies which were held as legally binding as marriage in church")   424 **affect'st** desirest, lovest   435 **Farre than Deucalion off** further back than Deucalion (legendary ancient king of Thessaly)

Worthy enough a herdsman—yea him, too,
440 That makes himself, but for our honor therein,
Unworthy thee°—if ever henceforth thou
These rural latches to his entrance open,
Or hoop his body more with thy embraces,
I will devise a death as cruel for thee
As thou art tender to 't.   *Exit.*

445 *Perdita.*   Even here undone!
I was not much afeard; for once or twice
I was about to speak and tell him plainly,
The selfsame sun that shines upon his court
Hides not his visage from our cottage, but
Looks on alike. [*To Florizel*] Will 't please you, sir,
450   be gone?
I told you what would come of this. Beseech you,
Of your own state take care: this dream of mine
Being now awake, I'll queen it no inch farther,
But milk my ewes, and weep.

Camillo.   Why, how now, father!
Speak ere thou diest.

455 *Shepherd.*   I cannot speak nor think,
Nor dare to know that which I know. [*To Florizel*]
      O sir,
You have undone a man of fourscore three,
That thought to fill his grave in quiet, yea,
To die upon the bed my father died,
460 To lie close by his honest bones; but now
Some hangman must put on my shroud, and lay me
Where no priest shovels in dust.° Oh cursèd wretch,
That knew'st this was the Prince, and wouldst ad-
      venture
To mingle faith with him! Undone, undone!
465 If I might die within this hour, I have lived
To die when I desire.   *Exit.*

Florizel.   Why look you so upon me?

439–41 **yea him ... Unworthy thee** indeed, you're worthy of Florizel—
whose conduct has made him, save for the fact of his being my son, unworthy
of you 462 **Where no priest shovels in dust** (before the Reformation, and
even in the First Prayer Book of Edward VI, the priest was directed to do this.
Felons were buried by the gallows)

I am but sorry, not afeard; delayed,
But nothing altered. What I was, I am;
More straining on, for plucking back; not following
My leash unwillingly.°

Camillo.   Gracious my lord,   470
You know your father's temper; at this time
He will allow no speech—which I do guess
You do not purpose to him—and as hardly
Will he endure your sight as yet, I fear;
Then, till the fury of his Highness settle,   475
Come not before him.

Florizel.   I not purpose it.
I think, Camillo?

Camillo.   Even he, my lord.

Perdita. How often have I told you 'twould be thus?
How often said my dignity would last
But till 'twere known?

Florizel.   It cannot fail, but by   480
The violation of my faith, and then
Let Nature crush the sides o' th' earth together,
And mar the seeds within.° Lift up thy looks;
From my succession wipe me, father, I
Am heir to my affection.

Camillo.   Be advised.   485

Florizel. I am, and by my fancy; if my reason
Will thereto be obedient, I have reason;
If not, my senses better pleased with madness,°
Do bid it welcome.

Camillo.   This is desperate, sir.

469–70 **More straining on ... unwillingly** (the image is of a hound. Florizel
continues on his chosen course, all the more strongly for having been dragged
back; he is not going to do as his father says against his will)   482–83 **Let
Nature ... the seeds within** (for this image of the end of creation compare
Macbeth 4.1.59 and *Lear* 3.2.8)   486–88 **fancy ... reason ... madness** if the
fancy, which makes images, is not obedient to the reason—a higher mental
power—the result is madness or dream (Florizel wants his reason to obey his
fancy; otherwise, he says, he'd rather be mad. For the psychology involved,
see *Midsummer Night's Dream* 5.1.2. ff.)

490 *Florizel.* So call it, but it does fulfill my vow;
  I needs must think it honesty. Camillo,
  Not for Bohemia, nor the pomp that may
  Be thereat gleaned; for all the sun sees or
  The close earth wombs or the profound seas hide
495 In unknown fathoms, will I break my oath
  To this my fair beloved. Therefore, I pray you,
  As you have ever been my father's honored friend,
  When he shall miss me, as in faith I mean not
  To see him any more, cast your good counsels
500 Upon his passion; let myself and Fortune
  Tug° for the time to come. This you may know,
  And so deliver: I am put to sea
  With her whom here I cannot hold on shore;
  And most opportune° to her need, I have
505 A vessel rides fast by, but not prepared
  For this design. What course I mean to hold
  Shall nothing benefit your knowledge, nor
  Concern me the reporting.

 Camillo.   O my lord,
  I would your spirit were easier for advice,
  Or stronger for your need.

510 *Florizel.*   Hark, Perdita——
  [*To Camillo*] I'll hear you by and by.

 Camillo.   He's irremovable,
  Resolved for flight. Now were I happy if
  His going I could frame to serve my turn,
  Save him from danger, do him love and honor,
515 Purchase the sight again of dear Sicilia,
  And that unhappy king, my master, whom
  I so much thirst to see.

 Florizel.   Now, good Camillo,
  I am so fraught with curious° business that
  I leave out ceremony.°

 Camillo.   Sir, I think

---

501 **Tug** contend, strive 504 **opportune** (accent on second syllable) 518 **curious** needing great care 519 **ceremony** (Florizel is apologizing for having broken away from Camillo to hold his urgent private talk with Perdita)

You have heard of my poor services i' th' love   520
That I have borne your father?

Florizel.   Very nobly
Have you deserved; it is my father's music
To speak your deeds, not little of his care
To have them recompensed, as thought on.

Camillo.   Well, my lord,
If you may please to think I love the King,   525
And through him what's nearest to him, which is
Your gracious self, embrace but my direction,°
If your more ponderous and settled project
May suffer alteration. On mine honor,
I'll point you where you shall have such receiving   530
As shall become your Highness, where you may
Enjoy your mistress; from the whom, I see
There's no disjunction to be made, but by—
As heavens forfend—your ruin; marry her;
And with my best endeavors, in your absence,   535
Your discontenting° father strive to qualify°
And bring him up to liking.

Florizel.   How, Camillo,
May this, almost a miracle, be done?
That I may call thee something more than man,
And after that trust to thee.

Camillo.   Have you thought on   540
A place whereto you'll go?

Florizel.   Not any yet;
But as th' unthought-on accident is guilty
To what we wildly do, so we profess
Ourselves to be the slaves of chance, and flies
Of every wind that blows.°

Camillo.   Then list° to me.   545
This follows, if you will not change your purpose,

---

527 **direction** advice   536 **discontenting** displeased   536 **qualify** appease,
moderate (used, for example, of tempering wine with water)   542–45 **But as . . .
wind that blows** since we are compelled to this wild behavior by a chance we
never foresaw, we think of ourselves as the slaves of chance, and will go where it
sends us, like flies in a wind   545 **list** listen

But undergo this flight: make for Sicilia,
And there present yourself and your fair princess
(For so I see she must be) 'fore Leontes.
550 She shall be habited as it becomes
The partner of your bed. Methinks I see
Leontes opening his free arms and weeping
His welcomes forth; asks thee, the son, forgiveness,
As 'twere i' th' father's person; kisses the hands
555 Of your fresh princess; o'er and o'er divides him
'Twixt his unkindness and his kindness: th' one
He chides to hell, and bids the other grow
Faster° than thought or time.

Florizel.   Worthy Camillo,
What color° for my visitation shall I
Hold up before him?

560 *Camillo.*   Sent by the King your father
To greet him, and to give him comforts. Sir,
The manner of your bearing towards him, with
What you, as from your father, shall deliver,
Things known betwixt us three, I'll write you down,
565 The which shall point you forth at every sitting
What you must say, that he shall not perceive,
But that° you have your father's bosom there,
And speak his very heart.

Florizel.   I am bound to you;
There is some sap° in this.

Camillo.   A course more promising
570 Than a wild dedication of yourselves
To unpathed waters, undreamed shores, most certain
To miseries enough: no hope to help you,
But as you shake off one, to take another;
Nothing so certain as your anchors, who
575 Do their best office if they can but stay° you,
Where you'll be loath to be. Besides, you know,
Prosperity's the very bond of love,

---

558 **Faster** firmer   559 **color** pretext   566–67 **perceive, / But that** know
otherwise than that   569 **sap** life fluid   575 **stay** hold

Whose fresh complexion and whose heart together
Affliction alters.

Perdita.   One of these is true:
I think affliction may subdue the cheek,   580
But not take in the mind.

Camillo.   Yea? Say you so?
There shall not at your father's house these seven
  years°
Be born another such.

Florizel.   My good Camillo,
She is as forward of her breeding as
She is i' th' rear 'our birth.°

Camillo.   I cannot say 'tis pity   585
She lacks instructions, for she seems a mistress
To most that teach.

Perdita.   Your pardon, sir; for this,
I'll blush you thanks.

Florizel.   My prettiest Perdita!
But O, the thorns we stand upon! Camillo—
Preserver of my father, now of me,   590
The medicine° of our house—how shall we do?
We are not furnished like Bohemia's son,
Nor shall appear° in Sicilia.

Camillo.   My lord,
Fear none of this. I think you know my fortunes
Do all lie there; it shall be so my care   595
To have you royally appointed,° as if
The scene you play were mine. For instance, sir,
That you may know you shall not want—one word.
          [*They talk aside.*]
          Enter Autolycus.
Autolycus. Ha, ha, what a fool° Honesty is! And

582 **these seven years** (used to signify a long, indefinite period)   584–85 **She
is as forward . . . our birth** she is as far in advance of the way of life she was
reared to as she is inferior to us in birth   591 **medicine** physician   593 **appear** appear so (the second word may have dropped out)   596 **royally appointed** equipped like a prince   599 **Ha, ha, what a fool . . .** (these lines echo
passages in Greene's *Second Part of Conny-catching* [1592]. The character of
Autolycus, and the account of the tricks of his trade, is indebted to this book)

600 Trust, his sworn brother, a very simple gentleman. I
have sold all my trumpery: not a counterfeit stone,
not a ribbon, glass, pomander, brooch, table-book,°
ballad, knife, tape, glove, shoe-tie, bracelet, horn-
ring, to keep my pack from fasting. They throng
605 who should buy first, as if my trinkets had been
hallowed,° and brought a benediction to the buyer;
by which means I saw whose purse was best in picture,° and what I saw to my good use I remembered. My clown, who wants but something to be
610 a reasonable man, grew so in love with the wenches'
song, that he would not stir his pettitoes° till he had
both tune and words, which so drew the rest of the
herd to me that all their other senses stuck in ears:
you might have pinched a placket, it was senseless;
615 'twas nothing to geld a codpiece of a purse; I would
have filed keys off that hung in chains. No hearing,
no feeling, but my sir's° song, and admiring the
nothing° of it. So that in this time of lethargy I
picked and cut most of their festival purses; and had
620 not the old man come in with a hubbub against his
daughter and the King's son, and scared my
choughs° from the chaff, I had not left a purse
alive in the whole army.

[*Camillo, Florizel, and Perdita come forward.*]

Camillo. Nay, but my letters, by this means being there
625 So soon as you arrive, shall clear that doubt.

Florizel. And those that you'll procure from King
Leontes?

Camillo. Shall satisfy your father.

Perdita.   Happy be you!
All that you speak shows fair.

Camillo. [*Seeing Autolycus*] Who have we here?
We'll make an instrument of this, omit

---

602 **table-book** notebook 606 **hallowed** sacred 607–608 **in picture** to
look at (?) 611 **pettitoes** toes (especially of a pig) 617 **my sir's** the
Clown's 618 **nothing** nothingness, nonsense (with perhaps, as Wilson suggests, a pun on "noting") 622 **choughs** fools

Nothing may give us aid.   630

Autolycus. If they have overheard me now—why, hanging.

Camillo. How now, good fellow, why shak'st thou so? Fear not, man; here's no harm intended to thee.

Autolycus. I am a poor fellow, sir.

Camillo. Why, be so still; here's nobody will steal that 635 from thee. Yet for the outside of thy poverty we must make an exchange; therefore discase° thee instantly—thou must think there's a necessity in 't —and change garments with this gentleman; though the pennyworth on his side be the worst, yet hold 640 thee, there's some boot.° [*Giving money.*]

Autolycus. I am a poor fellow, sir. [*Aside*] I know ye well enough.

Camillo. Nay, prithee dispatch; the gentleman is half flayed° already.   645

Autolycus. Are you in earnest, sir? [*Aside*] I smell the trick on 't.

Florizel. Dispatch, I prithee.

Autolycus. Indeed, I have had earnest,° but I cannot with conscience take it.   650

Camillo. Unbuckle, unbuckle.

[*Florizel and Autolycus exchange garments.*]

Fortunate mistress—let my prophecy°
Come home to ye—you must retire yourself
Into some covert; take your sweetheart's hat
And pluck it o'er your brows, muffle your face,   655
Dismantle you, and, as you can, disliken
The truth of your own seeming,° that you may

---

637 **discase** undress   641 **boot** extra reward   645 **flayed** skinned (undressed)
649 **earnest** money paid as installment, "deposit"   652 **prophecy** (the prophecy is the form of address, "Fortunate mistress!")   656–57 **disliken . . . seeming** (a complicated way of saying "alter your usual appearance," which may indicate Shakespeare's obsessive interest in problems related to "truth" and "seeming")

(For I do fear eyes over°) to shipboard
Get undescried.

Perdita.   I see the play so lies
That I must bear a part.

660 Camillo.   No remedy.
Have you done there?

Florizel.   Should I now meet my father,
He would not call me son.

Camillo.   Nay, you shall have no hat.

[*Giving hat to Perdita.*]

Come, lady, come; farewell, my friend.

Autolycus.   Adieu, sir.

Florizel. O Perdita, what have we twain forgot?
665   Pray you, a word.

Camillo. [*Aside*] What I do next shall be to tell the
        King
Of this escape, and whither they are bound;
Wherein my hope is, I shall so prevail
To force him after; in whose company
670 I shall re-view Sicilia, for whose sight
I have a woman's longing.

Florizel.   Fortune speed us!
Thus we set on, Camillo, to th' seaside.

Camillo. The swifter speed, the better.

        Exit [Camillo, with Florizel and Perdita].

Autolycus. I understand the business, I hear it. To have
675   an open ear, a quick eye, and a nimble hand, is
        necessary for a cutpurse; a good nose is requisite
        also, to smell out work for th' other senses. I see
        this is the time that the unjust man doth thrive. What
        an exchange had this been without boot! What a
680   boot is here, with this exchange! Sure, the gods do
        this year connive at° us, and we may do anything

658 **eyes over** watching; spying eyes   681 **connive at** close their eyes to

extempore. The Prince himself is about a piece of
iniquity—stealing away from his father, with his
clog° at his heels; if I thought it were a piece of
honesty to acquaint the King withal, I would not   685
do 't. I hold it the more knavery to conceal it; and
therein am I constant to my profession.

Enter Clown and Shepherd.

Aside, aside! Here is more matter for a hot brain.
Every lane's end, every shop, church, session,
hanging, yields a careful man work.   690

Clown. See, see, what a man you are now! There is
no other way but to tell the King she's a changeling,
and none of your flesh and blood.

Shepherd. Nay, but hear me.

Clown. Nay, but hear me.   695

Shepherd. Go to, then.

Clown. She being none of your flesh and blood, your
flesh and blood has not offended the King, and so
your flesh and blood is not to be punished by him.
Show those things you found about her, those   700
secret things, all but what she has with her. This
being done, let the law go whistle; I warrant you.

Shepherd. I will tell the King all, every word, yea, and
his son's pranks too; who, I may say, is no honest
man, neither to his father nor to me, to go about to   705
make me the King's brother-in-law.

Clown. Indeed brother-in-law was the farthest off you
could have been to him; and then your blood had
been the dearer by I know not how much an ounce.

Autolycus. [*Aside*] Very wisely, puppies!   710

Shepherd. Well, let us to the King; there is that in this
fardel° will make him scratch his beard.

Autolycus. [*Aside*] I know not what impediment this
complaint may be to the flight of my master.

684 **clog** hindrance (Perdita)   712 **fardel** bundle

715 *Clown.* Pray heartily he be at palace.°

Autolycus. [*Aside*] Though I am not naturally honest, I
    am so sometimes by chance. Let me pocket up my
    peddler's excrement.° [*Takes off false beard.*] How
    now, rustics, whither are you bound?

720 *Shepherd.* To th' palace, an it like your worship.

Autolycus. Your affairs there, what, with whom,° the
    condition of that fardel, the place of your dwelling,
    your names, your ages, of what having,° breeding,
    and anything that is fitting to be known, discover.

725 *Clown.* We are but plain fellows, sir.

Autolycus. A lie: you are rough, and hairy. Let me
    have no lying; it becomes none but tradesmen, and
    they often give us soldiers the lie, but we pay them
    for it with stamped coin, not stabbing steel; there-
730   fore they do not give us the lie.°

Clown. Your worship had like to have given us one,
    if you had not taken yourself with the manner.°

Shepherd. Are you a courtier,° an 't like you, sir?

Autolycus. Whether it like me or no, I am a courtier.
735   Seest thou not the air of the court in these enfold-
    ings? Hath not my gait in it the measure° of the
    court? Receives not thy nose court-odor from me?
    Reflect I not on thy baseness court-contempt?
    Think'st thou, for that I insinuate, or toaze° from
740   thee thy business, I am therefore no courtier? I am
    courtier cap-a-pé;° and one that will either push

---

715 **at palace** (the Clown speaks of the King being "at palace" as he might of an
ordinary man being "at home" [Cambridge editors])   718 **excrement** i.e., his
false beard (hair, beard, and nails were called "excrement," from L. *excrescere,* to
grow out)   721 **what, with whom** (parodying a form of legal questioning to ter-
rify the rustics)   723 **having** property   727–30 **it becomes none ... give us the
lie** (tradesmen give the lie by giving short measure, but the simple soldier nevertheless pays them for it with money, not with his sword—so the tradesmen
are not, after all, *giving* the lie; they are selling it [J. D. Wilson's explana-
tion])   732 **with the manner** in the act (at first Autolycus was about to lie by saying "give" instead of "sell" when speaking of the tradesmen; but he caught himself
in the act and changed his statement)   733 **courtier** (Autolycus is wearing
Florizel's festive clothes)   736 **measure** stately tread   739 **toaze** tease, worry,
comb out   741 **cap-a-pé** head-to-foot (of armor; here, thorough, complete)

on or pluck back thy business there; whereupon I
command thee to open thy affair.
Shepherd. My business, sir, is to the King.
Autolycus. What advocate hast thou to him?   745
Shepherd. I know not, an 't like you.
Clown. Advocate's the court-word for a pheasant;°
say you have none.
Shepherd. None, sir; I have no pheasant, cock nor hen.
Autolycus. How blessed are we that are not simple men!   750
Yet Nature might have made me as these are,
Therefore I will not disdain.
Clown. This cannot be but a great courtier.
Shepherd. His garments are rich, but he wears them
not handsomely.   755
Clown. He seems to be the more noble in being fan-
tastical. A great man, I'll warrant; I know by the
picking on 's teeth.°
Autolycus. The fardel there? What's i' th' fardel?
Wherefore that box?   760
Shepherd. Sir, there lies such secrets in this fardel and
box, which none must know but the King, and which
he shall know within this hour, if I may come to th'
speech of him.
Autolycus. Age, thou hast lost thy labor.   765
Shepherd. Why, sir?
Autolycus. The King is not at the palace; he is gone
aboard a new ship, to purge melancholy and air
himself; for if thou be'st capable of things serious,
thou must know the King is full of grief.   770
Shepherd. So 'tis said, sir—about his son, that should
have married a shepherd's daughter.
Autolycus. If that shepherd be not in handfast,° let
him fly; the curses he shall have, the tortures he
shall feel, will break the back of man, the heart of   775
monster.
Clown. Think you so, sir?

---

747 **Advocate's ... pheasant** (the Clown, misunderstanding the word,
thinks Autolycus is referring to the practice of bribing the judge with a
bird)   758 **picking on 's teeth** (regarded as an elegant practice)
773 **handfast** custody

Autolycus. Not he alone shall suffer what wit can
make heavy, and vengeance bitter; but those that
780   are germane° to him, though removed fifty times,
shall all come under the hangman; which, though
it be great pity, yet it is necessary. An old sheep-
whistling rogue, a ram-tender, to offer to have his
daughter come into grace! Some say he shall be
785   stoned; but that death is too soft for him, say I.
Draw our throne into a sheepcote! All deaths are
too few, the sharpest too easy.

Clown. Has the old man e'er a son, sir, do you hear, an
't like you, sir?

790 *Autolycus.* He has a son—who shall be flayed alive,
then 'nointed over with honey, set on the head of a
wasp's nest; then stand till he be three-quarters and a
dram dead; then recovered again with aqua-vitae or
some other hot infusion; then, raw as he is, and in
795   the hottest day prognostication° proclaims, shall he
be set against a brick wall, the sun looking with a
southward eye upon him, where he is to behold
him with flies blown to death. But what talk we of
these traitorly rascals, whose miseries are to be
800   smiled at, their offenses being so capital? Tell me,
for you seem to be honest plain men, what you have
to the King; being something gently considered,°
I'll bring you where he is aboard, tender° your
persons to his presence, whisper him in your be-
805   halfs; and if it be in man besides the King to effect
your suits, here is man shall do it.

Clown. He seems to be of great authority. Close with
him,° give him gold; and though authority be a
stubborn bear, yet he is oft led by the nose with
810   gold. Show the inside of your purse to the outside of
his hand, and no more ado. Remember—stoned, and
flayed alive.

Shepherd. An 't please you, sir, to undertake the busi-

---

780 **germane** related   795 **prognostication** weather forecast in the almanac for
the year   802 **being something gently considered** if you bribe me like a gentleman (handsomely)   803 **tender** present   807–08 **Close with him** accept his offer

ness for us, here is that gold I have; I'll make it as
much more, and leave this young man in pawn till *815*
I bring it you.

Autolycus. After I have done what I promised?

Shepherd. Ay, sir.

Autolycus. Well, give me the moiety.° Are you a
party in this business? *820*

Clown. In some sort, sir; but though my case be a
pitful one, I hope shall not be flayed° out of it.

Autolycus. Oh, that's the case of the shepherd's son:
hang him, he'll be made an example.

Clown. Comfort, good comfort! We must to the King, *825*
and show our strange sights; he must know 'tis none
of your daughter, nor my sister; we are gone else.
Sir, I will give you as much as this old man does
when the business is performed, and remain, as he
says, your pawn till it be brought you. *830*

Autolycus. I will trust you. Walk before toward the
seaside, go on the right hand; I will but look upon
the hedge,° and follow you.

Clown. We are blessed, in this man, as I may say, even
blessed. *835*

Shepherd. Let's before, as he bids us. He was provided
to do us good.

[Exeunt Shepherd and Clown.]

Autolycus. If I had a mind to be honest, I see Fortune
would not suffer me: she drops booties in my mouth.
I am courted now with a double occasion—gold, *840*
and a means to do the Prince, my master, good;
which who knows how that may turn back° to my
advancement? I will bring these two moles, these
blind ones, aboard him. If he think it fit to shore
them again, and that the complaint they have to the *845*
King concerns him nothing, let him call me rogue
for being so far officious; for I am proof against that
title, and what shame else belongs to 't. To him will I
present them, there may be matter in it. *Exit.*

819 **moiety** half 821–22 **caste ... flayed** (punning on case/skin)
832–33 **look upon the hedge** i.e., relieve himself 842 **turn back** redound

ACT 5

Scene 1. [*Sicilia, the Court of Leontes.*]

Enter Leontes, Cleomenes, Dion, Paulina, Servants.

Cleomenes. Sir, you have done enough, and have per-
formed
A saintlike sorrow. No fault could you make
Which you have not redeemed; indeed paid down
More penitence than done trespass. At the last,
Do as the heavens have done: forget your evil;
With them forgive yourself.

Leontes.   Whilst I remember
Her and her virtues, I cannot forget   .
My blemishes in them, and so still think of
The wrong I did myself; which was so much,
That heirless it hath made my kingdom, and
Destroyed the sweet'st companion that e'er man
Bred his hopes out of.

Paulina.   ' True, too true, my lord.
If one by one you wedded all the world,
Or from the all that are took something good
To make a perfect woman, she you killed
Would be unparalleled.

Leontes.   I think so. Killed?
She I killed! I did so; but thou strik'st me
Sorely, to say I did—it is as bitter
Upon thy tongue as in my thought. Now, good now,
Say so but seldom.

Cleomenes.   Not at all, good lady:

96

You might have spoken a thousand things that would
Have done the time more benefit, and graced°
Your kindness better.

Paulina.   You are one of those
Would have him wed again.

Dion.   If you would not so,
You pity not the state, nor the remembrance°   25
Of his most sovereign name; consider little
What dangers, by his Highness' fail° of issue,
May drop upon his kingdom, and devour
Incertain lookers-on.° What were more holy
Than to rejoice the former queen is well?   30
What holier than, for royalty's repair,
For present comfort, and for future good,
To bless the bed of majesty again
With a sweet fellow to 't?

Paulina.   There is none worthy,
Respecting her that's gone; besides, the gods   35
Will have fulfilled their secret purposes;
For has not the divine Apollo said—
Is 't not the tenor of his oracle—
That King Leontes shall not have an heir
Till his lost child be found? Which that it shall,   40
Is all as monstrous to our human reason
As my Antigonus to break his grave,
And come again to me; who, on my life,
Did perish with the infant. 'Tis your counsel
My lord should to the heavens be contrary,   45
Oppose against their wills. [*To Leontes*] Care not for issue,
The crown will find an heir. Great Alexander
Left his to th' worthiest: so his successor
Was like to be the best.

Leontes.   Good Paulina,
Who hast the memory of Hermione,   50

5.1.22 **graced** suited   25 **remembrance** (he means the perpetuation of the King's name in a son)   27 **fail** failure   29 **Incertain lookers-on** bystanders whose uncertainty makes them incapable of action

I know, in honor: O, that ever I
Had squared me to° thy counsel! Then, even now,
I might have looked upon my queen's full eyes,
Have taken treasure from her lips——

Paulina.   And left them
More rich for what they yielded.

55   *Leontes.*   Thou speak'st truth;
No more such wives, therefore no wife. One worse,
And better used, would make her sainted spirit
Again possess her corpse, and on this stage,
Where we offenders now appear,° soul-vexed,
And begin, "Why to me?"°

60   *Paulina.*   Had she such power,
She had just cause.

Leontes.   She had, and would incense me
To murder her I married.

Paulina.   I should so.
Were I the ghost that walked, I'd bid you mark
Her eye, and tell me for what dull part in 't
65   You chose her; then I'd shriek, that even your ears
Should rift to hear me, and the words that followed
Should be, "Remember mine."

Leontes.   Stars, stars,
And all eyes else, dead coals! Fear thou no wife;
I'll have no wife, Paulina.

Paulina.   Will you swear
70   Never to marry, but by my free leave?

Leontes. Never, Paulina, so be blessed my spirit.

Paulina. Then, good my lords, bear witness to his oath.

Cleomenes. You tempt him overmuch.

Paulina.   Unless another,

52 **squared me to** regulated myself by   59 **Where we offenders now appear**
(many attempts to emend this passage have given no better sense than the Folio.
The verb "appear" is needed both for the offenders and for the ghost of Hermione;
the obscurity arises from its doing duty for both. Compare the famous difficulty in
Hamlet 4.4.53: "Rightly to be great/Is not to stir without great argument . . .,"
where "not" stands for "not not")   60 **Why to me** Why do you offer such treat-
ment to me

As like Hermione as is her picture,
Affront° his eye.

Cleomenes.   Good madam——

Paulina.   I have done;   75
Yet if my lord will marry, if you will, sir—
No remedy but you will—give me the office
To choose you a queen; she shall not be so young
As was your former, but she shall be such
As, walked your first queen's ghost, it should take joy   80
To see her in your arms.

Leontes.   My true Paulina,
We shall not marry till thou bidd'st us.

Paulina.   That
Shall be when your first queen's again in breath;
Never till then.

Enter a Servant.

Servant. One that gives out himself Prince Florizel,   85
Son of Polixenes, with his princess——she
The fairest I have yet beheld——desires access
To your high presence.

Leontes.   What with him? He comes not
Like to his father's greatness; his approach,
So out of circumstance,° and sudden, tells us   90
'Tis not a visitation framed,° but forced
By need and accident. What train?°

Servant.   But few,
And those but mean.

Leontes.   His princess, say you, with him?

Servant. Ay, the most peerless piece of earth, I think,
That e'er the sun shone bright on.

Paulina.   O Hermione,   95
As every present time doth boast itself
Above a better, gone, so must thy grave

---

75 **affront** confront   90 **out of circumstance** lacking ceremony   91 **framed** planned   92 **train** attendants

Give way to what's seen now. Sir, you yourself
Have said, and writ so; but your writing now
Is colder than that theme:° "She had not been,
Nor was not to be equaled"; thus your verse°
Flowed with her beauty once; 'tis shrewdly ebbed,
To say you have seen a better.

Servant.   Pardon, madam:
The one I have almost forgot—your pardon—
The other, when she has obtained your eye,
Will have your tongue too. This is a creature,
Would she begin a sect, might quench the zeal
Of all professors° else; make proselytes
Of who she but bid follow.

Paulina.   How! Not women?

Servant. Women will love her that she is a woman
More worth than any man; men, that she is
The rarest of all women.

Leontes.   Go, Cleomenes,
Yourself, assisted with your honored friends,
Bring them to our embracement.

                              Exit [*Cleomenes with others*].
                              Still, 'tis strange,
He should thus steal upon us.

Paulina.   Had our prince,
Jewel of children, seen this hour, he had paired
Well with this lord; there was not full a month
Between their births.

Leontes. Prithee no more; cease; thou know'st
He dies to me again, when talked of. Sure
When I shall see this gentleman, thy speeches
Will bring me to consider that which may
Unfurnish me of reason. They are come.

     Enter Florizel, Perdita, Cleomenes, and others.
Your mother was most true to wedlock, Prince,

---

100 **theme** Hermione herself   101 **verse** (he had presumably written verses of
compliment to Hermione)   108 **professors** those who profess zeal for religion (especially Puritans)

For she did print your royal father off,   125
Conceiving you. Were I but twenty-one,
Your father's image is so hit in you,
His very air, that I should call you brother,
As I did him, and speak of something wildly
By us performed before. Most dearly welcome!   130
And your fair princess—goddess! Oh, alas!
I lost a couple that 'twixt heaven and earth
Might thus have stood begetting wonder as
You, gracious couple, do. And then I lost—
All mine own folly—the society,   135
Amity too, of your brave father, whom,
Though bearing misery, I desire my life
Once more to look on him.°

Florizel.   By his command
Have I here touched Sicilia, and from him
Give you all greetings that a king, at friend,°   140
Can send his brother; and but infirmity,
Which waits upon worn times,° hath something
    seized°
His wished ability, he had himself
The lands and waters 'twixt your throne and his
Measured to look upon you; whom he loves   145
(He bade me say so) more than all the scepters
And those that bear them living.

Leontes.   Oh, my brother—
Good gentleman!—the wrongs I have done thee stir
Afresh within me; and these thy offices,°
So rarely kind, are as interpreters   150
Of my behindhand slackness.° Welcome hither,
As is the spring to th' earth! And hath he too
Exposed this paragon to th' fearful usage,
At least ungentle, of the dreadful Neptune,

136–38 **whom … on him** I wish to go on living, however miserably, in order to
look on him again (the final "him" is dispensable, but the construction is
not unique in Shakespeare)   140 **at friend** being in friendship with   142 **worn
times** advanced years   142 **seized** arrested   149 **offices** kindnesses, compli-
ments   150–51 **interpreters … slackness** put into words feelings I've been too
slow in expressing

155　To greet a man not worth her pains, much less
　　Th' adventure° of her person?

Florizel.　　　　　　　　Good my lord,
　　She came from Libya.

Leontes.　　　　　Where the warlike Smalus,
　　That noble honored lord, is feared and loved?

Florizel. Most royal sir, from thence; from him, whose
　　　daughter
160　His tears proclaimed his, parting with her; thence,
　　A prosperous south wind friendly, we have crossed,
　　To execute the charge my father gave me,
　　For visiting your Highness. My best train
　　I have from your Sicilian shores dismissed;
165　Who for Bohemia bend, to signify
　　Not only my success in Libya, sir,
　　But my arrival and my wife's in safety
　　Here where we are.

Leontes.　　　　　The blessèd gods
　　Purge all infection from our air whilst you
170　Do climate° here! You have a holy father,
　　A graceful° gentleman, against whose person,
　　So sacred as it is, I have done sin;
　　For which, the heavens, taking angry note,
　　Have left me issueless; and your father's blessed,
175　As he from heaven merits it, with you,
　　Worthy his goodness. What might I have been,
　　Might I a son and daughter now have looked on,
　　Such goodly things as you!

Enter a Lord.

Lord.　　　　　　　　Most noble sir,
　　That which I shall report will bear no credit,
180　Were not the proof so nigh. Please you, great sir,
　　Bohemia greets you from himself, by me;
　　Desires you to attach° his son, who has—
　　His dignity and duty both cast off—

---

156 **adventure** risk　170 **climate** reside　171 **graceful** virtuous　182 **attach**
arrest

Fled from his father, from his hopes, and with
A shepherd's daughter.

Leontes.   Where's Bohemia? Speak.   185

Lord. Here in your city; I now came from him.
I speak amazedly, and it becomes
My marvel° and my message. To your court
Whiles he was hast'ning—in the chase, it seems,
Of this fair couple—meets he on the way   190
The father of this seeming lady, and
Her brother, having both their country quitted,
With this young prince.

Florizel.   Camillo has betrayed me;
Whose honor and whose honesty till now
Endured all weathers.

Lord.   Lay 't so to his charge;   195
He's with the King your father.

Leontes.   Who? Camillo?

Lord. Camillo, sir; I spake with him; who now
Has these poor men in question.° Never saw I
Wretches so quake; they kneel, they kiss the earth;
Forswear° themselves as often as they speak.   200
Bohemia stops his ears, and threatens them
With divers deaths in death.°

Perdita.   Oh my poor father!
The heaven sets spies upon us, will not have
Our contract celebrated.

Leontes.   You are married?

Florizel. We are not, sir, nor are we like to be;   205
The stars, I see, will kiss the valleys first;
The odds for high and low's alike.°

Leontes.   My lord,

187–88 **becomes/My marvel** suits my bewilderment   198 **in question** in
talk, in conference   200 **Forswear** deny on oath   202 **divers deaths in
death** various tortures   207 **The odds ... alike** (dicing terms. "Fortune is a
cheater who beguiles princes and shepherds alike with his false dice" [J. D.
Wilson])

Is this the daughter of a king?

Florizel.   She is,
When once she is my wife.

210 _Leontes._ That once, I see by your good father's speed,
Will come on very slowly. I am sorry,
Most sorry, you have broken from his liking,
Where you were tied in duty; and as sorry
Your choice is not so rich in worth° as beauty,
That you might well enjoy her.

215 _Florizel._   Dear, look up.
Though Fortune, visible an enemy,
Should chase° us, with my father, power no jot
Hath she to change our loves. Beseech you, sir,
Remember since you owed no more to Time
220 Than I do now; with thought of such affections,
Step forth mine advocate; at your request
My father will grant precious things as trifles.

Leontes. Would he do so, I'd beg your precious mis-
                                                 tress,
Which he counts but a trifle.

Paulina.   Sir, my liege,
225 Your eye hath too much youth in 't; not a month
'Fore your queen died, she was more worth such
                                                 gazes
Than what you look on now.

Leontes.   I thought of her,
Even in these looks I made. But your petition
Is yet unanswered. I will to your father.
230 Your honor not o'erthrown by your desires,°
I am friend to them and you: upon which errand
I now go toward him. Therefore follow me,
And mark what way I make.° Come, good my lord.
                                                 Exeunt.

---

214 **worth** rank   217 **chase** persecute   230 **Your honor ... desires** (a certain insistence on this point of prenuptial chastity is observable both in this
play and in _The Tempest_)   233 **what way I make** how far I succeed

Scene 2. [*Sicilia, before the palace of Leontes.*]

Enter Autolycus and a Gentleman.

Autolycus. Beseech you, sir, were you present at this relation?

First Gentleman. I was by at the opening of the fardel, heard the old shepherd deliver the manner how he found it; whereupon, after a little amazedness, we 5 were all commanded out of the chamber; only this, methought I heard the shepherd say, he found the child.

Autolycus. I would most gladly know the issue of it.

First Gentleman. I make a broken delivery of the 10 business, but the changes I perceived in the King and Camillo were very notes of admiration.° They seemed almost, with staring on one another, to tear the cases of their eyes.° There was speech in their dumbness, language in their very gesture; they 15 looked as they had heard of a world ransomed, or one destroyed. A notable passion of wonder appeared in them; but the wisest beholder that knew no more but seeing° could not say if th' importance° were joy, or sorrow—but in the extremity 20 of the one it must needs be.

Enter another Gentleman.

Here comes a gentleman that happily° knows more: the news, Rogero?

Second Gentleman. Nothing but bonfires. The oracle is fulfilled; the King's daughter is found; such a deal 25

5.2.12 **notes of admiration** exclamation points   14 **cases of their eyes** eyelids   19 **but seeing** but what he saw   19–20 **importance** significance
22 **happily** haply, perhaps

of wonder is broken out within this hour that ballad-
makers cannot be able to express it.

Enter another Gentleman.

Here comes the Lady Paulina's steward; he can
deliver you more. How goes it now, sir? This news,
30 which is called true, is so like an old tale that the
verity of it is in strong suspicion. Has the King found
his heir?

Third Gentleman. Most true, if ever truth were pregnant by circumstance;° that which you hear you'll
35 swear you see, there is such unity in the proofs. The
mantle of Queen Hermione; her jewel about the
neck of it; the letters of Antigonus found with it,
which they know to be his character;° the majesty
of the creature, in resemblance of the mother; the
40 affection° of nobleness, which nature shows above
her breeding and many other evidences—proclaim
her, with all certainty, to be the King's daughter. Did
you see the meeting of the two kings?

Second Gentleman. No.

45 *Third Gentleman.* Then have you lost a sight which
was to be seen, cannot be spoken of. There might
you have beheld one joy crown another, so and in
such manner that it seemed Sorrow wept to take
leave of them; for their joy waded in tears. There
50 was casting up of eyes, holding up of hands, with
countenance° of such distraction that they were to be
known by garment, not by favor.° Our king,
being ready to leap out of himself for joy of his
found daughter, as if that joy were now become a
55 loss, cries, "Oh, thy mother, thy mother"; then asks
Bohemia forgiveness, then embraces his son-in-law;
then again worries he his daughter with clipping°
her. Now he thanks the old shepherd, which stands

33–34 **truth ... circumstance** made evident by, filled out by circumstances
38 **character** handwriting   40 **affection** natural disposition   51 **countenance** (probably meant as a plural; a common orthographical feature in Shakespearean texts)   52 **favor** features   57 **clipping** embracing

by, like a weather-bitten conduit° of many kings'
reigns. I never heard of such another encounter,   60
which lames report to follow it, and undoes description to do it.°

Second Gentleman. What, pray you, became of Antigonus, that carried hence the child?

Third Gentleman. Like an old tale still, which will   65
have matter to rehearse, though credit° be asleep,
and not an ear open: he was torn to pieces with°
a bear. This avouches the shepherd's son, who has
not only his innocence° (which seems much) to
justify him, but a handkerchief and rings of his   70
that Paulina knows.

First Gentleman. What became of his bark and his
followers?

Third Gentleman. Wracked the same instant of their
master's death, and in the view of the shepherd: 75
so that all the instruments which aided to expose the
child were even then lost when it was found. But
oh, the noble combat, that 'twixt joy and sorrow was
fought in Paulina! She had one eye declined for the
loss of her husband, another elevated that the oracle   80
was fulfilled. She lifted the Princess from the earth,
and so locks her in embracing as if she would pin
her to her heart, that she might no more be in danger
of losing.°

First Gentleman. The dignity of this act was worth   85
the audience of kings and princes, for by such was
it acted.

Third Gentleman. One of the prettiest touches of all, and
that which angled for mine eyes—caught the
water though not the fish—was, when at the rela-   90
tion of the Queen's death, with the manner how she
came to 't bravely confessed and lamented by the
King, how attentiveness wounded his daughter; till,

59 **weather-bitten conduit** weather-worn fountain (the old man's tears make
him resemble a fountain in human shape)   62 **do it** describe it   66 **credit** belief   67 **with** by   69 **innocence** simplicity   84 **losing** being lost

from one sign of dolor to another, she did, with an
95 "Alas"—I would fain say—bleed tears; for I am
sure my heart wept blood. Who was most marble
there changed color; some swooned, all sorrowed.
If all the world could have seen 't, the woe had been
universal.

100 *First Gentleman.* Are they returned to the court?

Third Gentleman. No, the Princess, hearing of her
mother's statue, which is in the keeping of Paulina—
a piece many years in doing and now newly per-
formed° by that rare Italian master, Julio Ro-
105 mano,° who, had he himself eternity and could put
breath into his work, would beguile Nature of her
custom, so perfectly he is her ape:° he so near to
Hermione hath done Hermione, that they say one
would speak to her and stand in hope of answer.
110 Thither with all greediness of affection are they
gone, and there they intend to sup.

Second Gentleman. I thought she had some great matter there in hand, for she hath privately, twice or
thrice a day, ever since the death of Hermione,
115 visited that removed house. Shall we thither, and
with our company piece° the rejoicing?

First Gentleman. Who would be thence that has the
benefit of access? Every wink of an eye some new
grace will be born. Our absence makes us un-
120 thrifty to our knowledge.° Let's along.

                    Exit [*with the other Gentlemen*].

Autolycus. Now, had I not the dash of my former life
in me, would preferment drop on my head. I

103–04 **performed** completed 104–05 **Julio Romano** (Italian painter
[1492–1546]. This allusion has caused much debate, because of the anachro-
nism, and because Julio is remembered not as a sculptor but as a painter,
though he probably practiced sculpture as well) 105–07 **had he himself . . .
ape** had he this other attribute of God and could put breath into his statues, he
would cheat Nature of her trade, so closely can he imitate her (the sentiment is
a little confused) 116 **piece** i.e., add to 119–20 **unthrifty to our knowledge**
careless in the accumulation of knowledge

brought the old man and his son aboard the Prince;
told him I heard them talk of a fardel and I know
not what; but he at that time overfond of the shep-   125
herd's daughter (so he then took her to be), who
began to be much seasick, and himself little better,
extremity of weather continuing, this mystery remained undiscovered. But 'tis all one to me; for had
I been the finder-out of this secret, it would not have   130
relished° among my other discredits.

Enter Shepherd and Clown.

Here come those I have done good to against my
will, and already appearing in the blossoms of their
fortune.

Shepherd. Come, boy, I am past moe children; but thy   135
sons and daughters will be all gentlemen born.

Clown. You are well met, sir. You denied to fight with
me this other day, because I was no gentleman
born. See you these clothes? Say you see them not
and think me still no gentleman born; you were   140
best say these robes are not gentlemen born. Give
me the lie, do; and try whether I am not now a
gentleman born.

Autolycus. I know you are now, sir, a gentleman born.

Clown. Ay, and have been so any time these four   145
hours.

Shepherd. And so have I, boy.

Clown. So you have; but I was a gentleman born before my father; for the King's son took me by the
hand and called me brother; and then the two   150
kings called my father brother; and then the Prince,
(my brother) and the Princess (my sister) called
my father father; and so we wept; and there was the
first gentlemanlike tears that ever we shed.

Shepherd. We may live, son, to shed many more.   155

---

131 **relished** proved tasteful, acceptable

Clown. Ay; or else 'twere hard luck, being in so prepos-
terous° estate as we are.

Autolycus. I humbly beseech you, sir, to pardon me
all the faults I have committed to your worship, and
160   to give me your good report to the Prince, my master.

Shepherd. Prithee, son, do: for we must be gentle, now
we are gentlemen.

Clown. Thou wilt amend thy life?

165 *Autolycus.* Ay, an it like° your good worship.

Clown. Give me thy hand. I will swear to the Prince
thou art as honest a true° fellow as any is in Bohemia.

Shepherd. You may say it, but not swear it.

170 *Clown.* Not swear it, now I am a gentleman? Let
boors and franklins° say it, I'll swear it.

Shepherd. How if it be false, son?

Clown. If it be ne'er so false, a true gentleman may
swear it in the behalf of his friend; and I'll swear
175   to the Prince thou art a tall fellow of thy hands,°
and that thou wilt not be drunk; but I know thou art
no tall fellow of thy hands, and that thou wilt
be drunk; but I'll swear it, and I would thou
wouldst be a tall fellow of thy hands.

180 *Autolycus.* I will prove so, sir, to my power.°

Clown. Ay, by any means prove a tall fellow. If I do
not wonder how thou dar'st venture to be drunk, not
being a tall fellow, trust me not. Hark, the kings
and the princes, our kindred, are going to see the
185   Queen's picture. Come, follow us; we'll be thy good
masters.   *Exeunt.*

156–57 **preposterous** (malapropism for "prosperous")   165 **an it like** if it
please   167 **true** honest (as opposed to thieving)   171 **boors and franklins**
peasants and yeomen   175 **a tall fellow of thy hands** a man of
courage   180 **to my power** as far as I am able

Scene 3. [*Sicilia, a chapel in Paulina's house.*]

Enter Leontes, Polixenes, Florizel, Perdita, Camillo,
Paulina, Lords, etc.

Leontes. O grave and good Paulina, the great comfort
    That I have had of thee!

Paulina.   What, sovereign sir,
    I did not well, I meant well. All my services
    You have paid home.° But that you have vouch-
        safed,
    With your crowned brother and these your con-
        tracted°   5
    Heirs of your kingdoms, my poor house to visit,
    It is a surplus of your grace, which never
    My life may last to answer.

Leontes.   O Paulina,
    We honor you with trouble; but we came
    To see the statue of our queen. Your gallery   10
    Have we passed through, not without much content
    In many singularities;° but we saw not
    That which my daughter came to look upon,
    The statue of her mother.

Paulina.   As she lived peerless,
    So her dead likeness I do well believe   15
    Excels whatever yet you looked upon,
    Or hand of man hath done; therefore I keep it
    Lonely, apart. But here it is; prepare
    To see the life as lively mocked, as ever
    Still sleep mocked death: behold, and say 'tis well.   20

5.3.4 **paid home** paid in full   5 **your contracted** (this "your" should possibly
be omitted; the compositor could have caught it from "your crowned" or from
the next line)   12 **singularities** varieties

[Paulina draws a curtain and discovers] Hermione
[standing] like a statue.

I like your silence; it the more shows off
Your wonder; but yet speak, first you, my liege.
Comes it not something near?

Leontes.   Her natural posture!
Chide me, dear stone, that I may say indeed
25   Thou art Hermione; or rather, thou art she
In thy not chiding; for she was as tender
As infancy and grace. But yet, Paulina,
Hermione was not so much wrinkled, nothing
So agèd as this seems.

Polixenes.   Oh, not by much.

30   *Paulina.* So much the more our carver's excellence,
Which lets go by some sixteen years, and makes her
As she lived° now.

Leontes.   As now she might have done,
So much to my good comfort, as it is
Now piercing to my soul. Oh, thus she stood,
35   Even with such life of majesty—warm life,
As now it coldly stands—when first I wooed her.
I am ashamed: does not the stone rebuke me,
For being more stone than it? O royal piece!
There's magic in thy majesty, which has
40   My evils conjured to remembrance,° and
From thy admiring daughter took the spirits,
Standing like stone with thee.

Perdita.   And give me leave,
And do not say 'tis superstition that
I kneel, and then implore her blessing. Lady,
45   Dear queen, that ended when I but began,
Give me that hand of yours to kiss.

Paulina.   O, patience!
The statue is but newly fixed, the color's
Not dry.

32 **As she lived** as if she lived   39-40 **magic ... conjured ... remembrance** (the sight of the statue has called up his sins into his mind as a magi-
cian summons demons)

Camillo. My lord, your sorrow was too sore laid on,
    Which sixteen winters cannot blow away,   50
    So many summers dry. Scarce any joy
    Did ever so long live; no sorrow
    But killed itself much sooner.

Polixenes.   Dear my brother,
    Let him that was the cause of this have power
    To take off so much grief from you as he   55
    Will piece up° in himself.

Paulina.   Indeed, my lord,
    If I had thought the sight of my poor image
    Would thus have wrought you—for the stone is
       mine—
    I'd not have showed it.

Leontes.   Do not draw the curtain.

Paulina. No longer shall you gaze on 't, lest your fancy   60
    May think anon it moves.

Leontes.   Let be, let be!
    Would I were dead, but that methinks already°—
    What was he that did make it? See, my lord,
    Would you not deem it breathed? And that those
       veins
    Did verily bear blood?

Polixenes.   Masterly done!   65
    The very life seems warm upon her lip.

Leontes. The fixure° of her eye has motion in 't,
    As we are mocked with art.

Paulina.   I'll draw the curtain;
    My lord's almost so far transported that
    He'll think anon it lives.

Leontes.   O sweet Paulina,   70
    Make me to think so twenty years together!
    No settled° senses of the world can match
    The pleasure of that madness. Let 't alone.

---

56 **piece up** make his own   62 **Would . . . already** May I die if I do not think it moves already (Staunton)   67 **fixure** (early form of "fixture")   72 **settled** sane

    Paulina. I am sorry, sir, I have thus far stirred you;
        but
      I could afflict you farther.

75 *Leontes.*   Do, Paulina;
      For this affliction has a taste as sweet
      As any cordial° comfort. Still, methinks,
      There is an air comes from her. What fine chisel
      Could ever yet cut breath? Let no man mock me,
      For I will kiss her.

80 *Paulina.*   Good my lord, forbear!
      The ruddiness upon her lip is wet;
      You'll mar it if you kiss it; stain your own
      With oily painting. Shall I draw the curtain?

    Leontes. No, not these twenty years.

    Perdita.   So long could I
      Stand by, a looker-on.

85 *Paulina.*   Either forbear,
      Quit presently the chapel, or resolve you
      For more amazement. If you can behold it,
      I'll make the statue move indeed, descend,
      And take you by the hand—but then you'll think,
90   Which I protest against, I am assisted
      By wicked powers.

    Leontes.   What you can make her do,
      I am content to look on; what to speak,
      I am content to hear; for 'tis as easy
      To make her speak, as move.

    Paulina.   It is required
95   You do awake your faith; then, all stand still.
      Or those that think it is unlawful business
      I am about, let them depart.

    Leontes.   Proceed.
      No foot shall stir.

    Paulina.   Music, awake her: strike.
      'Tis time; descend; be stone no more; approach;

---

77 **cordial** heart-warming

Strike all that look upon with marvel; come;   *100*
I'll fill your grave up. Stir; nay, come away;
Bequeath to death your numbness, for from him
Dear life redeems you. You perceive she stirs.

[*Hermione comes down.*]

Start not; her actions shall be holy as
You hear my spell is lawful. Do not shun her   *105*
Until you see her die again, for then
You kill her double. Nay, present your hand.
When she was young, you wooed her; now, in age,
Is she become the suitor?

Leontes.   Oh, she's warm!
If this be magic, let it be an art   *110*
Lawful as eating.

Polixenes.   She embraces him.

Camillo. She hangs about his neck;
If she pertain to life, let her speak too.

Polixenes. Ay, and make it manifest where she has
lived,
Or how stol'n from the dead.

Paulina.   That she is living,   *115*
Were it but told you, should be hooted at
Like an old tale; but it appears she lives,
Though yet she speak not. Mark a little while:
Please you to interpose, fair madam; kneel,
And pray your mother's blessing; turn, good lady,   *120*
Our Perdita is found.

Hermione.   You gods look down,
And from your sacred vials pour your graces
Upon my daughter's head! Tell me, mine own,
Where hast thou been preserved? Where lived? How
found
Thy father's court? For thou shalt hear that I,   *125*
Knowing by Paulina that the oracle
Gave hope thou wast in being,° have preserved
Myself to see the issue.

127 **in being** alive

Paulina.   There's time enough for that,
       Lest they desire upon this push° to trouble
130   Your joys with like relation. Go together,
       You precious winners all; your exultation
       Partake° to every one. I an old turtle,
       Will wing me to some withered bough, and there
       My mate, that's never to be found again,
       Lament till I am lost.

135 *Leontes.*   O peace, Paulina!
       Thou shouldst a husband take by my consent,
       As I by thine a wife. This is a match,
       And made between 's by vows. Thou hast found mine,
       But how, is to be questioned; for I saw her,
140   As I thought, dead; and have in vain said many
       A prayer upon her grave. I'll not seek farre,°
       For him, I partly know his mind, to find thee
       An honorable husband. Come, Camillo,
       And take her by the hand, whose worth and honesty°
145   Is richly noted, and here justified
       By us, a pair of kings. Let's from this place
       What! Look upon my brother.° Both your pardons,
       That e'er I put between your holy looks
       My ill suspicion. This your son-in-law,
150   And son unto the King, whom, heavens directing,
       Is troth-plight to your daughter. Good Paulina,
       Lead us from hence, where we may leisurely
       Each one demand and answer to his part
       Performed in this wide gap of time since first
155   We were dissevered. Hastily lead away.   *Exeunt.*

                          FINIS

---

129 **upon this push** at this exciting moment   132 **Partake** communicate,
share   141 **farre** farther   144 **whose worth and honesty** i.e., Camillo's
147 **Look upon my brother** (Hermione has presumably shown some natural
embarrassment about greeting Polixenes)

Textual Note

The Winter's Tale was placed at the end of the section of Comedies in the Folio of 1623. There was no earlier edition, and so all subsequent editions derive from the Folio text. Bibliographical evidence shows that the play was added to the Folio late, when a number of the History plays had already been printed. Possibly no copy was available until then. The copy that eventually reached the printing house was almost certainly a transcript of the play made by Ralph Crane, whose hand is now well known to scholars. Crane did a good deal for Shakespeare's company, the King's Men, and the Folio texts of *The Tempest*, *The Two Gentlemen of Verona*—and possibly other plays too—are attributable to him. Certain of his characteristics—notably his fondness for brackets and his habit of placing all the entries at the head of the scene, whether or no they are repeated when the character actually comes in—are abundantly in evidence in the Folio text of *The Winter's Tale*.

The text is very deficient in stage directions, and Crane's copy was evidently not made for use in the playhouse. But he was an intelligent scribe, and doubtless gave the compositor clean copy. In fact, this is one of the cleanest of Shakespeare's texts, despite the difficulty of some of the verse. The present edition deletes the superfluous entries at heads of scenes and places them at the appropriate positions, modernizes spelling and punctuation, and translates from Latin into English the Folio's act and scene divisions. The list of characters, here prefixed to the play, in the Folio follows the play. Other material departures from the Folio text are listed below in italic type, followed by the Folio's reading (F) in roman; only in three or four places is there any real difficulty involved.

1.1.28 *have* hath

1.2.104 *And* A 158 *do* does 208 *you, they say* you say 276 *hobby-horse* Holy-horse 327–28 *sully/The purity* Sully the puritie 446–47 *thereon,/His execution sworn* Thereon his Execution sworne

2.1.25–26 *I have one/Of* I have one of

2.2.6 *whom* who 52 *let't* le't

2.3.38 *What* Who 52 *profess* professes 176 *its* it

3.2.1 *session* Sessions 10 *Silence* [F italicizes, as if s.d.] 32 *Who* Whom 107 *for* no

3.3.18 *awaking* a waking 119 *made* mad

4.3.10 *with heigh, with heigh* With heigh 57 *offends* offend

4.4.2 *do* Do's 12 *Digest it with* Digest with 13 *swoon* sworne 98 *your* you 160 *out* on't 365 *who* whom 423 *acknowledged* acknowledge 427 *who* whom 432 *shalt see* shalt neuer see 443 *hoop* hope 471 *your* my 494 *hide* hides 503 *whom* who 553 *asks thee, the son, forgiveness* asks thee there Sonne forgiuenesse 709 *know not* know 739 *or toaze* at toaze 849 *Exit* Exeunt

5.1.12 *True, too true* [F places the first "true" at the end of Leontes' previous speech] 61 *just cause* just such cause 75 *I have done* [F gives to Cleomenes]

5.2.36 *Hermione* Hermiones .

5.3.18 *Lonely* Louely 96 *Or* on

The Source of *The Winter's Tale*

Shakespeare's source was a *novella* by his old enemy Robert Greene. The title of the first edition reads:

> *Pandosto. The Triumph of Time.* Wherein is discouered by a pleasant Historie, that although by the meanes of sinister fortune, Truth may be concealed, yet by Time in spight of fortune it is most manifestly reuealed. Pleasant for age to auoyde drowsie thoughtes, profitable for youth to eschue other wanton pastimes, and bringing to both a desired content. *Temporis filia veritas.* By Robert Greene, Maister of Artes in Cambridge. *Omne tulit punctum qui miscuit vtile dulci.* Imprinted at London by Thomas Orwin for Thomas Cadman, dwelling at the Signe of the Bible, neere vnto the North doore of Paules, 1588.

The Short Title Catalogue records only one copy of this edition, in the British Museum; and that is imperfect. There were subsequent editions in 1592, 1595, 1607, and later. But although there was so recent an edition available, Shakespeare appears to have used the first. He seems for some reason to have been interested in Greene at this time, for he also drew on the pamphleteer's popular studies of the London underworld, especially *The Second Part of Conny-catching* (1591), useful for describing the tricks of Autolycus (especially the cheating of the Clown in 4.3); and although he rejected Greene's personal names, he replaced "Garinter" by "Mamillius," perhaps remembering Greene's "looking glass for the ladies of England," *Mamillia* (1583).

Shakespeare treats *Pandosto* in his usual way, freely changing it but often echoing its language and incidents. The following very brief summary uses the names Shakespeare gave the characters.

Shakespeare changes the countries about; Leontes is king of Bohemia, Polixenes of Sicily; and it is the wife of Polixenes who is daughter of the empress of Russia, not Hermione. Greene's Hermione, though perfectly innocent, gives more color to the suspicions of Leontes by the freedom of her conduct toward Polixenes. She does not discover her pregnancy till she is already in prison. Camillo shows more self-interest in the novel, and has no part in the return of Perdita to her father. The jealousy of Leontes, though not well founded, is less of a brainstorm in the original. He sends the new baby to sea in a little boat by herself; there is no Antigonus. After the trial he instantly accepts the word of the oracle, but his son and his wife both die. Perdita is cast ashore in Sicily and reared by shepherds interested in the gold that accompanies her. Years later, she is wooed by Florizel, but here the tone of the novel is very different from that of the play, despite suggestions that Shakespeare used in the sheep-shearing scene. Florizel is much more formal, and the relationship, until Perdita, properly suspicious, alters it by insisting on her virtue, is not much different from an ordinary seduction of a country girl by a courtier. But Florizel, appearing as a shepherd, establishes the honesty of his intentions and plans to amass money to elope with Perdita to Italy. The unhappy old shepherd is tricked into boarding the ship (but not by Autolycus, who does not exist in the novel). When the couple arrives in Bohemia, Leontes conceives a lustful desire for Perdita, and throws Florizel into prison. But when he hears the whole story from the ambassadors of Polixenes (who is alarmed to think of his son in the hands of an enemy), he frees Florizel and condemns Perdita and her father to death. But the old man now tells his tale; Perdita is proved to be Leontes' lost daughter. She returns to Sicily with Florizel, and they are married; but Leontes kills himself from remorse.

* * *

I have given no account of many changes that are simply a matter of dramaturgical economy. Despite the strong similarities in plot, there are important alterations in Shakespeare. The greatest of these, if the least tangible, is his substitution of Nature for Fortune as the deity presiding over the original story; and the consequent reconstruction in the statue scene, with Hermione restored and Leontes transported with joy at the recovery of his wife, his daughter, and his friend. For Shakespeare's Perdita and Florizel, Greene affords little more than hints, and the whole pastoral of the Fourth Act is similarly built on mere suggestions. Greene's Florizel knows better than to speak freely of his love; and Polixenes does not visit the sheepfold, let alone converse with Perdita on profound topics. The point at which the two works most closely concur is the scene of Hermione's trial, though the reader will see that other references to Greene's text are fairly frequent, so that it looks as if Shakespeare had the book on his desk. It was the story he wanted, to adapt as freely as he chose, and he shuns the Arcadianism of Greene's dialogue; yet once again the dead author might have found cause to complain, as he had eighteen years earlier, that the upstart "crow" had been "beautified with our feathers."

ROBERT GREENE

Selections from Pandosto

Among all the passions wherewith human minds are perplexed, there is none that so galleth with restless despite as the infectious sore of jealousy; for all other griefs are either to be appeased with sensible persuasions, to be cured with wholesome counsel, to be relieved in want, or by tract of time to be worn out, jealousy only excepted, which is so sauced with suspicious doubts and pinching mistrust, that whoso seeks by friendly counsel to raze out this hellish passion, it forthwith suspecteth that he giveth this advice to cover his own guiltiness. Yea, whoso is pained with this restless torment doubteth all, distrusteth himself, is always frozen with fear and fired with suspicion, having that wherein consisteth all his joy to be the breeder of his misery. Yea, it is such a heavy enemy to that holy estate of matrimony, sowing between the married couples such deadly seeds of secret hatred, as, love being once razed out by spiteful distrust, there oft ensueth bloody revenge, as this ensuing history manifestly proveth: wherein Pandosto, furiously incensed by causeless jealousy, procured the death of his most loving and loyal wife and his own endless sorrow and misery.

In the country of Bohemia, there reigned a king called Pandosto, whose fortunate success in wars against his foes, and bountiful courtesy toward his friends in peace, made him to be greatly feared and loved of all men. This Pandosto had to wife a lady called Bellaria, by birth royal, learned by education, fair by nature, by virtues famous, so that it was hard to judge whether her beauty, fortune, or virtue won the greatest commendations. These two, linked together in perfect love, led their lives with such fortunate content that their subjects greatly rejoiced to see their quiet disposition. They had not been married long, but Fortune, willing to increase their happiness, lent them a son, so adorned with the gifts of nature, as the perfection of the child greatly augmented the love of the parents and the joy of their commons. . . .

Fortune, envious of such happy success, willing to show some sign of her inconstancy, turned her wheel, and darkened their bright sun of prosperity with the misty clouds of mishap and misery. For it so happened that Egistus, king of Sicilia, who in his youth had been brought up with Pandosto, desirous to show that neither tract of time nor distance of place could diminish their former friendship, provided a navy of ships and sailed into Bohemia to visit his old friend and companion; who, hearing of his arrival, went himself in person and his wife Bellaria, accompanied with a great train of lords and ladies, to meet Egistus; and espying him, alighted from his horse, embraced him very lovingly, protesting that nothing in the world could have happened more acceptable to him than his coming, wishing his wife to welcome his old friend and acquaintance: who, to show how she liked him whom her husband loved, entertained him with such familiar courtesy as Egistus perceived himself to be very well welcome. . . .

Bellaria, who in her time was the flower of courtesy, willing to show how unfeignedly she loved her husband by his friend's entertainment, used him likewise so familiarly that her countenance bewrayed how her mind was affected towards him, oftentimes coming herself into his bedchamber to see that nothing should be amiss to mislike him. This honest familiarity increased daily more and more betwixt them; for Bellaria, noting in Egistus a princely and bountiful mind, adorned with sundry and excellent qualities, and Egistus, finding in her a virtuous and courteous disposition, there grew such a secret uniting of their affections, that the one could not well be without the company of the other: insomuch, that when Pandosto was busied with such urgent affairs that he could not be present with his friend Egistus, Bellaria would walk with him into the garden, where they two in private and pleasant devices would pass away the time to both their contents. This custom still continuing betwixt them, a certain melancholy passion entering the mind of Pandosto drave him into sundry and doubtful thoughts. First, he called to mind the beauty of his wife Bellaria, the comeliness and bravery of his friend Egistus, thinking that love was above all laws and, therefore, to be stayed with no law; that it was hard to put fire and flax together without burning; that their open pleasures might breed his secret displeasures. He considered with himself that Egistus was a man and must needs love, that his wife was a woman, and therefore, subject unto love, and that where fancy forced, friendship was of no force.

These and suchlike doubtful thoughts, a long time smothering in his stomach, began at last to kindle in his mind a secret mistrust, which, increased by suspicion, grew at last to a flaming jealousy that so tormented him as he could take no rest. He then began to measure all their actions, and to misconstrue of their too private familiarity, judging that it was not for honest affection, but for disordinate fancy, so that he began to watch them more narrowly to see if he could get any true or certain proof to confirm his doubtful suspicion. While thus he noted their looks and gestures and suspected their thoughts and meanings, they two silly souls, who doubted nothing of this his treacherous intent, frequented daily each other's company, which drave him into such a frantic passion, that he began to bear a secret hate to Egistus and a louring countenance to Bellaria; who marveling at such unaccustomed frowns, began to cast beyond the moon, and to enter into a thousand sundry thoughts, which way she should offend her husband: but finding in herself a clear conscience ceased to muse, until such time as she might find fit opportunity to demand the cause of his dumps. In the meantime Pandosto's mind was so far charged with jealousy, that he did no longer doubt, but was assured, as he thought, that his friend Egistus had entered a wrong point in his tables, and so had played him false play: whereupon, desirous to revenge so great an injury, he thought best to dissemble the grudge with a fair and friendly countenance, and so under the shape of a friend to show him the trick of a foe. Devising with himself a long time how he might best put away Egistus without suspicion of treacherous murder, he concluded at last to poison him; which opinion pleasing his humor he became resolute in his determination, and the better to bring the matter to pass he called unto him his cupbearer, with whom in secret he brake the matter, promising to him for the performance thereof to give him a thousand crowns of yearly revenues.

His cupbearer, either being of a good conscience or willing for fashion sake to deny such a bloody request, began with great reasons to persuade Pandosto from his determinate mischief, showing him what an offense murder was to the gods; how such unnatural actions did more displease the heavens than men, that causeless cruelty did seldom or never escape without revenge: he laid before his face that Egistus was his friend, a king, and one that was come into his kingdom to confirm a league of perpetual amity betwixt them; that he had and did show him a most friendly countenance; how Egistus was not only honored of his own people by obedience, but also loved of the Bohemians for his courtesy, and that if he now should without any just or manifest cause poison him, it would not only be a great dishonor to his majesty, and a means to sow perpetual enmity between the Sicilians and the Bohemians, but also his own subjects would repine at such treacherous cruelty. These and such-like persuasions of Franion—for so was his cupbearer called—could no whit prevail to dissuade him from his devilish enterprise, but, remaining resolute in his determination (his fury so fired with rage as it could not be appeased with reason), he began with bitter taunts to take up his man, and to lay before him two baits, preferment and death; saying that if he should poison Egistus, he would advance him to high dignities; if he refused to do it of an obstinate mind, no torture should be too great to requite his disobedience. Franion, seeing that to persuade Pandosto any more was but to strive against the stream, consented, as soon as opportunity would give him leave, to dispatch Egistus: wherewith Pandosto remained somewhat satisfied, hoping now he should be fully revenged of such mistrusted injuries, intending also as soon as Egistus was dead to give his wife a sop of the same sauce, and so be rid of those which were the cause of his restless sorrow. . . .

. . . Franion . . . seeing either he must die with a clear mind, or live with a spotted conscience, he was so cumbered with divers cogitations that he could take no rest, until at last he determined to break the matter to Egistus; but, fearing that the king should either suspect or hear of such matters, he concealed the device till opportunity would permit him to reveal it. Lingering thus in doubtful fear, in an evening he went to Egistus' lodging, and desirous to break with him of certain affairs that touched the king, after all were commanded out of the chamber, Franion made manifest the whole conspiracy which Pandosto had devised against him, desiring Egistus not to account him a traitor for bewraying his master's counsel, but to think that he did it for conscience: hoping that although his master, inflamed with rage or incensed by some sinister reports or slanderous speeches, had imagined such causeless mischief, yet when time should pacify his anger, and try those talebearers but flattering parasites, then he would count him as a faithful servant that with such care had kept his master's credit. Egistus had not fully heard Franion tell forth his tale, but a quaking fear possessed all his limbs, thinking that there was some treason wrought, and that Franion did but shadow his craft with these false colors: wherefore he began to wax in choler, and said that he doubted not Pandosto, sith he was his friend, and there had never as yet been any breach of amity. He had not sought to invade his lands, to conspire with his enemies, to dissuade his subjects from their allegiance; but in word and thought he rested his at all times: he knew not, therefore, any cause that should move Pandosto to seek his death, but suspected it to be a compacted knavery of the Bohemians to bring the king and him at odds.

Franion, staying him in the midst of his talk, told him that to dally with princes was with the swans to sing against their death, and that, if the Bohemians had intended any such mischief, it might have been better brought to pass than by revealing the conspiracy: therefore his majesty did ill to misconstrue of his good meaning, sith his intent was to hinder treason, not to become a traitor; and to confirm his promises, if it pleased his majesty to fly into Sicilia for the safeguard of his life, he would go with him, and if then he found not such a practice to be pretended, let his imagined treachery be repaid with most monstrous torments. Egistus, hearing the solemn protestation of Franion, began to consider that in love and kingdoms neither faith nor law is to be respected, doubting that Pandosto thought by his death to destroy his men, and with speedy war to invade Sicilia. These and such doubts throughly weighed, he gave great thanks to Franion, promising if he might with life return to Syracusa, that he would create him a duke in Sicilia, craving his counsel how he might escape out of the country. . . .

. . . Egistus, fearing that delay might breed danger, and willing that the grass should not be cut from under his feet, taking bag and baggage, by the help of Franion conveyed himself and his men out at a postern gate of the city, so secretly and speedily that without any suspicion they got to the seashore; where, with many a bitter curse taking their leave of Bohemia, they went aboard. Weighing their anchors and hoisting sail, they passed as fast as wind and sea would permit towards Sicilia, Egistus being a joyful man that he had safely passed such treacherous perils. But as they were quietly floating on the sea, so Pandosto and his citizens were in an uproar; for, seeing that the Sicilians without taking their leave were fled away by night, the Bohemians feared some treason, and the king thought that without question his suspicion was true, seeing his cupbearer had bewrayed the sum of his secret pretense. Whereupon he began to imagine that Franion and his wife Bellaria had conspired with Egistus, and that the fervent affection she bare him was the only means of his secret departure; insomuch that, incensed with rage, he commands that his wife should be carried to strait prison until they heard further of his pleasure. The guard, unwilling to lay their hands on such a virtuous princess and yet fearing the king's fury, went very sorrowful to fulfill their charge. Coming to the queen's lodging they found her playing with her young son Garinter, unto whom with tears doing the message, Bellaria, astonished at such a hard censure and finding her clear conscience a sure advocate to plead in her case, went to the prison most willingly, where with sighs and tears she passed away the time till she might come to her trial.

But Pandosto, whose reason was suppressed with rage and whose unbridled folly was incensed with fury, seeing Franion had bewrayed his secrets, and that Egistus might well be railed on, but not revenged, determined to wreak all his wrath on poor Bellaria. He, therefore, caused a general proclamation to be made through all his realm that the queen and Egistus had, by the help of Franion, not only committed most incestuous adultery, but also had conspired the king's death; whereupon the traitor Franion was fled away with Egistus, and Bellaria was most justly imprisoned. This proclamation being once blazed through the country, although the virtuous disposition of the queen did half discredit the contents, yet the sudden and speedy passage of Egistus and the secret departure of Franion induced them, the circumstances throughly considered, to think that both the proclamation was true, and the king greatly injured: yet they pitied her case, as sorrowful that so good a lady should be crossed with such adverse fortune. But the king, whose restless rage would admit no pity, thought that although he might sufficiently requite his wife's falsehood with the bitter plague of pinching penury, yet his mind should never be glutted with revenge till he might have fit time and opportunity to repay the treachery of Egistus with a fatal injury. But a curst cow hath ofttimes short horns, and a willing mind but a weak arm; for Pandosto, although he felt that revenge was a spur to war, and that envy always proffereth steel, yet he saw that Egistus was not only of great puissance and prowess to withstand him, but had also many kings of his alliance to aid him, if need should serve, for he married the emperor's daughter of Russia. These and the like considerations something daunted Pandosto his courage, so that he was content rather to put up a manifest injury with peace, than hunt after revenge, dishonor, and loss; determining, since Egistus had escaped scot-free, that Bellaria should pay for all at an unreasonable price.

Remaining thus resolute in his determination, Bellaria continuing still in prison and hearing the contents of the proclamation, knowing that her mind was never touched with such affection, nor that Egistus had ever offered her such discourtesy, would gladly have come to her answer, that both she might have known her just accusers, and cleared herself of that guiltless crime.

But Pandosto was so inflamed with rage and infected with jealousy, as he would not vouchsafe to hear her, nor admit any just excuse; so that she was fain to make a virtue of her need and with patience to bear those heavy injuries. As thus she lay crossed with calamities, a great cause to increase her grief, she found herself quick with child. . . .

. . . The jailer, pitying those her heavy passions, thinking that if the king knew she were with child he would somewhat appease his fury and release her from prison, went in all haste and certified Pandosto what the effect of Bellaria's complaint was; who no sooner heard the jailer say she was with child, but as one possessed with a frenzy he rose up in a rage, swearing that she and the bastard brat she was big withal should die if the gods themselves said no; thinking that surely by computation of time that Egistus and not he was the father to the child. This suspicious thought galled afresh this half-healed sore, insomuch as he could take no rest until he might mitigate his choler with a just revenge, which happened presently after. For Bellaria was brought to bed of a fair and beautiful daughter, which no sooner Pandosto heard, but he determined that both Bellaria and the young infant should be burnt with fire. His nobles hearing of the king's cruel sentence sought by persuasions to divert him from his bloody determination, laying before his face the innocency of the child, and virtuous disposition of his wife, how she had continually loved and honored him so tenderly that without due proof he could not, nor ought not, to appeach her of that crime. And if she had faulted, yet it were more honorable to pardon with mercy than to punish with extremity, and more kingly to be commended of pity than accused of rigor. And as for the child, if he should punish it for the mother's offense, it were to strive against nature and justice; and that unnatural actions do more offend the gods than men; how causeless cruelty nor innocent blood never scapes without revenge. These and suchlike reasons could not appease his rage, but he rested resolute in this, that Bellaria being an adultress the child was a bastard, and he would not suffer that such an infamous brat should call him father. Yet at last, seeing his noblemen were importunate upon him, he was content to spare the child's life, and yet to put it to a worse death. For he found out this device, that seeing, as he thought, it came by fortune, so he would commit it to the charge of fortune; and, therefore, he caused a little cockboat to be provided, wherein he meant to put the babe, and then send it to the mercies of the seas and the destinies. From this his peers in no wise could persuade him, but that he sent presently two of his guard to fetch the child. . . .

[Bellaria, hearing of her husband's intention, first faints, and then laments the fate of her child.] . . . Such and so great was her grief, that her vital spirits being suppressed with sorrow, she fell again down into a trance, having her senses so sotted with care that after she was revived yet she lost her memory, and lay for a great time without moving, as one in a trance. The guard left her in this perplexity, and carried the child to the king, who, quite devoid of pity, commanded that without delay it should be put in the boat, having neither sail nor rudder to guide it, and so to be carried into the midst of the sea, and there left to the wind and wave as the destinies please to appoint. . . .

[The child is taken away by sailors and put to sea in a storm.]

. . . But leaving the child to her fortunes, again to Pandosto, who not yet glutted with sufficient revenge devised which way he should best increase his wife's calamity. But first assembling his nobles and counselors, he called her for the more reproach into open court, where it was objected against her that she had committed adultery with Egistus, and conspired with Franion to poison Pandosto her husband, but their pretense being partly spied, she counseled them to fly away by night for their better safety. Bellaria, who standing like a prisoner at the bar, feeling in herself a clear conscience to withstand her false accusers, seeing that no less than death could pacify her husband's wrath, waxed bold and desired that she might have law and justice, for mercy she neither craved nor hoped for; and that those perjured wretches which had falsely accused her to the king might be brought before her face to give in evidence. But Pandosto, whose rage and jealousy was such as no reason nor equity could appease, told her that, for her accusers, they were of such credit as their words were sufficient witness, and that the sudden and secret flight of Egistus and Franion confirmed that which they had confessed; and as for her, it was her part to deny such a monstrous crime, and to be impudent in forswearing the fact, since she had past all shame in committing the fault: but her stale countenance should stand for no coin, for as the bastard which she bare was served, so she should with some cruel death be requited. Bellaria, no whit dismayed with this rough reply, told her husband Pandosto that he spake upon choler and not conscience, for her virtuous life had been ever such as no spot of suspicion could ever stain. And if she had borne a friendly countenance to Egistus, it was in respect he was his friend, and not for any lusting affection; therefore, if she were condemned without any further proof it was rigor and not law.

The noblemen, which sate in judgment, said that Bellaria spake reason, and entreated the king that the accusers might be openly examined and sworn, and if then the evidence were such as the jury might find her guilty (for seeing she was a prince she ought to be tried by her peers), then let her have such punishment as the extremity of the law will assign to such malefactors. The king presently made answer that in this case he might and would dispense with the law, and that the jury being once paneled they should take his word for sufficient evidence; otherwise he would make the proudest of them repent it. The noblemen seeing the king in choler were all whist; but Bellaria, whose life then hung in the balance, fearing more perpetual infamy than momentary death, told the king if his fury might stand for a law that it were vain to have the jury yield their verdict; and, therefore, she fell down upon her knees, and desired the king that for the love he bare to his young son Garinter, whom she brought into the world, that he would grant her a request; which was this, that it would please his majesty to send six of his noblemen whom he best trusted to the Isle of Delphos, there to inquire of the oracle of Apollo whether she had committed adultery with Egistus, or conspired to poison him with Franion? and if the god Apollo, who by his divine essence knew all secrets, gave answer that she was guilty, she were content to suffer any torment were it never so terrible. The request was so reasonable that Pandosto could not for shame deny it, unless he would be counted of all his subjects more willful than wise: he therefore agreed that with as much speed as might be there should be certain ambassadors dispatched to the Isle of Delphos, and in the mean season he commanded that his wife should be kept in close prison.

[The ambassadors arrive at Delphos.] ... They had not long kneeled at the altar, but Apollo with a loud voice said: "Bohemians, what you find behind the altar take, and depart." They forthwith obeying the oracle found a scroll of parchment, wherein was written these words in letters of gold—

THE ORACLE

SUSPICION IS NO PROOF: JEALOUSY IS AN UNEQUAL JUDGE: BEL-
LARIA IS CHASTE: EGISTUS BLAMELESS: FRANION A TRUE SUBJECT:
PANDOSTO TREACHEROUS: HIS BABE AN INNOCENT; AND THE KING
SHALL LIVE WITHOUT AN HEIR, IF THAT WHICH IS LOST BE NOT
FOUND.

As soon as they had taken out this scroll the priest of the god commanded them that they should not presume to read it before they came in the presence of Pandosto, unless they would incur the displeasure of Apollo. The Bohemian lords carefully obeying his command, taking their leave of the priest with great reverence, departed out of the temple, and went to their ships, and as soon as wind would permit them sailed toward Bohemia, whither in short time they safely arrived; and with great triumph issuing out of their ships went to the king's palace, whom they found in his chamber accompanied with other noblemen. Pandosto no sooner saw them but with a merry countenance he welcomed them home, asking what news? they told his majesty that they had received an answer of the god written in a scroll, but with this charge, that they should not read the contents before they came in the presence of the king, and with that they delivered him the parchment: but his noblemen entreated him that, sith therein was contained either the safety of his wife's life and honesty or her death and perpetual infamy, that he would have his nobles and commons assembled in the judgment hall, where the queen, brought in as prisoner, should hear the contents. If she were found guilty by the oracle of the god, then all should have cause to think his rigor proceeded of due desert: if her grace were found faultless, then she should be cleared before all, sith she had been accused openly. This pleased the king so, that he appointed the day, and assembled all his lords and commons, and caused the queen to be brought in before the judgment seat, commanding that the indictment should be read wherein she was accused of adultery with Egistus and of conspiracy with Franion. Bellaria hearing the contents was no whit astonished, but made this cheerful answer—

"If the divine powers be privy to human actions—as no doubt they are—I hope my patience shall make fortune blush, and my unspotted life shall stain spiteful discredit. For although lying report hath sought to appeach mine honor, and suspicion hath intended to soil my credit with infamy, yet where virtue keepeth the fort, report and suspicion may assail, but never sack: how I have led my life before Egistus' coming, I appeal, Pandosto, to the gods and to thy conscience. What hath passed betwixt him and me, the gods only know, and I hope will presently reveal: that I loved Egistus I cannot deny; that I honored him I shame not to confess: to the one I was forced by his virtues, to the other for his dignities. But as touching lascivious lust, I say Egistus is honest, and hope myself to be found without spot: for Franion, I can neither accuse him nor excuse him, for I was not privy to his departure; and that this is true which I have here rehearsed I refer myself to the divine oracle."

Bellaria had no sooner said but the king commanded that one of his dukes should read the contents of the scroll, which after the commons had heard they gave a great shout, rejoicing and clapping their hands that the queen was clear of that false accusation. But the king, whose conscience was a witness against him of his witless fury and false suspected jealousy, was so ashamed of his rash folly that he entreated his nobles to persuade Bellaria to forgive and forget these injuries; promising not only to show himself a loyal and loving husband, but also to reconcile himself to Egistus and Franion; revealing then before them all the cause of their secret flight, and how treacherously he thought to have practiced his death, if the good mind of his cupbearer had not prevented his purpose. As thus he was relating the whole matter, there was word brought him that his young son Garinter was suddenly dead, which news so soon as Bellaria heard, surcharged before with extreme joy and now suppressed with heavy sorrow, her vital spirits were so stopped that she fell down presently dead, and could be never revived. This sudden sight so appalled the king's senses, that he sank from his seat in a swound, so as he was fain to be carried by his nobles to his palace, where he lay by the space of three days without speech. His commons were, as men in despair, diversely distressed: there was nothing but mourning and lamentation to be heard throughout all Bohemia: their young prince dead, their virtuous queen bereaved of her life, and their king and sovereign in great hazard. This tragical discourse of fortune so daunted them, as they went like shadows, not men; yet somewhat to comfort their heavy hearts, they heard that Pandosto was come to himself, and had recovered his speech, who as in a fury brayed out these bitter speeches. . . .

[Pandosto reproaches himself, and is prevented from suicide. The story returns to Fawnia (Perdita).] . . . The little boat was driven with the tide into the coast of Sicilia, where sticking upon the sands it rested. Fortune minding to be wanton, willing to show that as she hath wrinkles on her brows so she hath dimples in her cheeks, thought after so many sour looks to lend a feigned smile, and after a puffing storm to bring a pretty calm, she began thus to dally. It fortuned a poor mercenary shepherd that dwelled in Sicilia, who got his living by other men's flocks, missed one of his sheep, and, thinking it had strayed into the covert that was hard by, sought very diligently to find that which he could not see, fearing either that the wolves or eagles had undone him (for he was so poor as a sheep was half his substance), wandered down toward the sea cliffs to see if perchance the sheep was browsing on the sea ivy, whereon they greatly do feed; but not finding her there, as he was ready to return to his flock he heard a child cry, but knowing there was no house near, he thought he had mistaken the sound and that it was the bleating of his sheep. Wherefore, looking more narrowly, as he cast his eye to the sea he spied a little boat, from whence, as he attentively listened, he might hear the cry to come. Standing a good while in a maze, at last he went to the shore, and wading to the boat, as he looked in he saw the little babe lying all alone ready to die for hunger and cold, wrapped in a mantle of scarlet richly embroidered with gold, and having a chain about the neck.

The shepherd, who before had never seen so fair a babe nor so rich jewels, thought assuredly that it was some little god, and began with great devotion to knock on his breast. The babe, who writhed with the head to seek for the pap, began again to cry afresh, whereby the poor man knew that it was a child, which by some sinister means was driven thither by distress of weather; marveling how such a silly infant, which by the mantle and the chain could not be but born of noble parentage, should be so hardly crossed with deadly mishap. The poor shepherd, perplexed thus with divers thoughts, took pity of the child, and determined with himself to carry it to the king, that there it might be brought up according to the worthiness of birth, for his ability could not afford to foster it, though his good mind was willing to further it. Taking therefore the child in his arms, as he folded the mantle together the better to defend it from cold there fell down at his foot a very fair and rich purse, wherein he found a great sum of gold; which sight so revived the shepherd's spirits, as he was greatly ravished with joy and daunted with fear; joyful to see such a sum in his power, and fearful, if it should be known, that it might breed his further danger. Necessity wished him at the least to retain the gold, though he would not keep the child: the simplicity of his conscience feared him from such deceitful bribery. Thus was the poor man perplexed with a doubtful dilemma until at last the covetousness of the coin overcame him; for what will not the greedy desire of gold cause a man to do? so that he was resolved in himself to foster the child, and with the sum to relieve his want. . . .

[He takes the child home, pacifies his suspicious wife, and swears her to secrecy. Later he buys the lease of a farm and stocks it with sheep, which Fawnia learns to tend.] . . . Fawnia thought Porrus had been her father and Mopsa her mother (for so was the shepherd and his wife called), honored and obeyed them with such reverence that all the neighbors praised the dutiful obedience of the child. Porrus grew in short time to be a man of some wealth and credit, for fortune so favored him in having no charge but Fawnia, that he began to purchase land, intending after his death to give it to his daughter, so that divers rich farmers' sons came as wooers to his house. For Fawnia was something cleanly attired, being of such singular beauty and excellent wit, that whoso saw her would have thought she had been some heavenly nymph and not a mortal creature, insomuch that, when she came to the age of sixteen years, she so increased with exquisite perfection both of body and mind, as her natural disposition did bewray that she was born of some high parentage; but the people thinking she was daughter to the shepherd Porrus rested only amazed at her beauty and wit; yea, she won such favor and commendations in every man's eye, as her beauty was not only praised in the country, but also spoken of in the court; yet such was her submiss modesty, that although her praise daily increased, her mind was no whit puffed up with pride, but humbled herself as became a country maid and the daughter of a poor shepherd. Every day she went forth with her sheep to the field, keeping them with such care and diligence as all men thought she was very painful, defending her face from the heat of the sun with no other veil but with a garland made of boughs and flowers, which attire became her so gallantly as she seemed to be the goddess Flora herself for beauty. . . .

[Now we meet Dorastus (Florizel), who angers his father by his unwillingness to marry.]

. . . It happened not long after this that there was a meeting of all the farmers' daughters in Sicilia, whither Fawnia was also bidden as the mistress of the feast, who, having attired herself in her best garments, went among the rest of her companions to the merry meeting, there spending the day in such homely pastimes as shepherds use. As the evening grew on and their sports ceased, each taking their leave at other, Fawnia, desiring one of her companions to bear her company, went home by the flock to see if they were well folded, and, as they returned, it fortuned that Dorastus, who all that day had been hawking, and killed store of game, encountered by the way these two maids, and, casting his eye suddenly on Fawnia, he was half afraid, fearing that with

Actaeon he had seen Diana; for he thought such exquisite
perfection could not be found in any mortal creature. As
thus he stood in a maze, one of his pages told him that the
maid with the garland on her head was Fawnia, the fair
shepherd whose beauty was so much talked of in the court.
Dorastus, desirous to see if nature had adorned her mind
with any inward qualities, as she had decked her body with
outward shape, began to question with her whose daughter
she was, of what age, and how she had been trained up? who
answered him with such modest reverence and sharpness of
wit that Dorastus thought her outward beauty was but a
counterfeit to darken her inward qualities, wondering how
so courtly behavior could be found in so simple a cottage,
and cursing fortune that had shadowed wit and beauty with
such hard fortune. As thus he held her a long while
with chat, beauty seeing him at discovert thought not to lose
the vantage, but struck him so deeply with an envenomed
shaft, as he wholly lost his liberty and became a slave to
love, which before contemned love, glad now to gaze on a
poor shepherd, who before refused the offer of a rich
princess. . . .

[Dorastus laments his choice of a low-born girl; Fawnia
knows he is above her station, but will not be his mistress.
When he comes dressed as a shepherd and woos her hon-
estly, she "yields up the fort."] . . . [Dorastus] embraced her
in his arms, swearing that neither distance, time, nor adverse
fortune should diminish his affection; but that, in despite of
the destinies, he would remain loyal unto death. Having thus
plighted their troth each to other, seeing they could not have
the full fruition of their love in Sicilia, for that Egistus' consent would never be granted to so mean a match, Dorastus
determined, as soon as time and opportunity would give
them leave, to provide a great mass of money and many rich
and costly jewels for the easier carriage, and then to trans-
port themselves and their treasure into Italy, where they
should lead a contented life, until such time as either he
could be reconciled to his father, or else by succession come
to the kingdom. . . .

[Fawnia approves the plan. The old shepherd (Porrus)

gets wind of the affair and fears the king's anger. He discusses the problem with his wife.] ... "If the king should know that Dorastus had begotten our daughter with child, as I fear it will fall out little better, the king's fury would be such as, no doubt, we should both lose our goods and lives. Necessity, therefore, hath no law, and I will prevent this mischief with a new device that is come in my head, which shall neither offend the king nor displease Dorastus. I mean to take the chain and the jewels that I found with Fawnia, and carry them to the king, letting him then to understand how she is none of my daughter, but that I found her beaten up with the water, alone in a little boat, wrapped in a rich mantle, wherein was enclosed this treasure. By this means, I hope the king will take Fawnia into his service, and we, whatsoever chanceth, shall be blameless." This device pleased the good wife very well, so that they determined, as soon as they might know the king at leisure, to make him privy to this case. ...

[Capnio, Dorastus' old servant, completes preparations for the lovers' flight, and gets them on board. The old shepherd sets out for the palace.] ... He met by chance in his way Capnio, who, trudging as fast as he could with a little coffer under his arm to the ship, and spying Porrus, whom he knew to be Fawnia's father, going towards the palace, being a wily fellow, began to doubt the worst, and, therefore, crossed him by the way, and asked him whither he was going so early this morning? Porrus, who knew by his face that he was one of the court, meaning simply, told him that the king's son Dorastus dealt hardly with him, for he had but one daughter who was a little beautiful, and that the neighbors told him the young prince had allured her to folly: he went, therefore, now to complain to the king how greatly he was abused.

Capnio, who straightway smelt the whole matter, began to soothe him in his talk, and said that Dorastus dealt not like a prince to spoil any poor man's daughter in that sort: he, therefore, would do the best for him he could, because he knew he was an honest man. "But," quoth Capnio, "you lose your labor in going to the palace, for the king means this day to take the air of the sea, and to go aboard of a ship that lies in the haven. I am going before, you see, to provide all things in a readiness, and, if you will follow my counsel, turn back with me to the haven, where I will set you in such a fit place as you may speak to the king at your pleasure." Porrus, giving credit to Capnio's smooth tale, gave him a thousand thanks for his friendly advice and went with him to the haven, making all the way his complaints of Dorastus, yet concealing secretly the chain and the jewels. . . .

[Capnio forces the shepherd to board the lovers' ship. Dorastus is sought by his anxious father, who discovers the affair with Fawnia. Dorastus and Fawnia are driven by tempest to the Bohemian coast, and proceed to Pandosto's court.] . . . Pandosto, amazed at the singular perfection of Fawnia, stood half astonished, viewing her beauty, so that he had almost forgot himself what he had to do: at last, with stern countenance he demanded their names, and of what country they were, and what caused them to land in Bohemia. "Sir," quoth Dorastus, "know that my name Meleagrus is, a knight born and brought up in Trapolonia, and this gentlewoman, whom I mean to take to my wife, is an Italian, born in Padua, from whence I have now brought her. The cause I have so small a train with me is for that, her friends unwilling to consent, I intended secretly to convey her to Trapolonia; whither, as I was sailing by distress of weather I was driven into these coasts: thus have you heard my name, my country, and the cause of my voyage." Pandosto, starting from his seat as one in choler, made this rough reply:

"Meleagrus, I fear this smooth tale hath but small truth, and that thou coverest a foul skin with fair paintings. No doubt, this lady by her grace and beauty is of her degree more meet for a mighty prince than for a simple knight, and thou, like a perjured traitor, hath bereft her of her parents, to their present grief and her ensuing sorrow. Till, therefore, I hear more of her parentage and of thy calling I will stay you both here in Bohemia."

Dorastus, in whom rested nothing but kingly valor, was not able to suffer the reproaches of Pandosto, but that he made him this answer:

"It is not meet for a king, without due proof, to appeach

any man of ill behavior, nor, upon suspicion, to infer belief: strangers ought to be entertained with courtesy, not to be entreated with cruelty, lest, being forced by want to put up injuries, the gods revenge their cause with rigor."

Pandosto, hearing Dorastus utter these words, commanded that he should straight be committed to prison, until such time as they heard further of his pleasure; but, as for Fawnia, he charged that she should be entertained in the court with such courtesy as belonged to a stranger and her calling. The rest of the shipmen he put into the dungeon.

Having, thus, hardly handled the supposed Trapolonians, Pandosto, contrary to his aged years, began to be somewhat tickled with the beauty of Fawnia. . . .

[Pandosto woos Fawnia, who resists him. Dorastus' father, hearing of the imprisonment of his son, sends an embassy to request his release and the execution of Fawnia and the old shepherd. Pandosto consents, but the old shepherd saves the situation by relating the discovery of Fawnia.] . . . Pandosto would scarce suffer him to tell out his tale but that he inquired the time of the year, the manner of the boat, and other circumstances; which when he found agreeing to his count, he suddenly leaped from his seat and kissed Fawnia, wetting her tender cheeks with his tears, and crying, "My daughter Fawnia! ah sweet Fawnia! I am thy father, Fawnia." This sudden passion of the king drave them all into a maze, especially Fawnia and Dorastus. But, when the king had breathed himself a while in this new joy, he rehearsed before the ambassadors the whole matter, how he had entreated his wife Bellaria for jealousy, and that this was the child, whom he had sent to float in the seas. . . .

[Great rejoicing follows. Then . . .] Pandosto, willing to recompense old Porrus, of a shepherd made him a knight; which done, providing a sufficient navy to receive him and his retinue, accompanied with Dorastus, Fawnia, and the Sicilian ambassadors, he sailed towards Sicilia, where he was most princely entertained by Egistus; who, hearing this most comical event, rejoiced greatly at his son's good hap, and without delay (to the perpetual joy of the two young lovers) celebrated the marriage: which was no sooner ended, but

Pandosto, calling to mind how first he betrayed his friend Egistus, how his jealousy was the cause of Bellaria's death, that contrary to the law of nature he had lusted after his own daughter, moved with these desperate thoughts, he fell into a melancholy fit, and, to close up the comedy with a tragical stratagem, he slew himself. . . .

Commentaries

SIMON FORMAN

The Winter's Tale at the Globe, 1611, the 15 of May

Observe there how Leontes, the King of Sicilia, was over-come with jealousy of his wife with the King of Bohemia his friend, that came to see him; and how he contrived his death and would have had his cupbearer to have poisoned, who gave the King of Bohemia warning thereof and fled with him to Bohemia.

Remember also how he sent to the Oracle of Apollo, and the answer of Apollo, that she was guiltless and that the King was jealous, etc., and how except the child was found again that was lost, the King should die without issue; for the child was carried into Bohemia and there laid in a forest and brought up by a shepherd. And the King of Bohemia his son married that wench, and how they fled into Sicilia to Leontes, and the shepherd having showed the letter of the nobleman by whom Leontes sent away that child and the jewels found about her, she was known to be Leontes' daughter, and was then sixteen years old.

Remember also the Rogue that came in all tattered like coll pixci,[1] and how he feigned him sick and to have been robbed of all that he had, and how he cozened the poor man

From Forman's *Booke of Plaies*.
1. A doubtful reading, of doubtful significance.

of all his money, and after came to the sheep-shear with a peddler's pack, and there cozened them again of all their money. And how he changed apparel with the King of Bohemia his son, and then how he turned courtier, etc. Beware of trusting feigned beggars or fawning fellows.

SAMUEL TAYLOR COLERIDGE

[Comments on *The Winter's Tale*]

At the commencement of the fourth lecture last evening, Mr. Coleridge combated the opinion held by some critics, that the writings of Shakespeare were like a wilderness, in which were desolate places, most beautiful flowers, and weeds; he argued that even the titles of his plays were appropriate and showed judgment, presenting as it were a bill of fare before the feast. This was peculiarly so in *The Winter's Tale*—a wild story, calculated to interest a circle around a fireside. He maintained that Shakespeare ought not to be judged of in detail, but on the whole. A pedant differed from a master in cramping himself with certain established rules, whereas the master regarded rules as always controllable by and subservient to the end. The passion to be delineated in *The Winter's Tale* was *jealousy*. Shakespeare's description of this, however, was perfectly philosophical: the mind, in its first harboring of it, became mean and despicable, and the first sensation was perfect shame, arising from the consideration of having possessed an ob-

In 1813–14 Coleridge delivered a series of lectures at Bristol. They do not survive, but the reports of them in the *Bristol Gazette* provide an idea of their gist. The first passage contains all that was reported of the lecture on *The Winter's Tale*. The scrappier material printed beneath this report is from Coleridge's marginalia. All of this Coleridge material is drawn from 2nd ed., ed. Thomas Middleton Raysor (New York: E. P. Dutton & Company, Inc., 1960; London: J. M. Dent & Sons, Ltd., 1961), 2 vols.

ject unworthily, of degrading a person to a thing. The mind that once indulges this passion has a predisposition, a vicious weakness, by which it kindles a fire from every spark, and from circumstances the most innocent and indifferent finds fuel to feed the flame. This he exemplified in an able manner from the conduct and opinion of Leontes, who seized upon occurrences of which he himself was the cause, and when speaking of Hermione, combined his anger with images of the lowest sensuality, and pursued the object with the utmost cruelty. This character Mr. Coleridge contrasted with that of Othello, whom Shakespeare had portrayed the very opposite to a jealous man: he was noble, generous, open-hearted; unsuspicious and unsuspecting.

* * *

Although on the whole exquisitely respondent to its title, and even in the fault I am about to mention, still a winter's tale, yet it seems a mere indolence of the great bard not to have in the oracle provided some ground for Hermione's seeming death and fifteen years concealment, voluntary concealment. This might have been easily affected by some obscure sentence of the oracle, as, *ex. gr.,* "Nor shall he ever recover an heir if he have a wife before that recovery."

[IV.IV.445–54]

> *Perdita.*   Even here undone!
> I was not much afeard; for once or twice
> I was about to speak and tell him plainly,
> The selfsame sun that shines upon his court
> Hides not his visage from our cottage, but
> Looks on alike. [*To Florizel*] Will 't please you, sir, be
>   gone?
> I told you what would come of this. Beseech you,
> Of your own state take care: this dream of mine
> Being now awake, I'll queen it no inch farther,
> But milk my ewes, and weep.

O how more than exquisite is this whole speech,—and that profound nature of noble pride and grief venting themselves in a momentary peevishness of resentment toward Florizel—

Will 't please you, sir, be gone?

Difference of style in the first scene between two chit-chatters [Camillo and Archidamus], and the rise of diction on the introduction of the kings and Hermione [in the second scene].

Admirable preparation in Polixenes' obstinate refusal to Leontes—

There is no tongue that moves, none, none i' th' world

and yet his after-yielding to Hermione, which is at once perfectly natural from mere courtesy of sex and the exhaustion of the will by the former effort, and yet so well calculated to set in nascent action the jealousy of Leontes. And this, once excited, [is] increased by Hermione—

yet, good deed, Leontes,
[I love thee not a jar o' th' clock behind
What lady she her lord]

accompanied (as a good actress ought to represent it) by an expression and recoil of apprehension that she had gone too far. The first working of this—

At my request he would not.

This [should be] judiciously introduced accompanied by a definition of *jealousy*, not of all so-called by persons imperfectly acquainted with the circumstances, but of what really is so; i.e., [jealousy] as a *vice* of the mind, a culpable despicable tendency.

The natural effects and concomitants of this passion.

1. Excitability by the most inadequate causes [as in Leontes' aside], "Too hot, too hot." Eagerness to snatch at proofs. . . .

2. Grossness of conception, and a disposition to degrade the object of it. Sensual fancies and images. . . .

3. Shame of his own feelings exhibited in moodiness and soliloquy.

4. And yet from the violence of the passion forced to *utter* itself, and, therefore, catching occasion to ease the mind by ambiguities, equivoques, talking to those who cannot and who are known not to be able to understand what is said—a soliloquy in the mask of dialogue. [1.2.120–27]. Hence confused, broken manner, fragmentary, in the dialogue with the little boy.

5. The dread of vulgar ridicule, as distinct from the high sense of honor—

They're here with me already: whispering, rounding
[I.II.217]

and out of this, selfish vindictiveness. How distinguished from the feeling of high honor (as in Othello), a mistaken sense of duty.

E. M. W. TILLYARD

From Shakespeare's Last Plays

In *The Winter's Tale* Shakespeare omitted all the irrelevancies that had clotted *Cymbeline* and presented the whole tragic pattern, from prosperity to destruction, regeneration, and still fairer prosperity, in full view of the audience. This is a bold, frontal attack on the problem, necessitating the complete disregard of the unity of time; but it succeeded, as far as success was possible within the bounds of a single play. One difference in plot from *Cymbeline* is that there is little overlap between the old and the new life. In Guiderius and Arviragus the new life had been incubating for years while the old life held sway in Cymbeline and his court. But Perdita, chief symbol of the new life, has not lived many hours before Leontes begins his own conversion.

Unlike *Cymbeline,* the first half of the play is seriously tragic and could have included Hermione's death, like Greene's *Pandosto.* Leontes's obsession of jealousy is terrifying in its intensity. It reminds us not of other Shakespearian tragic errors, but rather of the god-sent lunacies of Greek drama, the lunacies of Ajax and Heracles. It is as scantily motivated as these, and we should refrain from demanding any motive. Indeed, it is as much a surprise to the characters in the play as it is to the reader, and its nature is that of an

From *Shakespeare's Last Plays* by E. M. W. Tillyard (London: Chatto & Windus, Ltd., 1938; New York: Hillary House Publishers, Ltd.) Reprinted by permission of Chatto & Windus, Ltd.

earthquake or the loss of the *Titanic* rather than of rational human psychology. And equally terrifying is Leontes's cry, when, after defying the oracle, he hears of his son's death:

> Apollo's angry, and the heavens themselves
> Do strike at my injustice.   (3.2.143–44)

Hermione's character is far more firmly based on probability than Imogen's. There is nothing strained or hectic about her love for her husband: it is rooted in habit. And when at her trial, addressing Leontes, she says:

> To me can life be no commodity.
> The crown and comfort of my life, your favor,
> I do give lost, for I do feel it gone,
> But know not how it went,   (91–94)

we accept the statement as sober truth. While for distilled pathos no poet, not even Euripides, has excelled her final soliloquy, when she realizes Leontes's fixed hostility:

> The Emperor of Russia was my father:
> Oh that he were alive, and here beholding
> His daughter's trial! That he did but see
> The flatness of my misery; yet with eyes
> Of pity, not revenge!   (117–21)

In sum, the first half of the play renders worthily, in the main through a realistic method, the destructive portion of the tragic pattern.

Now, although Leontes and Hermione live on to give continuity to the play and although the main tragic pattern is worked out nominally in Leontes, the royal person, it is not they in their reconciliation who most create the feeling of rebirth. At the best they mend the broken vessel of their fortunes with glue or seccotine; and our imaginations are not in the least stirred by any future life that we can conceive the pair enjoying together. Were the pattern of destruction and regeneration the sole motive of the play, the statue scene would have little point and be, as Middleton Murry calls it, a theatrical trick. But the continued existence of Leontes and Hermione is a matter of subordinate expediency; and it is Florizel and Perdita and the countryside where they meet which make the new life.

And here I must plead as earnestly as I can for allowing more than the usual virtue and weight to the fourth act of *The Winter's Tale*. There are several reasons why it has been taken too lightly. It has been far too much the property of vague young women doing eurythmics at Speech Days or on vicarage lawns; and, when it is acted professionally, the part of Perdita is usually taken by some pretty little fool or pert suburban charmer. Also, it is usually thought that joy and virtue are inferior as poetic themes to suffering and vice; or that the earthly paradise taxed the resources of Dante less than Ugolino's tower. It would seem that the truth is the other way round, because convincing pictures of joy and virtue are extremely rare, while those of suffering and vice are comparatively common. Shelley succeeds in describing the sufferings of Prometheus; the earthly bliss brought on by them is, except in patches, a shoddy affair in comparison. Shakespeare never did anything finer, more serious, more evocative of his full powers, than his picture of an earthly paradise painted in the form of the English countryside. The old problem of adjusting realism and symbol is so well solved that we are quite unconscious of it. The country life is given the fullest force of actuality, as when the old shepherd describes his wife's hospitality at the shearing feast:

> . Fie, daughter! When my old wife lived, upon
> This day she was both pantler, butler, cook;
> Both dame and servant; welcomed all, served all;
> Would sing her song and dance her turn; now here,
> At upper end o' the table, now i' the middle;
> On his shoulder, and his; her face o' fire
> With labor and the thing she took to quench it,
> She would to each one sip.
>
> (4.4.55–62)

Yet the whole country setting stands out as the cleanest and most elegant symbol of the new life into which the old horrors are to be transmuted.

It is the same with the characters. Shakespeare blends the realistic and the symbolic with the surest touch. Florizel, who is kept a rather flat character the more to show up Perdita, one would call a type rather than a symbol; but for the play's purposes he is an efficient type of chivalry and generosity. He will not let down Perdita, but defies his father at the risk of losing a kingdom:

> I am not sorry, not afeard; delayed
> But nothing altered. What I was, I am;
> More straining on for plucking back; not following
> My leash unwillingly.
>
> (467–70)

Perdita, on the other hand, is one of Shakespeare's richest characters; at once a symbol and a human being. She is the play's main symbol of the powers of creation. And rightly, because, as Leontes was the sole agent of destruction, so it is fitting, ironically fitting, that the one of his kin whom he had thrown out as bastard should embody the contrary process. Not that Leontes, as a character, is the contrary to Perdita. His obsession is not a part of his character but an accretion. Her true contrary is Iago. It is curious that Iago should ever have been thought motiveless. The desire to destroy is a very simple derivative from the power instinct, the instinct which in its evil form goes by the name of the first of the deadly sins, Pride. It was by that sin that the angels fell, and at the end of *Othello* Iago is explicitly equated with the Devil. Shakespeare embodied all his horror of this type of original sin in Iago. He was equally aware of original virtue, and he pictured it, in Perdita, blossoming spontaneously in the simplest of country settings. There is little direct reference to her instincts to create; but they are implied by her sympathy with nature's lavishness in producing flowers, followed by her own simple and unashamed confession of wholesome sensuality. The whole passage, so often confined to mere idyllic description, must be quoted in hopes that the reader will allow the profounder significance I claim for it. Perdita is talking to her guests, to Polixenes, Camillo, and Florizel in particular:

> *Perdita.* Here's flow'rs for you:
>   Hot lavender, mints, savory, marjoram,
>   The marigold, that goes to bed wi' th' sun
>   And with him rises weeping, these are flow'rs
>   Of middle summer, and I think they are given
>   To men of middle age. You're very welcome.

> *Camillo.* I should leave grazing, were I of your flock,
>   And only live by gazing.

> *Perdita.*   Out, alas!
>   You'd be so lean, that blasts of January
>   Would blow you through and through. Now, my fair'st friend,
>   I would I had some flowers o' th' spring that might
>   Become your time of day; and yours, and yours,
>   That wear upon your virgin branches yet
>   Your maidenheads growing. O Proserpina,
>   For the flow'rs now, that, frighted, thou let'st fall
>   From Dis's wagon! Daffodils,
>   That come before the swallow dares, and take
>   The winds of March with beauty; violets dim,
>   But sweeter than the lids of Juno's eyes,
>   Or Cytherea's breath; pale primroses,
>   That die unmarried ere they can behold
>   Bright Phoebus in his strength (a malady
>   Most incident to maids); bold oxlips, and
>   The crown imperial; lilies of all kinds,
>   The flower-de-luce being one. O, these I lack,
>   To make you garlands of, and my sweet friend,
>   To strew him o'er and o'er!

> *Florizel.*   What, like a corse?

> *Perdita.* No, like a bank for Love to lie and play on;
>   Not like a corse; or if, not to be buried,
>   But quick and in mine arms.

(103–32)

The great significance of Perdita's lines lies partly in the verse, which (especially at the close) is leisurely, full, as-

sured, matured, suggestive of fruition, and acutely contrasted to the tortured, arid, and barren ravings of Leontes,
and which reinforces that kinship with nature and healthy
sensuality mentioned above. But it lies also in the references to the classical Pantheon. The gods of Greece and
Rome occur very frequently in the last plays of Shakespeare and are certainly more than mere embroidery.
Apollo is the dominant god in *The Winter's Tale*, and his
appearance in Perdita's speech is meant to quicken the
reader to apprehend some unusual significance. He appears
as the bridegroom, whom the pale primroses never know,
but who visits the other flowers. Not to take the fertility
symbolism as intended would be a perverse act of caution.
Perdita should be associated with them as symbol both of
the creative powers of nature, physical fertility, and of healing and re-creation of the mind. She is like Milton's youthful Ceres,

> Yet virgin of Proserpina from Jove,

or his Eve, mistress of the flowers of Paradise.

The health of Perdita's natural instincts not only helps her
symbolic force; it helps to make her a realistic character.
Other parts of her character are a deep-seated strength and
ruthless common sense. She argues coolly with Polixenes
about art and nature, and is not frightened by his later fulmi-
nations, saying when he has gone:

> I was not much afeard; for once or twice
> I was about to speak and tell him plainly,
> The selfsame sun that shines upon his court
> Hides not his visage from our cottage, but
> Looks on alike.   (446–50)

At the same time she shows that she has been all the time
quite without illusions about the danger she runs in loving
Florizel, the Prince, and when the shock comes with the discovery of their plighted love she is prepared without fuss to
accept her fate. Turning to Florizel, she goes on:

> Will 't please you, sir, be gone?
> I told you what would come of this. Beseech you,
> Of your own state take care: this dream of mine
> Being now awake, I'll queen it no inch farther,
> But milk my ewes and weep.

(450–54)

It is through Perdita's magnificence that we accept as valuable the new life into which the play is made to issue. The disadvantage of centering the creative processes in her and Florizel is structural. There is a break in continuity; for though Perdita is born in the first half of the play, as characters the pair are new to the last half. And we have juxtaposition, not organic growth. There is no Orestes to lead from the *Choephoroe* to the *Eumenides*. On the other hand, I find this juxtaposition easy enough to accept; and it is mitigated by Perdita's parentage. She is Hermione's true daughter and prolongs in herself those regenerative processes which in her mother have suffered a temporary eclipse.

The common praise of Autolycus as a character is well justified. It is likely that he is organic to the whole country scene, and that it would collapse into an oversweetness of sentiment without him. Though he comes and goes with the aloofness of an elf among humans, he is united with the other characters in his admirable adjustment to the country life. His delinquencies, like the pastoral realism, keep the earthly paradise sufficiently earthly without disturbing the paradisiac state; for they are antitoxic, harmless to vigorous health, and an efficient prophylactic against the lotus fruit which, as a drug, has so greatly impaired the health of most earthly paradises.

*   *   *   *   *   *

If *The Winter's Tale* succeeded better than *Cymbeline* with the tragic pattern, so did it with the planes of reality also. No blurring, but clean contrast. The paranoiac world of Leontes is set against the everyday world of the courtiers and the world, still of everyday but intensified, of Hermione. Leontes's world is marvelously expressed by the hot and twisted language he uses. Another world is introduced at the beginning of the third act by the short scene where Cleomenes and Dion speak of their visit to the Oracle. Here the words are cool and pellucid: we are in the realm of contemplation.

> *Cleomenes.* The climate's delicate, the air most sweet,
>   Fertile the isle, the temple much surpassing
>   The common praise it bears.
>
> *Dion.*   I shall report,
>   For most it caught me, the celestial habits
>   (Methinks I so should term them,) and the reverence
>   Of the grave wearers. O, the sacrifice!
>   How ceremonious, solemn, and unearthly
>   It was i' th' off'ring.   (1–8)

And this "ceremonious, solemn, and unearthly" note is repeated in the great scene, in itself fantastically unreal, where Leontes kisses Hermione's statue and it comes to life. It would be tedious to speak of every transition in this play from one world to another. I will confine myself to noting the most violent of all, and one which the greatest skeptic of my argument would hardly consider accidental. Antigonus, on the coast of Bohemia, carrying the infant Perdita, sends the mariner back to his ship and proceeds to describe in a soliloquy how Hermione appeared to him in a dream. There is nothing in the play so melodramatic, so remote from ordinary life as this speech:

>   She did approach
> My cabin where I lay; thrice bowed before me,
> And gasping to begin some speech, her eyes
> Became two spouts, the fury spent, anon
> Did this break from her—   (3.3.22–26)

and when she had done speaking, "with shrieks, she melted into air" (35–36). From this strained, impossible world we are abruptly recalled by the stage direction *exit, pursued by a bear*, and the entry of the old shepherd, whose first words put us at the very center of common humanity:

I would there were no age between ten and three-and-twenty, or
that youth would sleep out the rest; for there is nothing in the between but getting wenches with child, wronging the ancientry,
stealing, fighting.
                                                                    (58–62)

It is worth noting, in parenthesis, that the above abrupt
transition not only expresses the sense of different worlds
but has an important technical work to do, that of throwing a
bridge across the two halves of the play. Shakespeare has to
present us in the country scenes with a new kind of serious
writing, with re-creation after destruction. Now it is easy
enough to set the farcical or the grotesque against tragedy
without fear of misunderstanding. But to set the serious
world of Perdita abruptly against the other serious world of
Leontes and Hermione might make trouble. Perdita might
appear too slight, set against the earlier violence. Shakespeare's solution is to drive the tortured world of Leontes
and Hermione to a ridiculous extreme in Antigonus' vision.
In so doing he really puts an end to it. Any return to it would
court ridicule. But the ridiculousness of Antigonus' vision
prepares us for any kind of the ridiculous; and Shakespeare
proceeds to give us good earthy comedy, and we take it. Out
of this comedy grows the serious, sane, and transfigured
earthiness of the Perdita scenes, which we now never dream
of confusing with the world of Leontes and Hermione. This
transition has obvious analogies with music.

G. WILSON KNIGHT

From The Crown of Life

[Mr. Knight uses as his text 4.4.79–112.] Of this one could say much. Notice first, the continued emphasis on seasons at the opening and concluding lines of my quotation; the strong physical realism (recalling Hermione's defense) in Perdita's use of "breed"; and the phrase "great creating nature" (to be compared with "great nature" earlier, at 2.2.59).

The speakers are at cross purposes, since one is referring to art, the other to artificiality, itself a difficult enough distinction. The whole question of the naturalist and transcendental antinomy is accordingly raised. The art concerned is called natural by Polixenes in that either (i) human invention can never do more than direct natural energy, or (ii) the human mind and therefore its inventions are nature-born: both meanings are probably contained. Human civilization, art and religion are clearly in one sense part of "great creating nature," and so is everything else. But Perdita takes her stand on natural simplicity, growing from the unforced integrity of her own country upbringing, in opposition to the artificialities of, we may suggest, the court: she is horrified at dishonoring nature by human trickery. Observe that both alike reverence "great creating

From *The Crown of Life* by G. Wilson Knight, 2nd. ed. (London: Methuen & Co., Ltd., 1948; New York: British Book Centre, 1952) Reprinted by permission of Methuen & Co., Ltd.

nature," though differing in their conclusions. No logical deduction is to be drawn; or rather, the logic is dramatic, made of opposing statements, which serve to conjure up an awareness of nature as an all-powerful presence, at once controller and exemplar. The dialogue forms accordingly a microcosm of our whole drama.

There is a certain irony, too, in Polixenes' defense of exactly the type of love-mating which Florizel and Perdita are planning for themselves. Polixenes is, perhaps, setting a trap; or may be quite unconsciously arguing against his own later behavior. Probably the latter.

Perdita next turns to Florizel:

> *Perdita.*   Now, my fair'st friend,
>   I would I had some flow'rs o' th' spring that might
>   Become your time of day; and yours, and yours,
>   That wear upon your virgin branches yet
>   Your maidenheads growing: O Proserpina,
>   For the flow'rs now that, frighted, thou let'st fall
>   From Dis's wagon! Daffodils
>   That come before the swallow dares, and take
>   The winds of March with beauty; violets dim,
>   But sweeter than the lids of Juno's eyes,
>   Or Cytherea's breath; pale primroses,
>   That die unmarried ere they can behold
>   Bright Phoebus in his strength (a malady
>   Most incident to maids); bold oxlips, and
>   The crown imperial; lilies of all kinds,
>   The flower-de-luce being one. O, these I lack
>   To make you garlands of, and my sweet friend,
>   To strew him o'er and o'er!
>
> *Florizel.*   What, like a corse?
>
> *Perdita.* No, like a bank for Love to lie and play on;
>   Not like a corse; or if, not to be buried,
>   But quick and in mine arms. Come, take your flowers;
>   Methinks I play as I have seen them do
>   In Whitsun pastorals; sure this robe of mine
>   Does change my disposition.   (4.4.112–35)

Reference to the season-myth of Proserpine is natural enough; indeed, almost an essential. You might call Perdita herself a seed sowed in winter and flowering in summer. "Take" = "charm," or "enrapture." Though Autolycus' first entry suggested spring, we are already, as the nature of our festival and these lines declare, in summer. Note the fine union, indeed identity, of myth and contemporary experience, finer than in earlier Shakespearian pastorals: Dis may be classical, but his "wagon" is as real as a wagon in Hardy. See, too, how classical legend and folklore coalesce in the primroses and "bright Phoebus in his strength," a phrase pointing the natural poetic association of sun fire and mature love (as in *Antony and Cleopatra*): the sun corresponding, as it were, to physical fruition (as the moon to the more operatic business of wooing) and accordingly raising in Perdita, whose poetry is strongly impregnated with fertility suggestion (the magic here is throughout an earth magic, a sun magic), a wistful aside, meant presumably for herself. Perdita's flower poetry reaches a royal impressionism in "crown imperial" and "garland" suiting the speaker's innate, and indeed actual, royalty. The contrasting suggestion of "corse" quickly merging into a love embrace (reminiscent of the love and death associations in *Antony and Cleopatra* and Keats) finally serves to heighten the pressure of exuberant, buoyant, life. The "Whitsun pastorals," like our earlier puritans, though perhaps historically extraneous, may be forgiven for their lively impact, serving to render the speech vivid with the poet's, and hence, somehow, our own, personal experience.

Perdita's royalty is subtly presented: her robes as mistress of the feast have, as she said, made her act and speak strangely. Florizel details each of her graces (135–43), wishing her in turn to speak, to sing, to dance—as "a wave o' th' sea"—forever. He would have her every action perpetuated, the thought recalling Polixenes' recollections of himself and Leontes as "boy eternal" (1.2.65). Florizel has expressed a delight in the given instant of youthful grace so sacred that it somehow deserves eternal status; when she moves he would have her, in a phrase itself patterning the blend of motion and stillness it describes, "move still, still so." Watching her, he sees the universe completed, crowned, at each moment of her existence:

> Each your doing,
> So singular in each particular,
> Crowns what you are doing in the present deeds,
> That all your acts are queens.   (4.4.143–46)

As once before, we are reminded, this time more sharply, of Blake's "minute particulars." The royalistic tonings here and in the "crown imperial" of her own speech (126) not merely hint Perdita's royal blood, but also serve to stamp her actions with eternal validity; for the crown is always to be understood as a symbol piercing the eternity dimension. We are, it is true, being forced into distinctions that Shakespeare, writing from a royalistic age, need not actually have surveyed; but Florizel's lines certainly correspond closely to those in *Pericles* imaging Marina as a palace "for the crown'd Truth to dwell in" and again as monumental Patience sitting "above kings' graves" and "smiling extremity out of act" (*Pericles*, 5.1.123,140). Perdita is more lively; time, creation, nature, earth, all have more rights here than in *Pericles*; but the correspondence remains close.

Perdita's acts are royal both in their own right and also because she is, in truth, of royal birth:

> This is the prettiest low-born lass that ever
> Ran on the greensward; nothing she does or seems
> But smacks of something greater than herself,
> Too noble for this place.   (4.4.156–59)

But this is not the whole truth. Later, after Polixenes' outburst, she herself makes a comment more easily appreciated in our age than in Shakespeare's:

> I was not much afeard; for once or twice
> I was about to speak and tell him plainly,
> The selfsame sun that shines upon his court
> Hides not his visage from our cottage, but
> Looks on alike.   (446–50)

The lovely New Testament transposition (with "sun" for "rain") serves to underline the natural excellence and innate worth of this simple rustic community; and only from some such recognition can we make full sense of the phrase "queen of curds and cream" (161). We may accordingly regroup our three royalties in terms of (i) Perdita's actual descent, (ii) her natural excellence and (iii) that more inclusive category from which both descend, or to which both aspire, in the eternity-dimension. A final conclusion would reach some concept of spiritual royalty corresponding to Wordsworth's (in his *Immortality Ode*); with further political implications concerning the expansion of sovereignty among a people.

The lovers are, very clearly, felt as creatures of "rare"—the expected word recurs (32)—excellence, and their love, despite its strong fertility contacts, is correspondingly pure. Perdita, hearing Florizel's praises, fears he woos her "the false way" (151); while Florizel is equally insistent that his "desires run not before his honor," nor his "lusts burn hotter" than his "faith" (33–35). The statement, which appears, as in *The Tempest* later, a trifle labored, is clearly central: Perdita, as mistress of the feast, insists that Autolycus "use no scurrilous words in's tunes" (215). Our first tragedy was precipitated by suspicion of marital infidelity; and our young lovers express a corresponding purity. . . .

. . . Now, as the resurrection draws near, we are prepared for it by Perdita's restoration. St. Paul once seems, perhaps justly, to consider resurrection as no more remarkable than birth (see Romans 4:17 in Dr. Moffatt's translation).[1] Certainly here the safeguarding of Perdita is considered scarcely less wonderful than the resurrection of the dead. That the child should be found, says Paulina,

> Is all as monstrous to our *human reason*
> As my Antigonus to break his grave
> And come again to me.
>
> (5.1.41–43)

---

[1] It must, however, be noted that the birth here concerned seems to be one of an abnormal, semimiraculous, sort; but the Pauline doctrine of resurrection holds strong fertility suggestion elsewhere, as in the great passage on immortality at I Corinthians, XV, where the dead body is compared to a grain of wheat buried in earth.

Yet she is restored, as the Gentlemen recount, and human reason accordingly negated. Scattered throughout are dim foreshadowings of the miraculous. Nevertheless, death looms large enough still, in poetry's despite: Paulina sees to that. When a gentleman praises Perdita she remarks:

> O Hermione!
> As every present time doth boast itself
> Above a better, gone, so must thy grave
> Give way to what's seen now.   (95–98)

The temporal order demands that the past slip away, that it lose reality; the more visible present always seems *superior.* Paulina resents this; and her remark may be aligned with both our early lines on boyhood never dreaming of any future other than to be "boy eternal" (1.2.65) and Florizel's desire to have Perdita's every act in turn—speaking, dancing, etc.—perpetuated. All these are strivings after eternity. Paulina, moreover, here suggests that the gentleman concerned, who seems to be a poet, is himself at fault: his verse, which "flowed with her [i.e., Hermione's] beauty once," is now "shrewdly ebbed" (5.1.102). The complaint is, not that Hermione has gone, but that the gentleman has failed in some sense to keep level. Death is accordingly less an objective reality than a failure of the subject to keep abreast of life. This may seem to turn an obvious thought into meaningless metaphysics, but the lines, in their context, can scarcely be ignored. Throughout *Troilus and Cressida* (especially at 3.3.145–84, an expansion of Paulina's comment) Shakespeare's thoughts on time are highly abstruse (see my essay in *The Wheel of Fire*); so are they in the Sonnets. Wrongly used time is as intrinsic to the structure of *Macbeth* as is "eternity" to that of *Antony and Cleopatra* (see my essays on both plays in *The Imperial Theme*). As so often in great poetry, the philosophical subtlety exists within or behind a speech, or plot, of surface realism and simplicity. Now *The Winter's Tale* is hammering on the threshold of some extraordinary truth related to both "nature" and "eternity." Hence its emphasis on the seasons, birth and childhood, the continual molding of new miracles on the pattern of the old; hence, too, the desire expressed for youthful excellence perpetuated and eternal; the thought of Perdita's every action as a "crowned" thing, a "queen," in its own eternal right (4.4.145–6); and also of art as improving or distorting nature, in the flower-dialogue, in Julio Romano's uncanny, eternity-imitating, skill. And yet no metaphysics, no natural philosophy or art, satisfy the demand that the lost thing, in all its nature-born warmth, be preserved; that it, not only its descendant, shall live; that death be revealed as a sin-born illusion; that eternity be flesh and blood.

The action moves to the house of the "grave and good Paulina" (5.3.1). The scene is her "chapel," recalling the chapel of death at 3.2.237, where Leontes last saw Hermione's dead body. Paulina shows them the statue, which excels anything "the hand of man hath done" (5.3.17); and they are quickly struck with—again the word—"wonder" (22). Leontes gazes; recognizes Hermione's "natural posture" (23); asks her to chide him, yet remembers how she was tender "as infancy and grace" (27):

> Oh, thus she stood,
> Even with such life of majesty—warm life,
> As now it coldly stands—when first I wooed her.
> I am ashamed: does not the stone rebuke me,
> For being more stone than it? O royal piece!   (34–38)

Sweet though it be, it remains cold and withdrawn, like Keats' Grecian Urn. Yet its "majesty" exerts a strangely potent "magic" (39) before which Perdita kneels almost in "superstition" (43). Leontes' grief is so great that Camillo reminds him how "sixteen winters" and "so many summers" should by now alternately have blown and dried his soul clean of "sorrow"; why should that prove more persistent than short-lived "joy"? (49–53). Leontes remains still, his soul pierced (34) by remembrance. Paulina, however, speaks realistically of the statue as art, saying how its color is not dry yet (47); half apologizing for the way it moves him, her phrase "for the stone is mine" (58) re-emphasizing her peculiar office. She offers to draw the curtain, fearing lest

Leontes' "fancy may think anon it moves" (60–61). The excitement generated, already intense, reaches new impact and definition in Paulina's sharp ringing utterance on "moves."

But Leontes remains quiet, fixed, in an otherworldly consciousness, a living death not to be disturbed, yet trembling with expectance:

> Let be, let be!
> Would I were dead, but that, methinks, already—
> What was he that did make it?   (61–63)

A universe of meaning is hinted by that one word "already" and the subsequent, tantalizing, break. Now the statue seems no longer cold:

> See, my lord,
> Would you not deem it breathed? And that those veins
> Did verily bear blood?   (63–65)

As the revelation slowly matures, it is as though Leontes' own grief and love were gradually infusing the thing before him with life. He, under Paulina, is laboring, even now, that it may live. The more visionary, paradisal, personal wonder of Pericles (who alone hears the spheral music) becomes here a crucial conflict, an *agon*, in which many persons share; dream is being forced into actuality. "Masterly done," answers Polixenes, taking us back to common sense, and yet again noting that "the very life seems warm upon her lip" (65–66). We are poised between motion and stillness, life and art:

> The fixture of her eye has motion in't,
> As we are mocked with art.   (67–68)

The contrast drives deep, recalling the balancing of art and nature in Perdita's dialogue with Polixenes; and, too, the imaging of the living Marina as "crown'd Truth" or monumental Patience (*Pericles*, 5.1.124,140). Paulina reiterates her offer to draw the curtain lest Leontes be so far "transported" (cf. 3.2.155; a word strongly toned in Shakespeare with magical suggestion) that he actually think it "lives"—

thus recharging the scene with an impossible expectation.
To which Leontes replies:

> No settled senses of the world can match
> The pleasure of that madness. Let't alone.   (72–73)

He would stand here, spellbound, forever; forever gazing on
this sphinxlike boundary between art and life.

Paulina, having functioned throughout as the Oracle's
implement, becomes now its priestess. Her swift changes
key the scene to an extraordinary pitch, as she hints at new
marvels:

> I am sorry, sir, I have thus far stirred you; but
> I could afflict you farther.   (74–75)

She has long caused, and still causes, Leontes to suffer
poignantly; and yet his suffering has undergone a subtle
change, for now this very "affliction has a taste as sweet as
any cordial comfort" (76–77). Already (at 5.2.20 and 78,
and 5.3.51–53) we have found joy and sorrow in partner-
ship, as, too, in the description of Cordelia's grief (*King
Lear*, 4.3.17–26). So Leontes endures a pain of ineffable
sweetness as the mystery unfolds:

>   Still, methinks,
> There is an air comes from her. What fine chisel
> Could ever yet cut breath?   (77–79)

However highly we value the eternity phrased by art (as in
Yeats' "monuments of unaging intellect" in "Sailing to
Byzantium"[2] and Keats' "Grecian Urn"), yet there is a frontier
beyond which it and all corresponding philosophies fail: they
lack one thing, breath. With a fine pungency of phrase, more
humanly relevant than Othello's "I know not where is that
Promethean heat. . . ." (5.2.12), a whole world of human
idealism is dismissed. The supreme moments of earlier
tragedy—Othello before the "monumental alabaster" (5) of

---

[2] A yet more relevant comparison with Yeats might adduce his drama
Resurrection. Compare also the statue-interest of Ibsen's latest plays.

the sleeping Desdemona, Romeo in Capulet's monument, Juliet and Cleopatra blending sleep and death—are implicit in Leontes' experience; more, their validity is at stake, as he murmurs, "Let no man mock me" (79), stepping forward for an embrace; as old Lear, reunited with Cordelia, "a spirit in bliss," says "Do not laugh at me" (4.7.68); as Pericles fears lest his reunion with Marina be merely such a dream as "mocks" man's grief (5.1.144,164). Those, and other, supreme moments of pathos are here re-enacted to a stronger purpose. Leontes strides forward; is prevented by Paulina; we are brought up against a cul-de-sac. But Paulina herself immediately releases new impetus as she cries, her voice quivering with the Sibylline power she wields:

> Either forbear,
> Quit presently the chapel, or resolve you
> For more amazement. If you can behold it,
> I'll make the statue move indeed, descend,
> And take you by the hand—but then you'll think,
> Which I protest against, I am assisted
> By wicked powers. (85–91)

The "chapel" setting is necessary, for we attend the resurrection of a supposedly buried person; the solemnity is at least half funereal. Much is involved in the phrase "wicked powers": we watch no act of necromancy. The "magic" (39), if magic it be, is a white magic; shall we say, a natural magic; the living opposite of the Ghost in *Hamlet* hideously breaking his tomb's "ponderous and marble jaws" (1.4.50). The difference is that between Prospero's powers in *The Tempest* and those of Marlowe's Doctor Faustus or the Weird Sisters in *Macbeth*. The distinction in Shakespeare's day was important and further driven home by Paulina's:

> It is required
> You do awake your faith; then, all stand still.
> Or those that think it is unlawful business
> I am about, let them depart. (94–97)

The key word "faith" enlists New Testament associations, but to it Paulina adds a potency more purely Shakespearean: music. Shakespeare's use of music, throughout his main antagonist to tempestuous tragedy, reaches a newly urgent precision at Cerimon's restoration of Thaisa and Pericles' reunion with Marina. Here it functions as the specifically releasing agent:

> *Paulina.* Music, awake her: strike. [*music sounds*]
> 'Tis time; descend; be stone no more; approach;
> Strike all that look upon with marvel; come;
> I'll fill your grave up. Stir; nay, come away;
> Bequeath to death your numbness, for from him
> Dear life redeems you. You perceive she stirs.
>
> > [*Hermione comes down*]
>
> Start not; her actions shall be holy as
> You hear my spell is lawful. Do not shun her
> Until you see her die again, for then
> You kill her double. Nay, present your hand.
> When she was young, you wooed her; now, in age
> Is she become the suitor?
>
> *Leontes.*   Oh, she's warm!
> If this be magic, let it be an art
> Lawful as eating.
>
> > (98–111)

"Redeems" (cf. "ransomed" at 5.2.16), "holy" and "lawful" continue earlier emphases. The concreteness of "fill your grave up" has analogies in Shelley's *Witch of Atlas* (LXIX–LXXI) and the empty sepulcher of the New Testament. Such resurrections are imaged as a reinfusing of the dead body with life. Hermione's restoration not only has nothing to do with black magic; it is not even transcendental. It exists in warm human actuality (cf. *Pericles*, 5.1.154): hence our earlier emphases on warmth and breath; and now on "eating" too. It is, indeed, part after all of "great creating nature"; no more, and no less; merely another miracle from the great power, the master artist of creation, call it what you will, nature or eternity, Apollo or—as in the New Testament—"the living God"....

... *The Winter's Tale* may seem a rambling, perhaps an untidy, play; its anachronisms are vivid, its geography disturbing. And yet Shakespeare offers nothing greater in tragic psychology, humor, pastoral, romance, and that which tops them all and is, except for *Pericles*, new. The unity of thought is more exact than appears: it was Sicily, at first sight ill suited to the somber scenes here staged, that gave us the myth of Proserpine or Persephone. The more profound passages are perhaps rather evidence of what is beating behind or within the creative genius at work than wholly successful ways of printing purpose on an average audience's, or an average reader's, mind; but the passages are there, and so is the purpose, though to Shakespeare it need not have been defined outside his drama. That drama, however, by its very enigma, its unsolved and yet uncompromising statement, throws up—as in small compass did the little flower-dialogue too—a vague, numinous sense of mighty powers, working through both the natural order and man's religious consciousness, that preserve, in spite of all appearance, the good. Orthodox tradition is used, but it does not direct; a pagan naturalism is used too. The Bible has been an influence; so have classical myth and Renaissance pastoral;[3] but the greatest influence was Life itself, that creating and protecting deity whose superhuman presence and powers the drama labors to define.

[3]And, it would seem, Greek drama too, especially Sophocles', wherein a tyrant is punished like Leontes by the sudden loss of his son (*Antigone*) and a child exposed like Perdita (*Oedipus*).

CAROL THOMAS NEELY

The Winter's Tale: Women and Issue

Many readers have seen the final reconciliations in *The Winter's Tale* as the triumph of nature, art, the gods, time: these large impersonal forces inform every aspect of the play. But the play's central miracle—birth—is human, personal, physical, and female, and its restorations are achieved by the rich presence and compelling actions of its women: Hermione, Paulina, and Perdita. They are more active, central, and fully developed than the women in the other romances. Through their acceptance of "issue" and of all that this central idea implies—sexuality and delivery, separation and change, growth and decay—they bring the play's men and the play's audience to embrace life's rhythms fully. In this romance, incest is most extensively and fruitfully transformed and the ruptures in marriage most fully manifested and healed.

Childbirth is the literal and symbolic center of the play. Hermione's pregnancy, delivery, recovery, and nursing receive close attention. Pervasive imagery of breeding, pregnancy, and delivery transforms many actions and scenes into analogues of birth with emotional and symbolic ties to the literal birth of Perdita:

From *Broken Nuptials in Shakespeare's Plays* (New Haven: Yale University Press, 1985), pp. 191–209, condensed by author.

This child was prisoner to the womb and is
By law and process of great Nature thence
Freed, and enfranchised.   (2.2.58–60)

Birth is proscribed in Antigonus' threat to geld his daughters so they will not "bring false generations" (2.1.148),
parodied when the Shepherd and Clown become "gentlemen born" in the last act, and corrupted in the gestation
of jealousy in Leontes' "Affection! Thy intention stabs
the center" speech (1.2.138–46). Images of birth resonate
through many other significant speeches and crucial scenes:
the messengers' return from Delphos with the wish that
"something rare / Even then will rush to knowledge . . . /
And gracious be the issue" (3.1.20–22); the penance that is
Leontes' "recreation"; the old shepherd's central line—
"Thou met'st with things dying, / I with things new born"
(3.3.112–13); Time's description of his role as father-
creator; Polixenes' grafting scheme for the purpose of conceiving new stock; the narrated reunion where, in spite of
the broken delivery, "Truth" is "pregnant by circumstance;" (5.2.33–34), and "every wink of an eye / some new
grace will be born" (118–19); and the reanimation of the
statue which imitates labor and delivery. The metaphors
emphasize the fundamental components of the process
of reproduction: union and fullness, labor and separation,
creation and loss, risk and fulfillment, enclosure and
enfranchisement.

In spite of this imagery, *The Winter's Tale* begins in a
static, masculine world that appears self-sufficient and
self-sustaining without the violent trauma of birth. It pur-
ports to control time and space through the unchanged
boyhood friendship of Leontes and Polixenes and through
Leontes' son, Mamillius, who "makes old hearts fresh"
(1.1.41) and will perpetuate Leontes' kingdom. Women are
strikingly absent from the idyllic picture, and when
Hermione enters in Scene 2, visibly pregnant, she becomes
the "matter" that first "alter[s]," then revitalizes this brittle
harmony (1.1.35).

The catalyst for this disruption is the possessive misogyny that fuels Leontes' jealousy. This sudden jealousy

reveals itself first in a sour memory of his courtship, develops into Leontes' fantasy of Hermione "paddling palms and pinching fingers" with Polixenes (1.2.115), and erupts finally in debased imagery of intercourse and gestation which "proves" her infidelity and his cuckoldry:

> Affection! Thy intention stabs the center.
> Thou dost make possible things not so held,
> Communicat'st with dreams—how can this be?—
> With what's unreal thou coactive art,
> And fellow'st nothing.
>
> (138–42)

The pseudo-logic and metaphoric substratum of this speech[1] show that Leontes' jealousy joins together the self-conscious conventionality and folly of the comedy heroes with the profound sexual revulsion of the heroes of tragedy. At the root of Leontes' folly is his divorce of sexuality from love, his pernicious swerve—resembling Hamlet's, Othello's, and Antony's—from the idealization of women to their degradation. The sexual disgust that leads Leontes to condemn and imprison Hermione corrupts and destroys his relations with Polixenes and Mamillius as well.

These latter relationships have protected Leontes against full participation in his marriage. Both Leontes and Polixenes are nostalgic for their innocent, presexual boyhood when each had a "dagger muzzled, / Lest it should bite its master" (156–57), and their "weak spirits" were not yet "higher reared / With stronger blood" (72–73). Both blame their "fall" into sexuality on women who are "devils" (82), seductive and corrupting. Both wish to remain "boy eternal," preserving their brotherhood as identical, innocent, "twinned lambs." The boyhood friendship, continued unchanged across time and space, is a protection against women, sex, change, and difference.[2] It is no wonder Leontes wants Polixenes to stay longer in Sicily!

The kings' intimacy with their sons is likewise defensive. They imagine their children as copies of themselves, extensions of their own egos, guarantees of their own innocence. Leontes repeatedly insists that his son is "like me" (129), and Polixenes describes his use of his son to regenerate himself:

> He makes a July's day short as December,
> And with his varying childness, cures in me
> Thoughts that would thick my blood.   (169–71)

Despite Polixenes' claim, the children cannot "cure" their fathers, for the men's corrupted views of sexuality are projected onto their offspring. Mamillius dies not only because of his connection with his threatened mother but because Leontes projects corruption onto him and repudiates the physical integrity of mother and son: "Conceiving the dishonor of his mother, / He straight declined, drooped, took it deeply, / Fastened, and fixed the shame on't himself; / Threw off his spirit, his appetite, his sleep, / And downright languished" (2.3.12–16). Leontes cannot split wife from son, repudiating Hermione and possessing Mamillius.[3] Later, in Bohemia, Polixenes—astonishingly—views his son's rebelliousness as a loss comparable to Mamillius' death: "Kings are no less unhappy, their issue not being gracious, than they are in losing them when they have approved their virtues" (4.2.28–30). Attacking Florizel and Perdita at the moment of their betrothal, Polixenes threatens to eliminate Florizel from his blood by disinheriting him as Leontes has already eliminated Hermione, Perdita, and Mamillius. Ironically, by denying their children freedom, difference, and sexual maturity, the two men deny themselves the potency, regeneration, and continuity that they desire but which cannot be achieved by their own return, through their friendship or their children, to a changeless childhood innocence.

The three women in the play serve, along with the pastoral scenes, as the "cure" for the "thoughts" that "thick" the men's "blood" (1.2.170–71). They are witty and realistic whereas the men are solemnly fantastic; they are at ease with sex whereas the kings are uneasy about it; and they take for granted change, difference, separation.

The extraordinary dignity and subdued control with which Hermione responds to Leontes' accusations has tended to obscure her earlier vivacity and its roots in her realistic attitudes toward sexuality, marriage, and children. She takes pleasure in competing verbally with men—"A lady's 'Verily' is / As potent as a lord's" (50–51). She denies the notion that marital sex implies "offenses" (83) and goes on to counsel Leontes in the appropriately tender management of it—"you may ride's / With one soft kiss a thousand furlongs, ere / With spur we heat an acre" (94–96). She affirms her physical connection with her children and her differences from them. Mamillius is the "first fruits of my body" (3.2.95), and Perdita, her babe, is "from my breast, / The innocent milk in its most innocent mouth / Haled out to murder" (97–99). But she does not identify herself with her children or assume their perpetual innocence. At the beginning of Act 2, Scene 1, in one of the most apt of the play's numerous realistic touches, she is quite simply tired of Mamillius: "he so troubles me, / 'Tis past enduring" (1–2).

But in spite of Hermione's down-to-earth wit, her long absence and her mock death have the effect of purifying and idealizing her. Like the earlier mock deaths of Hero in *Much Ado About Nothing* and Helena in *All's Well That Ends Well*, this one is engineered by the woman and her confidante for the purpose of self-protection and self-preservation as well as for the punishment and rehabilitation of the man. But Shakespeare—uniquely in the canon—withholds the crucial information of the deception from the audience until the last scene of the play; even then Hermione comes alive as gradually for the audience as she does for Leontes. The belief that the death is actual enhances the sanctification of Hermione as ideal wife and mother, enabling her to acquire near mythic status. In her absence, her power is extended through Paulina's defense of her, through Perdita's recreation of her, and through Antigonus' dream in which she becomes the play's very human deity.

This dream, in which Hermione appears, weeping, "In pure white robes, / Like very sanctity" (3.3.21–22) is, like the dream visions of Diana in *Pericles* and of Jupiter in

Cymbeline, "an emblematic recognition scene, in which we are shown the power that brings about the comic resolution" and in which "the controlling deity appears with an announcement of what is to conclude the action."[4] The figure of Hermione instructs Antigonus as Diana instructs Pericles, and narrates the conclusion of the first part of the play as Jupiter does the conclusion of *Cymbeline*; she protects her child and ensures its future. Like the other recipients of these visions, Antigonus misinterprets his. Although he takes the dream to mean that Hermione is guilty and dead, it is emblematic, rather, of her persistent, fierce love and grief for her daughter, and connects her with the maternal fertility goddess, Ceres, with whom she is explicitly linked when Perdita associates herself with Ceres' daughter, Proserpina.

Like *The Winter's Tale*, Ovid's tale focuses on the mother's desperate grief, on her frantic efforts to be reunited with the lost Proserpina, and on the consequences of their separation. Having learned that Proserpina has been stolen by Pluto, "Stonelike stood Ceres at this heavy newes; / And, staring, long continued in this muse."[5] (Perhaps this story, as well as that of Pygmalion, suggested the statue scene to Shakespeare.) When unable to find her daughter, Ceres takes vengeance on the land, especially on Sicily, where the abduction occurred:

> Therefore there shee brake
> The furrowing plough; the Oxe and owner strake
> Both with one death; then, bade the fields beguile
> The trust impos'd, shrunk seeds corrupts. That soile,
> So celebrated for fertilitie,
> Now barren grew: corne in the blade doth die.   (lines 478–83)

When reunited with her daughter, Ceres is rejuvenated and regenerates the earth; when Perdita returns to Sicily, its barren winter ends, its air is purged of "infection" (5.1.169), and Hermione is brought back to life. In the myth, because of the consummation of the rape, Proserpina cannot become completely a daughter again; she is required to spend six months with her mother and six months in the underworld with Pluto, a grim allegory of a daughter's enforced separation from and continuing ties to her mother upon reaching sexual maturity. Similarly, Perdita longs for reunion with her lost mother, although happily betrothed.

Throughout *The Winter's Tale*, and especially during Hermione's long absence, Paulina is present as the heroine's double, defender, and surrogate; her role is crucial to the transformations enacted in the play. Like Beatrice in *Much Ado About Nothing*, and Emilia in *Othello*, she is Hermione's shrewishly outspoken and vehement defender, asserting her mistress's chastity more vociferously than the slandered woman can. Like Emilia, she expresses the audience's rage at the heroine's "death." After this death, Paulina is a mediator both dramatically and psychologically. Her role shifts from that of comic shrew to wise counselor as, after castigating Leontes' folly, she engineers the penance that will transform his tragic actions to a comic conclusion.

The penance is fruitful in part because Paulina, who shares many of Hermione's qualities and is present when she is absent, is a surrogate for her mistress. She can lead Leontes toward a reunion with Hermione as Hermione herself cannot because she assumes an unthreatening, asexual role. At first, Paulina takes an assertive masculine role, defending Hermione and Perdita when Leontes' timid counselors fear to do so. But after Leontes has accepted Hermione's innocence and Paulina's tutelage, Paulina changes her strategy, and identifies herself as a woman subordinate to Leontes—"Now, good my liege, / Sir, royal sir, forgive a foolish woman" (3.2.224–25). By Act 5, Scene 1, Paulina and Leontes have achieved understanding and reciprocity; their long, intimate, chaste friendship is a transformation and vindication of that of Hermione and Polixenes.

As Hermione's virtues are regenerated for Leontes by Paulina, they are regenerated for the audience in Perdita. In her flower speeches with their embrace of change and pity for maidenhood, in her image of Florizel as "a bank for Love to lie and play on" (4.4.130), and in her easy assumption that he should "Desire to breed by me" (103), Perdita expresses a frank and wholehearted acceptance of sexuality that recalls Hermione's in the opening scenes. She wittily deflates men's exaggerated rhetoric and vapid generalizations, boldly embraces the risk of loving the son of the king, and participates in healthy relations with her lover and father that transform the infected ones in Sicily. Florizel, a joyous and confident lover, acknowledges Perdita's sexuality and his own while controlling his burning "lusts" (34). He delights in Perdita's frankness, her beauty, her wit, in her "blood" which "look[s] out" (160) and praises her unconventionally:

> Each your doing,
> So singular in each particular,
> Crowns what you are doing in the present deeds,
> That all your acts are queens.   (143–46)

As Florizel is a transformation of Leontes as lover, so the old shepherd is a transformation of Leontes as father. Like all the inhabitants of the Bohemian countryside, he views youth as a period of wantonness, not innocence, and accepts this fact now wryly, now warmly. He contemplates with exasperated tolerance the age "between ten and three-and-twenty," occupied with "getting wenches with child, wronging the ancientry, stealing, fighting" (3.3.58–62). He makes Perdita mistress of the feast and urges her to "lay it on" (4.3.42), to behave with the boldness, warmth, and flirtatiousness embodied in his remarkable, affectionate reminiscence of his dead wife (4.4.55–62). Appreciating his wife's sexual vitality, he accepts Perdita's and encourages her romance and betrothal.

In the pastoral world sexuality is represented as natural, inevitable, comic; female chastity is viewed as temporary and unnatural and aggressive male sexuality is celebrated. We find these attitudes in Florizel's courting, Perdita's flower speeches, in the rough dance by the "men of hair" (4.4.330), but especially in Autolycus's songs and ballads. In these "the red blood reigns in the winter's pale" (4.3.4); a "delicate burden" urges, "Jump her, and thump her" (4.4.195–96); Autolycus peddles: "Pins and poking-sticks of steel; / What maids lack from head to heel!" (228–29); and it is implied that it is better to be the "usurer's wife ... brought to bed of twenty money-bags at a burden" (264–65) than to be the woman "turned into a cold fish for she would not exchange flesh with one that loved her" (281–82).

In his role as parodic double of Leontes, Autolycus transmutes into comedy the conflicts and motives of the first three acts in other ways too.[6] Leontes' dangerous fantasies are translated into Autolycus' tall tales, his cruel manipulations into benign comic routines. Leontes' delusion of the deceit of those he makes victims is parodied in Autolycus' pretense of victimization as he robs the clown. Leontes' revulsion from sexuality and fatherhood is incorporated comically into Autolycus' ballads with their rejected lover, their grotesque childbirth, and their love triangle of "two maids wooing a man"—a happy reversal (from the male perspective) of the triangle of Leontes' imagination. Leontes' need to take revenge against his family is displaced in Autolycus' exaggerated threats to the shepherd and clown of Polixenes' likely revenge for their kinship with Perdita. In contrast to Leontes, Autolycus is an outsider, unencumbered by social or familial ties. (He does give himself a wife in his autobiographical sketch, but we cannot know if she is authentic; maybe she is dead!) His merry marginality is a positive version of Leontes' isolation in paranoia and penance. In the last act, Autolycus' repentance and promised incorporation into an all-male social hierarchy by the shepherd and clown parallel Leontes' repentance and restoration to his family.

Leontes' isolation in Sicily issues in a yet more fruitful conclusion. He has not simply been worn down by a winter of abstinence and penance, but has been regenerated. His transformation is apparent in his continuing acknowledgment of guilt, his chastened rhetoric, but most of all in his new apprehension of Hermione. She is seen no longer as a conventional abstraction, but as a unique woman—"no more such wives, therefore no wife" (5.1.56). He now honors her sexuality; he longs to see and touch and kiss her: "Then, even now, / I might have looked upon my queen's full eyes, / Have taken treasure from her lips" (52–54).

Leontes' resuscitation of the image of a wife who is peerless, sexual, and human—"the sweet'st companion that e'er man / Bred his hopes out of" (11–12)—prepares him to enter into a transformed relationship with Polixenes and Perdita and Florizel and makes possible the climactic recovery of Hermione herself.[7] When Perdita and Florizel flee to Sicily, Leontes can become "advocate" (220–23) to the couple's love because of his own transformed attitudes toward sexual "affections." He can acknowledge the incestuous component of his admiration for the youthfully peerless Perdita, but differentiates it from the longing he once felt—and still feels—for his wife: "I thought of her / Even in these looks I made" (227–28).

Leontes' advocacy precipitates the multiple-recognition scene. At the center of its joy is the grief of Leontes and Perdita for the absence of Hermione. This grief, the narrators' emphasis on "delivery," and the detailed description of Hermione's statue issue into the final scene. The scene is generated by Leontes' restored vision of Hermione, by his recovery of Perdita, and by the longing of the daughter, though blessed now with three fathers, a brother, and a beloved, to be united with the mother who "ended when I but began" (5.3.45). This longing is reciprocated by Hermione, who has not been "content to die" but has "desire[d]" her life to "see" Perdita a woman (1.1.42–43).

The final scene, like the preceding recognition scene, is communal; all of the characters need to recover Hermione. Paulina shapes the desires of the participants into a shared verbal ritual, so that their speech gradually imbues the statue with life—for them and for the play's audience. The statue, first an "it," becomes a "she" (5.3.61–80). The on-lookers' remarks move toward greater verbal certainty: from questions, to a possibility, to a fact qualified by a comparison (61–88). They recreate Hermione bit by bit, pointing first to fragmented physical attributes like "blood" and "hand" and "lip," and then invoking integrated processes like "motion: and speech." Leontes' earlier reduction of Hermione to her physical parts and his repudiation of these is thus reversed.

Leontes, at the beginning of the play, had wanted to possess a Hermione who was, in effect, a statue; he had distrusted her wit, her warmth, her blood. Now he explicitly longs for her "warm life," her "blood," her "breath," her speech (35,65,79). His determination to kiss the statue signals Paulina that he is ready for reunion with Hermione the woman.

The moment of reunion is as painful, laborious, and exhilarating as the moment of birth. Both Hermione and Leontes must experience constriction, separation, and transformation. Hermione, as she moves from being hated to being loved, must break out of her own entombed emotions while Leontes must embrace the living woman in place of his fantasy. Both must begin again. Hence Paulina, acting as midwife, entices Hermione out of her numbness with her reference to "time" and her image of fulfillment:

> 'Tis time; descend; be stone no more; approach;
> Strike all that look on you with marvel; come;
> I'll fill your grave up.   (99–101)

She then must stop Leontes from rejecting Hermione again:

>   Do not shun her
> Until you see her die again, for then
> You kill her double. Nay, present your hand.
> When she was young, you wooed her; now, in age,
> Is she become the suitor?   (105–09)

The action repeats and reverses the inception of their nuptials, when Leontes wooed painfully. Now Hermione must "become the suitor" and embrace him, and he must "open" his hand to her, abandoning possessiveness and delighting in her embrace: "Oh, she's warm! / If this be magic, let it be an art / Lawful as eating" (109–11). This reunion, like those in the other romances, recalls, as it reverses, the original rupture. The gradual theatrical regeneration of the Hermione whom Leontes had "killed" dramatizes most explicitly the reversal of the process of destruction, the undoing of loss.

But the reunion with Leontes is not the final, indeed, not

the central one for Hermione. Her own renewal is completed only when she speaks to Perdita, bestowing on her the blessing the daughter wishes for and reassuming her own motherhood:

> You gods look down,
> And from your sacred vials pour your graces
> Upon my daughter's head! Tell me, mine own,
> Where hast thou been preserved? Where lived? How found
> Thy father's court? For thou shalt hear that I,
> Knowing by Paulina that the oracle
> Gave hope thou wast in being, have preserved
> Myself to see the issue.   (121–28)

Leontes has been preserved and renewed by Paulina. Perdita has been preserved by time and nature and her foster family in the Bohemian countryside. But Hermione, like Paulina bereft of husband and future, has preserved herself to see both Perdita and "the issue" in a wider sense: the outcome, "Time's news," which is "known when 'tis brought forth" (4.1.26–27).

NOTES

1. For extended analyses of this speech and of the statue scene, see my "*The Winter's Tale*: The Triumph of Speech," *Studies in English Literature* 15 (1975): 324–27, 335–37.
2. Cf. C. L. Barber, " 'Thou that beget'st him / That did thee beget': Transformation in *Pericles* and *The Winter's Tale*," *Shakespeare Survey* 22 (1966): 59–67, who interprets Leontes' jealousy psychoanalytically as a projection onto Hermione of his affection for Polixenes and explores the transformation of this motif; and Murray M. Schwartz, "Leontes' Jealousy in *The Winter's Tale*," *American Imago* 30 (1973): 250–73 and "*The Winter's Tale*: Loss and Transformation," *American Imago* 32 (1975): 149–99, who ar-

gues in his two-part essay that *The Winter's Tale* is "a play about how this fantasy of perfect mutuality can be made to survive the impact of 'great difference' (1.1.3) and yet remain itself" (30:256).

3. See Schwartz, "Loss and Transformation," pp. 154–55; Richard P. Wheeler, *Shakespeare's Development and the Problem Comedies* (Berkeley: U. of California Press, 1981), p. 217; and Coppélia Kahn, *Man's Estate: Masculine Identity in Shakespeare* (Berkeley: U. of California Press, 1981), pp. 216–17 for related analyses of Mamillius' death.

4. Northrop Frye, "Recognition in *The Winter's Tale*," in *Essays on Shakespeare and Elizabethan Drama in Honour of Hardin Craig*, ed. Richard Hosley (Columbia: U. of Missouri Press, 1962), p. 238.

5. George Sandys, trans. *Ovid's Metamorphosis, Englished, Mythologized, and Represented in Figures* (1632), ed. Karl Hulley and Stanley T. Vandersall (Lincoln: U. of Nebraska Press, 1970), bk. V, lines 510–11.

6. Compare the discussions of Autolycus' parodic and mediating functions in Charles Frey, *Shakespeare's Vast Romance: A Study of The Winter's Tale* (Columbia: U. of Missouri Press, 1976), pp. 148–49 and Joan Hartwig, "Cloten, Autolycus, and Caliban: Bearers of Parodic Burdens," in *Shakespeare's Romances Reconsidered*, ed. Carol McGinnis Kay and Henry E. Jacobs (Lincoln: U. of Nebraska Press, 1978), pp. 91–103.

7. In contrast, C. L. Barber in "Thou that beget'st" and Peter Erickson in "Patriarchal Structure in *The Winter's Tale*," *PMLA* 97 (1982): 819–29; both claim that it is the restored friendship with Polixenes that makes Hermione's recovery possible.

COPPÉLIA KAHN

Twinned Lambs and the Pastoral Daughter in *The Winter's Tale*

Shakespeare rarely portrays a hero outside a filial context. Only Timon has neither kith nor kin, but through compulsive generosity he tries to make Athens his family. Even that most pathologically solitary hero, Richard III, defines himself by systematically exterminating his family. In fact, an intense ambivalence toward the family runs through all of Shakespeare's works. Characters must break out of their families in order to grow up, and when they have founded their own families, must then relinquish the future to their children. Leontes, hero of *The Winter's Tale*, is a father who must struggle to accept his difference from and dependence on women, and take fatherhood as the measure of his mortality. Shakespeare resolves Leontes' crisis through the father-daughter relationship, configuring the daughter's chaste sexuality and capacity to produce heirs as the foundation of the hero's hard-won paternal identity.[1]

In an illuminating essay, C. L. Barber says, "The primary motive which is transformed in *The Winter's Tale* . . . is the

From Coppélia Kahn, *Man's Estate: Masculine Identity in Shakespeare* (University of California Press, 1981), revised for the Signet Classic Edition of *The Winter's Tale*. Used by permission of the publisher and the author.

[1]For a penetrating analysis of patriarchal structurations of the father-daughter relationship, see Lynda E. Boose, "The Father's House and the Daughter in It," in *Daughters and Fathers*, ed. Lynda E. Boose and Betty S. Flowers (Baltimore: Johns Hopkins Press, 1989), pp. 19–74.

affection of Leontes for Polixenes, whatever name one gives it."[2] Though Leontes is a mature man—king, husband, father—the nine-months' visit of his boyhood friend reveals that he is still split between two identities, the boy of the past and the father of the present. Following J.I.M. Stewart (who follows Freud) in interpreting Leontes' jealousy, I would argue that the hero's belief that his wife loves his best friend is his way of defending against the horrified realization that he too still loves that friend, his way of saying, "Indeed, I do not love him, she loves him!"[3] Recall the appealing imagery used to describe the affection "rooted" between Leontes and Polixenes in their boyhoods. It portrays a paradise of sameness and oneness, the complete untroubled identity of each with the other:

> We were as twinn'd lambs that did frisk i' th' sun,
> And bleat the one at th'other; what we chang'd
> Was innocence for innocence; we knew not
> The doctrine of ill-doing, nor dreamed
> That any did.   (1.2.67–71)

Clearly, Polixenes is Leontes' double, one of the same sex and age who only mirrors him; loving Polixenes is depicted as guiltless, Edenic, and asexual, as opposed to loving a woman. It is also a love which denies time; Leontes and his friend were

> Two lads that thought there was no more behind
> But such a day tomorrow as today,
> And to be boy eternal.   (63–65)

[2] C. L. Barber, " 'Thou that beget'st him that did thee beget': Transformation in *Pericles* and *The Winter's Tale*," *Shakespeare Survey* 22 (1969): 59–68. See also the discussion of Leontes' affection for and jealousy of Polixenes as oedipally configured in C. L. Barber and Richard P. Wheeler, *The Whole Journey: Shakespeare's Power of Development* (Berkeley: University of California Press, 1986), pp. 328–34.

[3] J. I. M. Stewart, *Character and Motive in Shakespeare* (London and New York: Longmans, Green, 1949), p. 34. See also Sigmund Freud, "Some Neurotic Mechanisms in Jealousy, Paranoia, and Homosexuality" (1922), *Standard Edition* 18, pp. 221–33.

The homosexual implications of this nostalgic fantasy are less important than what it suggests about Leontes' attitude toward his mature sexuality, his manliness. He would like to escape and repudiate it, because being a husband and father means entrusting one's sexual dignity to a daughter of Eve, ceding the future to one's children, and facing death. Being "boy eternal," on the other hand, means being free of sexual desire, with its risks, its complications, and its implication in the procreative cycle, and being, though only in fantasy, immortal. In Polixenes' idyllic picture of boyhood, childish innocence is contrasted with adult sinfulness, and that sinfulness is then specifically associated with the women he and Leontes married, the "temptations" later "born to" them. The association of sin with the carnal pleasure legitimized by marriage betokens a guilt-ridden reluctance to accept, let alone appreciate, the natural desire of men for women; a reluctance soon rationalized into the violent misogyny through which Leontes voices his jealousy, the conviction that women are false through and through.

Having lost the mirror of his masculine identity in Polixenes, Leontes then seeks it in Mamillius, as he normally would in the patriarchal Shakespearean world. But his jealousy provokes him, ironically, to misinterpret the strong physical resemblance between himself and Mamillius. While Shakespeare makes it clear that this resemblance is the legitimate confirmation of Leontes' sexual union with Hermione, and the proof of her fidelity, Leontes finds Hermione's assertion of it another indication of female treachery:

> . . . they say we are
> Almost as like as eggs; women say so,
> That will say anything.
>
> (129–31)

In several significant ways, Shakespeare makes Mamillius a symbol of the union of male and female. While his name associates him with the maternal function of nursing, and he is shown in the female company of his mother and her attendants, he is also "a gentleman of the greatest promise" and universally acknowledged as the future ruler of Sicily,

Leontes' heir. The news of his death arrives immediately upon Leontes' denial of the oracle, an act which spells Hermione's doom. That is, Mamillius dies when Leontes denies most absolutely his natural and legitimate sexual union with the feminine, with Hermione, of which Mamillius is the sign and seal. And he is driven to deny it because he cannot sustain it. Despite his age, his kingship and his fatherhood, emotionally he is stuck at the developmental stage preceding the formation of identity, the stage of undifferentiated oneness with the mother, on which his oneness with Polixenes was modeled.[4] He cannot sustain a relationship with a woman based on the union of his and her separate identities, in which trust and reciprocity mediate that separateness.

Fittingly, Mamillius' death, in robbing Leontes of an heir, deprives him of a supremely important aspect of his male identity. Just as Macbeth cannot rest content with kingship so long as he lacks heirs to pass it on to, so Leontes is incomplete without an heir, and his lack of one is the direct result of his inability to accept his dependence on feminine power and to sustain a trusting union with Hermione.[5] With the deaths of Mamillius and (seemingly) Hermione, Leontes' delusion lifts, and he enters into a period of realiza-

[4]See Sigmund Freud, "Leonardo da Vinci and a Memory of His Childhood," *Standard Edition* 11; "On Narcissism: An Introduction," *Standard Edition* 14; and Murray Schwartz, "Leontes' Jealousy in *The Winter's Tale*," *American Imago* 30 (Fall 1973): 250–73, and "*The Winter's Tale*: Loss and Transformation," *American Imago* 32 (Summer 1975): 145–99. Arguing that Leontes is motivated by a "fear of separation from idealized others" and that he attempts "to reunite himself with a fantasized ideal maternal figure," Schwartz analyzes the paranoia of the hero's jealousy as a radical denial of separation, and sees the second half of the play as a successful reconstitution of continuity and union rooted ontogenetically in the mother-son symbiosis. His interpretation of the play's psychology is rigorous, comprehensive, and brilliant; I am greatly indebted to it.

[5]For an illuminating interpretation centering on "issue" as a pivotal factor in male perspectives on women's sexuality in the romances especially, see Carol Thomas Neely, *Broken Nuptials in Shakespeare's Plays* (New Haven: Yale University Press, 1986), pp. 191–209. For a reading of *The Winter's Tale* that interweaves and richly extends those of Barber and Wheeler and Neely, see Janet Adelman, *Suffocating Mothers: Fantasies of Maternal Origin in Shakespeare's Plays, Hamlet to The Tempest* (London: Routledge, 1992), pp. 320–38.

tion and repentance. At this point Shakespeare makes explicit, through the figure of Time, connections between the human experience of time in the life cycle, women, and the formation of masculine identity that have been implicit in the first half of the play.

Inga-Stina Ewbank shows how Leontes, crazy in his jealousy, acts with feverish haste, "goes against time and is therefore blind to truth." In the tradition of Renaissance iconography appropriated by Shakespeare in this play, time is a father, an old man, just what Leontes does not want to be. Ironically, in defying Father Time, he denies his own fatherhood and deprives himself of a son and a future. He is plunged into seemingly endless mourning for his past actions. As Ewbank says, now Leontes "has to become aware of truth in a wider sense . . . through subjection to Time the Revealer."[6] It is in this second half of the play that women, Paulina and Perdita, gain effective dramatic power to nurture men; while concurrently, time becomes the revealer, whose daughter is truth rather than the destroyer, *tempus edax*, who seized Mamillius and Hermione. The play moves to "a world ransomed"—Bohemia, and through a number of parallels in dramatic structure and action, Shakespeare keeps alive his "primary motive," Leontes' feeling for Polixenes, now changed into the wide gap of enmity dividing the once "twinn'd" brothers. But this time the younger generation, the sons and daughters, are to redeem or, in Shakespeare's metaphor, "beget" their fathers, restoring them to new identities as fathers.

Camillo's plot to present Florizel as his father's ambassador to Leontes provides the middle term by which the breaches between father and son, and brother and brother (Leontes and Polixenes), can both be healed at once. As Murray Schwartz argues, "By impersonating his father, Florizel can replace him without really replacing him."[7] But more important for the play's main action, the trans-

[6]Inga-Stina Ewbank, "The Triumph of Time in *The Winter's Tale*," in *Shakespeare's Later Comedies*, ed. D. J. Gordon (Harmondsworth, England: Penguin, 1971).
[7]Schwartz, "*The Winter's Tale*: Loss and Transformation," p. 178.

formation of Leontes' affection for Polixenes, Florizel in the latter's place bridges the gap between the two men and makes them friends again, not as "twinn'd lambs" but as men who have erred, suffered, and lost. The king's greeting to his future son-in-law makes this change clear:

> Your mother was most true to wedlock, Prince,
> For she did print your royal father off,
> Conceiving you. . . .
>   Most dearly welcome!
> And your fair princess—goddess! Oh, alas!
> I lost a couple that 'twixt heaven and earth
> Might thus have stood, begetting wonder as
> You, gracious couple, do. And then I lost—
> All mine own folly—the society,
> Amity too, of your brave father, whom,
> Though bearing misery, I desire my life
> Once more to look on him.   (5.1.123–25, 129–37)

Florizel and Perdita represent complementary modes of mediating separation and difference from significant others, a crucial task in identity formation. He fights his father; then reconciles with him. Perdita, on the other hand, does not fight, but subsumes opposites into a transcendent reality. On the sexual level, she reconciles virginity and erotic appeal, modesty and abandonment; mythically, through the imagery and ambiance of Bohemia, she is associated with "things dying" and "things newborn," with mother earth, the womb and tomb of all. She combines the qualities of the chaste preoedipal mother and the sexually desirable oedipal mother, symbolically uniting Leontes' divided attitudes toward women.

Significantly, though, Leontes' recognition of Florizel precedes his recognition of Perdita; he gains a son before he regains a daughter, thus recasting his relationship with his "brother," Polixenes, before he goes on to recognize and recast his relationship with the feminine in Perdita and then Hermione. This sequence of reunions recapitulates the sequence of identity development for which I am arguing. The total identity of like with like Leontes found with Polixenes was an effort to repeat the mother-child symbiotic unity and to avoid male identity. When Leontes "takes" Florizel "for" Polixenes as well as "for" Mamillius, he is accepting paternity, his and Polixenes', as the crucial component of his male identity—and paternity is equally based upon his separateness from the feminine and his union with it. To acknowledge Perdita as his daughter is to accept the sexuality he had wanted to repudiate; to acknowledge her as his heir is to accept the mortality he had wanted to escape. It is fitting that Leontes, as he clasps Hermione's hand (that crucial gesture again), characterizes his reunion with her in terms of the most primitive, elemental human activity, begun at the mother's breast:

> Oh, she's warm!
> If this be magic, let it be an art
> Lawful as eating.

(5.3.109–11)

SYLVAN BARNET

The Winter's Tale on Stage and Screen

Between 1611 and 1634 there are a few references to performances of *The Winter's Tale* at court, but these references tell us nothing more than that the play was done. The only mention of a public performance is Simon Forman's report (printed on pages 143–44) of a visit to the Globe on May 15, 1611. Forman very briefly summarizes part of the plot, dwells a moment on "the Rogue that came in all tattered" (i.e. Autolycus), and concludes with a warning to himself: "Beware of trusting feigned beggars or fawning fellows."

It's interesting to notice Forman making so close a connection between the play and his own experience (no nonsense about art for art's sake here), but anyone interested in stage history must wish that Forman had reported more fully what he had seen. For one thing, he does not report the scene in which the statue comes to life, a scene so striking—so memorable, one would have thought—that some scholars have conjectured, on the basis of Forman's neglect of the episode, that it may not have been in the play when *The Winter's Tale* was first produced. On balance, however, it seems more reasonable to recognize that Forman's omission of any given detail is, in so brief an account, of no significance.

It is tempting to think, especially after we see a performance that does not satisfy us, that there is, or was, one

right way to stage a play, or, indeed, to deliver any given
speech, and we would give much to know how *The Winter's Tale* was done at the Globe in Shakespeare's day.
What are some of the things we wish Forman had reported? For one, there is the most famous stage direction in
all of Shakespeare's work, "Exit, pursued by a bear"
(3.3.57). Was the bear a real bear, or a man on all fours in
a bear costume, or perhaps a man in a bear costume but
walking on two legs, imitating a bear rampant? (A real
bear would have been available to players at the Globe
from the nearby bear-baiting house, but bears are notoriously unpredictable, and it seems most unlikely that an acting company would dare to rely on a real one.) In Trevor
Nunn's 1969 Royal Shakespeare Company production, the
bear was a towering affair draped over a frame supported
by a walking actor. In the 1976 RSC production the bear
was represented symbolically by a masked actor, who then
removed the mask and was seen to be the Chorus who
spoke the role of Time.

Or, to take a larger issue, what about Leontes' jealousy,
which erupts in 1.2.108, with "Too hot, too hot!" as he
watches his wife, Hermione, chat genially with their visitor,
Polixenes. There has been much discussion among critics
about Leontes' motivation—or lack of motivation. He ex-
plodes soon after Polixenes agrees to stay longer when
Hermione urges him to do so. Is Leontes suddenly over-
come by jealousy, or has he been jealous all along? Early in
the nineteenth century Samuel Taylor Coleridge found
Polixenes' change of mind "perfectly natural from mere
courtesy of sex and the exhaustion of the will by former effort," but this sudden change of mind, according to Coleridge, is "well-calculated to set in nascent action the
jealousy of Leontes." Those who have looked for signs that
Leontes has from the start been jealous point out that before
the outburst his speeches are short—evidence that he is re-
pressing his feelings?—and that in fact he says very little in
the early part of the scene; Polixenes has about twice as
many lines as Leontes, and Hermione has still more. Further, Hermione says to Leontes, "You / Charge him too

coldly." Does she perceive that Leontes is acting oddly? Or is her remark merely the good-natured teasing of a wife? Insofar as we can tell how earlier actors played the scene, nothing was made of a smoldering Leontes who is jealous from the start until John Gielgud played the role that way in 1951, in Peter Brook's production. Earlier actors apparently presented the outburst as a sudden and rather crazy attack.

Gielgud's interpretation, now often followed, is sometimes supported by presenting Hermione as evidently pregnant. Polixenes' innocent opening speech in this scene, with its reference to nine months, and with such words as "burden," "perpetuity," "rich place," and "multiply," is regarded as unintentionally fueling Leontes' thoughts that Polixenes may be the father of the child Hermione is so obviously carrying:

> Nine changes of the wat'ry star hath been
> The shepherd's note since we have left our throne
> Without a burden: time as long again
> Would be filled up, my brother, with our thanks,
> And yet we should for perpetuity
> Go hence in debt. And therefore, like a cipher,
> Yet standing in rich place, I multiply
> With one "We thank you," many thousands moe
> That go before it.
>
> (1.2.1–9)

Against this interpretation that Leontes is jealous from the start and is further enraged both by the sight of his pregnant wife and by Polixenes' language of fertility, it can, of course, be argued that the text does not mention Hermione's pregnancy until the next act, in 2.1, when the First Lady says to Mamillius, "The Queen, your mother, rounds apace," and the Second Lady adds that Hermione "is spread of late / Into a goodly bulk." A director can at the start show us a visibly pregnant Hermione, but, if so, it should be remembered that this is a directorial decision. The text does not require it. And perhaps only a super-subtle spectator (or, more likely, a super-subtle reader) could hear in Polixenes' opening lines in 1.2 any suggestions of pregnancy.

It's all very well for us to feel that directors and actors should simply give us Shakespeare's play—the play that Forman saw at the Globe in 1611—and should keep their subtle interpretations to themselves, but in fact directors and actors simply cannot behave this way. For instance, when Leontes speaks his early lines, he must either smolder or not; and the text does not provide conclusive evidence about how the lines are to be given. This said, it does not follow that all interpretations are equally valid; surely one can object to Jeremy Irons's interpretation, in Terry Hands's production at Stratford-upon-Avon in 1986, in which a capricious Irons played Leontes' bawdy lines for laughs. After the explosion in 1.2.108ff ("too hot, too hot! / . . . / I have tremor cordis on me; my heart dances, / But not for joy, not joy"), with its obsessive repetition of "not for joy, not joy," and the ensuing vision of "paddling palms and pinching fingers," when we get such a passage as the following, one can hardly say that Leontes is a genial cynic talking about adultery:

> Inch-thick, knee-deep, o'er head and ears a forked
>   one!
> Go play, boy, play: thy mother plays, and I
> Play too—but so disgraced a part, whose issue
> Will hiss me to my grave; contempt and clamor
> Will be my knell. Go play, boy, play. There have been,
> Or I am much deceived, cuckolds ere now,
> And many a man there is, even at this present,
> Now, while I speak this, holds his wife by th' arm,
> That little thinks she has been sluiced in 's absence,
> And his pond fished by his next neighbor, by
> Sir Smile, his neighbor.   (1.2.186–96)

Again, the obsessive repetitions ("Go play, boy, play"; "Go play, boy, play"; "even at this present, / Now, while I speak this") and the vulgarity ("sluiced," "his pond fished") surely make a playful interpretation impossible. Still, one cannot easily say that such and such an interpretation is right or wrong. For instance, what of Michael Kahn's production at Stratford, Connecticut, in 1975, in which the bear was played by the actor who later (4.1) played Time; as the bear Time wore not a bear's costume but a golden bear-mask. Given the fact that the appearance of Time in 4.1 obviously takes us beyond realism into the realm of myth (it is also noteworthy that Time's pairs of rhymed lines are the only rhymes in the play, aside from the songs), is this a legitimate dramatic way of calling attention to what Shakespeare in one of his sonnets characterizes as "devouring time"?

And what of the idea of doubling the roles of Hermione and her daughter Perdita? Obviously such doubling can, if apparent to the audience, emphasize the unity of the two parts of the play, and can emphasize the idea of renewal, or, so to speak, of winter turning into spring. The first recorded instance of such doubling is in 1887, when Mary Anderson played the two parts, though it is possible that the parts were also doubled in Shakespeare's day. (There is, however, one obstacle to such doubling; both characters appear in 5.3, and indeed in lines 42–46 Perdita speaks, so at least in this scene two actresses are needed, unless lines 42–46 are cut.)

Or, to take one last example, how much explicit emphasis should be put on Time and renewal? Michael Kahn in 1975 made much use of circular symbolism to indicate loss and restoration. The stage was a circular platform, over which was suspended a disk on which Time marked off the hours, at first (in the "wintry" part of the play) with a bare branch, later (when the action shifts to Bohemia and to springtime) with a leafy bough, and finally with a golden branch bearing golden fruit.

It is time to return to the earliest productions, and to reiterate that, unfortunately, we know almost nothing about them, beyond what the text of the play itself tells us, for instance that in 4.4 there is "a dance of Shepherds and Shepherdesses," and that later in the scene, certain performers having "made themselves all hair" (i.e. having dressed like satyrs or the wild men of medieval art), there is "a dance of twelve Satyrs."

The first revival we hear of is Henry Giffard's, in London in 1741, at his theater in Goodman's Fields. A little later in the year the play was given a short run at Covent Garden, but even the addition of "a new Grand Ballet called the Rural Assembly" in the pastoral scene apparently could not ensure success. In 1754 Macnamara Morgan adapted *The Winter's Tale* into a work called *The Sheep-Shearing*. He cut the first half of the play heavily (Leontes and Hermione do not appear in *The Sheep-Shearing,* but Antigonus does, and indeed, since there is no bear, Antigonus survives), and put all of the emphasis on Florizel and Perdita. The work was a popular success in London and in Dublin, and was performed at Covent Garden as late as 1798.

Morgan's version of 1754 was followed in 1756 by David Garrick's version, called *Florizel and Perdita, A Dramatic Pastoral.* Garrick retained more of Shakespeare's text than Morgan did, but like Morgan he avoided the "wide gap of time" in the play, and began in Bohemia, *after* the sixteen years which divide the two halves of Shakespeare's play. Except for the scene in which the Clown and the Shepherd discover Perdita (Shakespeare's 3.3), Garrick used only acts 4 and 5, and conveyed the gist of the first three acts by means of newly invented dialogue spoken by Camillo and a Gentleman. By this expository device, and by bringing Leontes, Hermione, and Paulina to Bohemia, he preserved the allegedly classical "unities" of time, place, and action. Although he retained a fair amount of dialogue from the second half of Shakespeare's play, he also cut, altered, and added. Given the modern emphasis on Perdita's and Polixenes' dialogue on art and nature (4.4.85ff), it comes as a shock to find that Garrick omitted the lines. It also comes as a shock to learn that *Florizel and Perdita* was highly popular, enduring well into the first half of the nineteenth century, even after John Philip Kemble in 1802 had brought a fairly complete version of Shakespeare's play back to the stage.

Although it is fair to say that Kemble restored Shakespeare's play, he also made cuts, rearranged some of Shakespeare's material, and kept some of Garrick's additions, including a song for Perdita in 4 and an emotional speech for Leontes in 5. One of the most conspicuous cuts is that of Time; probably Time's direct address to the audience seemed naive and inartistic to an eighteenth-century audience. In any case, without the help of Time the audience simply had to conclude that the infant left at the end of the first half of the play had grown to the young adult who appeared at the start of the second half.

Because Kemble's production took place on a proscenium stage with painted flats in grooves, a very different stage from the platform stage of Shakespeare's day, some rearrangements of scenes were therefore necessary. For instance, in Shakespeare's text a short scene (3.1) between Cleomenes and Dion intervenes between the scene in which Leontes orders Antigonus to dispose of the infant (2.3) and the trial scene (3.2). It intervenes, that is, between two big court scenes, and it provides a notable change of atmosphere, for the two men talk of their visit to the oracle at Delos: "The climate's delicate, the air most sweet, / Fertile the isle." But when fairly elaborate scenery is used, it is difficult to strike a set and then resurrect it a little later, so Kemble put this brief lyrical scene after 2.2 (the scene with the jailer) and before the scene in which Antigonus takes the infant from the court. He began the next act with the trial scene, which was set up during the interval. This sequence was adopted by several productions later in the nineteenth century, for instance sometimes by William Macready and Samuel Phelps.

Kemble did not worry about a consistent setting. How could he, since the play includes references to the Delphic oracle, the Renaissance painter Julio Romano, the Empress of Russia, and the English countryside? Kemble's sets in the first half of the play evoked both the Classical and the Gothic world, the prison evoked the etchings of Piranese (mid-eighteenth century), and the scene with the statue (Hermione's apparent resurrection in the last scene) evoked the world of Greek sculpture, or at least of Greek sculpture as it was then understood. Kemble's Hermione (his sister, the great actress Sarah Siddons) wore impressive royal robes in the first part of the play; later, as the statue, she appeared in white, leaning on a column. Lamps behind the pedestal provided her with the appropriate radiance.

Although Kemble deserves great credit for restoring much of Shakespeare's text, the most famous production of the nineteenth century was that of Charles Kean, which opened in 1856 and ran for a hundred and two consecutive nights. The cult of Hellenism, which had begun in the late eighteenth century and is known to every schoolchild today through such works as Keats's "Ode on a Grecian Urn" and Poe's "To Helen," was by the middle of the nineteenth century in full bloom. And so, too, was the passion for historical accuracy. For Kean, Kemble's mixture of what was supposed to be Greek with what was supposed to be Gothic was unthinkable. The costumes and sets, as accurate as the latest research could determine, were derived from images on Greek vases. Even the toy cart with which little Mamillius played was a copy of a toy painted on a Greek vase. Kean decided that the play was set in the late fourth century B.C., which of course meant that the references to Julio Romano and the Empress of Russia had to be deleted, and so too did the allusion to Judas, in "My name / Be yoked with his, that did betray the Best!" (1.2.420). In his acting edition of the play Kean explained:

> The pivot on which the story revolves is in fact the decision pronounced by the oracle of Delphi; and taking this incident as the corner-stone of the whole fabric, I have adopted a period when Syracuse according to Thucydides, had from a mere Doric colony, increased in magnificence to a position in no way inferior to that of Athens herself.

And what of the other locale, Bohemia—to which Shakespeare (less scrupulous than Kean in his research) had attributed a seacoast? Kean accepted Thomas Hanmer's emendation (1744) of Bohemia to Bithynia, and chose to present this realm, in which Polixenes ruled, as somewhat more ornate and opulent than the Greek world of Leontes.

Kean feasted the eye not only with sets and costumes that were thought to be historically accurate, but also with elaborate spectacles. J. W. Cole, in his *Life . . . of Charles Kean* (1859), describes the opening:

> As the curtain rose, we saw before us Syracuse at the epoch of her highest prosperity, about 330 B.C., and gazed on the fountains of Arethusa and the temple of Minerva. After the short introductory scene between Camillo and Archidamus, we passed to the banqueting-hall in the royal palace, where Leontes, Polixenes, Hermione, and guests were discovered reclining on couches, after the manner of the ancient Greeks. Musicians were playing the hymn to Apollo, and slaves supplied wine and garlands. Thirty-six resplendently handsome young girls, representing youths in complete warlike panoply, entered, and performed the evolutions of the far-famed Pyrrhic dance. The effect was electrical, and established at the commencement an impression of what might be expected as the play advanced.

Other spectacles included an extremely elaborate allegory with Time (it began with Luna appearing in a chariot, surrounded by women who represented star deities), and an elaborate pastoral dance which turned into a Bacchic revel with some three hundred participants. Because all of this took a good deal of time, the text had to be fairly heavily cut. A few additional cuts were made on grounds of propriety, for instance the allusions to Hermione's visible pregnancy.

Most subsequent revivals in the nineteenth century sought to emulate Kean's, which means that there was not only great concern with historical accuracy but also with spectacle—that is, with making this historical accuracy very evident to the audience. When the play was presented at the Lyceum in 1886–1887, for instance, with Mary Anderson as Hermione and Forbes-Robertson as Leontes, the costumes were designed by the painter Alma-Tadema, who was well known for his concern with historical detail. The production resembled Kean's in other ways, too; bawdry was deleted, and so were the anachronistic Julio Romano and the Empress of Russia. One other point, already mentioned, should be repeated; in this production, Mary Anderson doubled the roles of Hermione and Perdita, beginning a tradition (or perhaps unknowingly reviving one that had died in the early seventeenth century) that continues to find favor.

The tradition of Kean came to an end with Herbert Beerbohm Tree, who gave a spectacular production of *The Winter's Tale* in 1906, Ellen Terry's fiftieth year on the stage. Because Ellen Terry had begun her career fifty years earlier when she played Mamillius in Kean's 1856 production of *The Winter's Tale*, Tree invited her to play Hermione to celebrate her anniversary. Again the text was heavily cut, in order to allow for the time consumed by the elaborate spectacle. Spectacle—in particular, spectacle that reproduced a recognizable scene in amazing detail—was at the heart of Tree's conception of drama. The aim of drama, he said in *Thoughts and After-Thoughts*, is illusion, and illusion is achieved by "accuracy of detail." To those new voices who protested that the best way to stage Shakespeare's plays was with little or no scenery, on a stage that resembled Shakespeare's, Tree replied:

> . . . the trend of [the public's] taste has undoubtedly been towards putting Shakespeare upon the stage as worthily and munificently as the manager can afford.

And so Tree's productions were noted for their great crowd scenes, their picturesque and illusionistic settings (for instance, a flowing brook), and their elaborate pantomimes. One quotation from the promptbook will serve to indicate the sort of thing Tree did:

> At cue from orchestra, first note of Perdita theme,—Curtain— Perdita is heard singing from cottage. Enter Florizel from back L.E., crosses stepping stones to front of cottage, moves down bank to first tree; there stands listening to Perdita's song. At end of song, Florizel turns, moves up to cottage and throws flowers in at cottage window, then moves back to first tree. Perdita ap-

pears in at cottage window. Florizel beckons her to come out, which she does. Perdita runs down bank to Florizel and takes both his hands. Florizel leads her up bank and across stepping stones, then off L U E. When thoroughly off, Autolycus is seen rising from bank of rushes C, yawning, stretching. Autolycus moves around bank and down to C. humming melody (viz:— "will you buy any lace and tape" etc.), turns, sees water. Moves on to 1st stepping stone, kneels, washes hands and arms then splashes water over face. Crawls on to the bank L., rises, takes handkerchief from pocket and while drying himself begins his speech.

Soon the Clown enters, leading a live donkey. (Tree had made a great hit in 1900 when he had introduced live rabbits in his production of *A Midsummer Night's Dream*, so why not an ass now?) Of course, since all of this stage business took considerable time, extensive cuts had to be made throughout the play, minimizing some characters, simplifying many complicated passages, and deleting bawdry. And because sets could not easily be dismantled and then raised again, some scenes were transposed and three scenes (1.1, 3.2, and 5.2) were completely deleted.

But Tree represented the end of a tradition; those who, like William Poel, in one way or another were trying to revive Elizabethan principles of staging, were making headway. In 1910 Winthrop Ames in New York produced *The Winter's Tale* (though in a heavily cut text) on a platform stage built out over the orchestra pit. Actors thus were fairly close to the audience and could directly address it, in defiance of the principles of illusionistic staging. The set— dark paneling in the Elizabethan style—was permanent, with an alcove at the rear. Changes of scene were indicated by changes of properties in the alcove, and the shift from Sicily to Bohemia was boldly indicated by a change of arms in the alcove. When the alcove was not used, for instance at Autolycus's first appearance, it was obscured with a curtain. Benches served as thrones, but the element of spectacle was not neglected since the costumes were elaborate.

Ames's production was important, but even more important was the version put on by Harley Granville-Barker in London in 1912. This was the first of his three productions (the other two were *Twelfth Night* in 1912 and *A Midsummer Night's Dream* in 1914) that revolutionized the staging of Shakespeare. Barker rejected the realistic illusionism of Tree on the grounds that illusionism was contrary to the nature of the play (after all, how illusionistic can a play be if it includes a character called Time?) and that illusionism (as Tree's practice demonstrated) requires heavy cutting of Shakespeare's lines. (Barker cut only a few lines; the promptbook does not survive, but various witnesses claim that the number did not exceed fifteen, and may have been as small as six.) Further, an illusionistic presentation requires that the actors remain in a world behind the proscenium, whereas some parts of the play call for direct address to the audience.

Barker's stage had three acting areas. At the rear was a sort of alcove, a small inset stage framed by classical white columns; in front of it, four steps lower, was a larger area, the proscenium stage; and in front of this was a forestage twelve feet deep at the center, eleven feet at the sides, built over the orchestra pit. There were no footlights; the forestage was illuminated by projectors at the front of the dress circle. Barker brought the action forward as much as possible, and, not worrying about illusionism, sometimes had his characters address the audience. (Following this tradition, Jonathan Miller said of the BBC television version, "Since this is a fairy story, we've used a stylized production, with the bare minimum of scenery, so that you can focus on the hard reality of the emotions." Kean and Tree would not have understood.) The court was indicated by the columns; rural Bohemia was indicated by a simple, stylized cottage. But in some ways the stage was richly adorned, for the courtly characters wore spangled clothing and gold and silver boots, inspired not by any particular historical period but by Bakst, Beardsley, and the Russian ballet. The peasants of Bohemia, on the other hand, were dressed rather like characters out of Thomas Hardy's countryside, though when Perdita impersonated Flora she looked like a character from Botticelli's *Primavera* as seen by Beardsley.

Probably no later production of *The Winter's Tale* has been as influential as Barker's—its influence was evident, for instance, in the highly stylized production of the Royal Shakespeare Company at Stratford-upon-Avon in 1981—but there have nevertheless been impressive productions. Chief among them was Peter Brook's (1951), with John Gielgud as Leontes, Diana Wynyard as Hermione, Flora Robson as Paulina, and George Rose as Autolycus. All four of these performances were acknowledged as masterful, but, as has already been mentioned, Gielgud's was especially interesting because it presented Leontes as jealous from the start, rather than as a man overcome by a sudden and crazy suspicion. Somewhat in Barker's style, a simple white box set was used: elegant arches at the sides for the court scenes were transformed into more rustic structures for the pastoral scene. The costumes were Tudor in the first half, and (as in Barker) Thomas Hardy in the second half. "Tudor" music, composed by the playwright Christopher Fry, accompanied the action.

Trevor Nunn's production at Stratford-upon-Avon in 1969 continued the Barker tradition, at least insofar as its sets were symbolic (or, to use Barker's word, "decorative") rather than illusionistic. The play began with Time speaking part of his speech from 4.1, while flashes of stroboscopic light illuminated Leontes, who, arms outstretched as if crucified, was seen in a tall box with mirrored walls. The problem of the origin of Leontes' jealousy was thus avoided. Judi Dench doubled in the roles of Hermione and Perdita, though there was some difficulty when she slipped off stage as Perdita and displaced the momentarily concealed statue of Hermione, which, by the way, was in the same box that Leontes had been in. The effect was too tricky, or perhaps not tricky enough, a sort of trick that the audience saw through and did not care for. Nunn's version was given again, co-directed by John Barton, in 1976.

Finally, something should be said about the BBC TV version, directed by Jonathan Miller (1980). Miller follows the text closely, making only a few very small cuts, though one conspicuous cut is of the dance of satyrs in 4.4. The set consists chiefly of expressionistic cones and pyramids, light gray for wintry Sicilia, where the people wear furs—Leontes in fur hat and fur coat seems bearlike—and yellow in springtime Bohemia, where a green floor and leaves on a tree that had been barren in Sicilia also tell viewers that they have moved from a realm of "things dying" to "things new born" (3.3.113). The return to Sicilia includes a sign of life, too, in Paulina's garden, where the statue comes to life.

The televised version, now almost a thing of the remote past, remains quite serviceable, but persons interested in seeing (as opposed to reading) *The Winter's Tale* do not have to rely on it. No year now goes by without several worthy productions of *The Winter's Tale*. When Henry Giffard staged the play in 1741 he said, probably accurately, that it had not been acted for a hundred years. We have changed all that; although it is still easier to find a production of *Hamlet* than of *The Winter's Tale*, theatergoers interested in seeing *The Winter's Tale* now can probably find a nearby production in almost any year.

Bibliographic Note: The fullest account of the play in the theater is Dennis Bartholomeusz, *"The Winter's Tale" in Performance in England and America, 1611–1976* (1982), a detailed and well-illustrated study with an extensive bibliography. Much briefer, and much narrower in scope, but still very useful, is R. P. Draper, *"The Winter's Tale": Text and Performance* (1985), which concentrates on four productions by the Royal Shakespeare Company (1969, directed by Trevor Nunn; 1976, directed by John Barton and Nunn; 1981, directed by Ronald Eyre; 1980, directed by Jane Howell for BBC television). W. Moelwyn Merchant's essay on Charles Kean's production, in *Shakespeare and the Artist* (1959), includes interesting illustrations from several eighteenth- and nineteenth-century sources. For a chronological survey of the movement away from illusionistic staging of

Shakespeare, concentrating on the first half of the twentieth century, see J. L. Styan, *The Shakespeare Revolution* (1977). For reviews of productions since about 1950, consult *Shakespeare Survey* (an annual publication) and *Shakespeare Quarterly*.

Suggested References

The number of possible references is vast and grows alarmingly. (The *Shakespeare Quarterly* devotes one issue each year to a list of the previous year's work, and *Shakespeare Survey*—an annual publication—includes a substantial review of biographical, critical, and textual studies, as well as a survey of performances.) The vast bibliography is best approached through James Harner, *The World Shakespeare Bibliography on CD-Rom: 1900–Present*. The first release, in 1996, included more than 12,000 annotated items from 1990–93, plus references to several thousand book reviews, productions, films, and audio recordings. The plan is to update the publication annually, moving forward one year and backward three years. Thus, the second issue (1997), with 24,700 entries, and another 35,000 or so references to reviews, newspaper pieces, and so on, covered 1987–94.

Though no works are indispensable, those listed below have been found especially helpful. The arrangement is as follows:

1. Shakespeare's Times
2. Shakespeare's Life
3. Shakespeare's Theater
4. Shakespeare on Stage and Screen
5. Miscellaneous Reference Works
6. Shakespeare's Plays: General Studies
7. The Comedies
8. The Romances
9. The Tragedies
10. The Histories
11. *The Winter's Tale*

The titles in the first five sections are accompanied by brief explanatory annotations.

1. Shakespeare's Times

Andrews, John F., ed. *William Shakespeare: His World, His Work, His Influence*, 3 vols. (1985). Sixty articles, dealing not only with such subjects as "The State," "The Church," "Law," "Science, Magic, and Folklore," but also with the plays and poems themselves and Shakespeare's influence (e.g., translations, films, reputation)

Byrne, Muriel St. Clare. *Elizabethan Life in Town and Country* (8th ed., 1970). Chapters on manners, beliefs, education, etc., with illustrations.

Dollimore, John, and Alan Sinfield, eds. *Political Shakespeare: New Essays in Cultural Materialism* (1985). Essays on such topics as the subordination of women and colonialism, presented in connection with some of Shakespeare's plays.

Greenblatt, Stephen. *Representing the English Renaissance* (1988). New Historicist essays, especially on connections between political and aesthetic matters, statecraft and stagecraft.

Joseph, B. L. *Shakespeare's Eden: the Commonwealth of England 1558–1629* (1971). An account of the social, political, economic, and cultural life of England.

Kernan, Alvin. *Shakespeare, the King's Playwright: Theater in the Stuart Court 1603–1613* (1995). The social setting and the politics of the court of James I, in relation to *Hamlet*, *Measure for Measure*, *Macbeth*, *King Lear*, *Antony and Cleopatra*, *Coriolanus*, and *The Tempest*.

Montrose, Louis. *The Purpose of Playing: Shakespeare and the Cultural Politics of the Elizabethan Theatre* (1996). A poststructuralist view, discussing the professional theater "within the ideological and material frameworks of Elizabethan culture and society," with an extended analysis of *A Midsummer Night's Dream*.

Mullaney, Steven. *The Place of the Stage: License, Play, and Power in Renaissance England* (1988). New Historicist analysis, arguing that popular drama became a cultural institution "only by . . . taking up a place on the margins of society."

Schoenbaum, S. *Shakespeare: The Globe and the World*

(1979). A readable, abundantly illustrated introductory book on the world of the Elizabethans.

Shakespeare's England, 2 vols. (1916). A large collection of scholarly essays on a wide variety of topics, e.g., astrology, costume, gardening, horsemanship, with special attention to Shakespeare's references to these topics.

2. Shakespeare's Life

Andrews, John F., ed. *William Shakespeare: His World, His Work, His Influence,* 3 vols. (1985). See the description above.

Bentley, Gerald E. *Shakespeare: A Biographical Handbook* (1961). The facts about Shakespeare, with virtually no conjecture intermingled.

Chambers, E. K. *William Shakespeare: A Study of Facts and Problems,* 2 vols. (1930). The fullest collection of data.

Fraser, Russell. *Young Shakespeare* (1988). A highly readable account that simultaneously considers Shakespeare's life and Shakespeare's art.

————. *Shakespeare: The Later Years* (1992).

Schoenbaum, S. *Shakespeare's Lives* (1970). A review of the evidence and an examination of many biographies, including those of Baconians and other heretics.

————. *William Shakespeare: A Compact Documentary Life* (1977). An abbreviated version, in a smaller format, of the next title. The compact version reproduces some fifty documents in reduced form. A readable presentation of all that the documents tell us about Shakespeare.

————. *William Shakespeare: A Documentary Life* (1975). A large-format book setting forth the biography with facsimiles of more than two hundred documents, and with transcriptions and commentaries.

3. Shakespeare's Theater

Astington, John H., ed. *The Development of Shakespeare's Theater* (1992). Eight specialized essays on theatrical companies, playing spaces, and performance.

Beckerman, Bernard. *Shakespeare at the Globe, 1599–1609* (1962). On the playhouse and on Elizabethan dramaturgy, acting, and staging.

Bentley, Gerald E. *The Profession of Dramatist in Shakespeare's Time* (1971). An account of the dramatist's status in the Elizabethan period.

———. *The Profession of Player in Shakespeare's Time, 1590–1642* (1984). An account of the status of members of London companies (sharers, hired men, apprentices, managers) and a discussion of conditions when they toured.

Berry, Herbert. *Shakespeare's Playhouses* (1987). Usefully emphasizes how little we know about the construction of Elizabethan theaters.

Brown, John Russell. *Shakespeare's Plays in Performance* (1966). A speculative and practical analysis relevant to all of the plays, but with emphasis on *The Merchant of Venice*, *Richard II*, *Hamlet*, *Romeo and Juliet*, and *Twelfth Night*.

———. *William Shakespeare: Writing for Performance* (1996). A discussion aimed at helping readers to develop theatrically conscious habits of reading.

Chambers, E. K. *The Elizabethan Stage*, 4 vols. (1945). A major reference work on theaters, theatrical companies, and staging at court.

Cook, Ann Jennalie. *The Privileged Playgoers of Shakespeare's London, 1576–1642* (1981). Sees Shakespeare's audience as wealthier, more middle-class, and more intellectual than Harbage (below) does.

Dessen, Alan C. *Elizabethan Drama and the Viewer's Eye* (1977). On how certain scenes may have looked to spectators in an Elizabethan theater.

Gurr, Andrew. *Playgoing in Shakespeare's London* (1987). Something of a middle ground between Cook (above) and Harbage (below).

———. *The Shakespearean Stage, 1579–1642* (2nd ed., 1980). On the acting companies, the actors, the playhouses, the stages, and the audiences.

Harbage, Alfred. *Shakespeare's Audience* (1941). A study of the size and nature of the theatrical public, emphasizing the representativeness of its working class and middle-class audience.

Hodges, C. Walter. *The Globe Restored* (1968). A conjectural restoration, with lucid drawings.

Hosley, Richard. "The Playhouses," in *The Revels History of Drama in English*, vol. 3, general editors Clifford Leech and T. W. Craik (1975). An essay of a hundred pages on the physical aspects of the playhouses.

Howard, Jane E. "Crossdressing, the Theatre, and Gender Struggle in Early Modern England," *Shakespeare Quarterly* 39 (1988): 418–40. Judicious comments on the effects of boys playing female roles.

Orrell, John. *The Human Stage: English Theatre Design, 1567–1640* (1988). Argues that the public, private, and court playhouses are less indebted to popular structures (e.g., innyards and bear-baiting pits) than to banqueting halls and to Renaissance conceptions of Roman amphitheaters.

Slater, Ann Pasternak. *Shakespeare the Director* (1982). An analysis of theatrical effects (e.g., kissing, kneeling) in stage directions and dialogue.

Styan, J. L. *Shakespeare's Stagecraft* (1967). An introduction to Shakespeare's visual and aural stagecraft, with chapters on such topics as acting conventions, stage groupings, and speech.

Thompson, Peter. *Shakespeare's Professional Career* (1992). An examination of patronage and related theatrical conditions.

———. *Shakespeare's Theatre* (1983). A discussion of how plays were staged in Shakespeare's time.

4. Shakespeare on Stage and Screen

Bate, Jonathan, and Russell Jackson, eds. *Shakespeare: An Illustrated Stage History* (1996). Highly readable essays on stage productions from the Renaissance to the present.

Berry, Ralph. *Changing Styles in Shakespeare* (1981). Discusses productions of six plays (*Coriolanus, Hamlet, Henry V, Measure for Measure, The Tempest,* and *Twelfth Night*) on the English stage, chiefly 1950–1980.

————. *On Directing Shakespeare: Interviews with Contemporary Directors* (1989). An enlarged edition of a book first published in 1977, this version includes the seven interviews from the early 1970s and adds five interviews conducted in 1988.

Brockbank, Philip, ed. *Players of Shakespeare: Essays in Shakespearean Performance* (1985). Comments by twelve actors, reporting their experiences with roles. See also the entry for Russell Jackson (below).

Bulman, J. C., and H. R. Coursen, eds. *Shakespeare on Television* (1988). An anthology of general and theoretical essays, essays on individual productions, and shorter reviews, with a bibliography and a videography listing cassettes that may be rented.

Coursen, H. P. *Watching Shakespeare on Television* (1993). Analyses not only of TV versions but also of films and videotapes of stage presentations that are shown on television.

Davies, Anthony, and Stanley Wells, eds. *Shakespeare and the Moving Image: The Plays on Film and Television* (1994). General essays (e.g., on the comedies) as well as essays devoted entirely to *Hamlet*, *King Lear*, and *Macbeth*.

Dawson, Anthony B. *Watching Shakespeare: A Playgoer's Guide* (1988). About half of the plays are discussed, chiefly in terms of decisions that actors and directors make in putting the works onto the stage.

Dessen, Alan. *Elizabethan Stage Conventions and Modern Interpretations* (1984). On interpreting conventions such as the representation of light and darkness and stage violence (duels, battles).

Donaldson, Peter. *Shakespearean Films/Shakespearean Directors* (1990). Postmodernist analyses, drawing on Freudianism, Feminism, Deconstruction, and Queer Theory.

Jackson, Russell, and Robert Smallwood, eds. *Players of Shakespeare 2: Further Essays in Shakespearean Performance by Players with the Royal Shakespeare Company* (1988). Fourteen actors discuss their roles in productions between 1982 and 1987.

————. *Players of Shakespeare 3: Further Essays in Shakespearean Performance by Players with the Royal
Shakespeare Company* (1993). Comments by thirteen
performers.

Jorgens, Jack. *Shakespeare on Film* (1977). Fairly detailed
studies of eighteen films, preceded by an introductory
chapter addressing such issues as music, and whether to
"open" the play by including scenes of landscape.

Kennedy, Dennis. *Looking at Shakespeare: A Visual History of Twentieth-Century Performance* (1993). Lucid
descriptions (with 170 photographs) of European, British,
and American performances.

Leiter, Samuel L. *Shakespeare Around the Globe: A Guide
to Notable Postwar Revivals* (1986). For each play there
are about two pages of introductory comments, then discussions (about five hundred words per production) of ten
or so productions, and finally bibliographic references.

McMurty, Jo. *Shakespeare Films in the Classroom* (1994).
Useful evaluations of the chief films most likely to be
shown in undergraduate courses.

Rothwell, Kenneth, and Annabelle Henkin Melzer. *Shakespeare on Screen: An International Filmography and
Videography* (1990). A reference guide to several hundred films and videos produced between 1899 and 1989,
including spinoffs such as musicals and dance versions.

Sprague, Arthur Colby. *Shakespeare and the Actors* (1944).
Detailed discussions of stage business (gestures, etc.)
over the years.

Willis, Susan. *The BBC Shakespeare Plays: Making the
Televised Canon* (1991). A history of the series, with
interviews and production diaries for some plays.

5. Miscellaneous Reference Works

Abbott, E. A. *A Shakespearean Grammar* (new edition,
1877). An examination of differences between Elizabethan and modern grammar.

Allen, Michael J. B., and Kenneth Muir, eds. *Shakespeare's
Plays in Quarto* (1981). One volume containing facsimi-

les of the plays issued in small format before they were collected in the First Folio of 1623.

Bevington, David. *Shakespeare* (1978). A short guide to hundreds of important writings on the subject.

Blake, Norman. *Shakespeare's Language: An Introduction* (1983). On vocabulary, parts of speech, and word order.

Bullough, Geoffrey. *Narrative and Dramatic Sources of Shakespeare*, 8 vols. (1957–75). A collection of many of the books Shakespeare drew on, with judicious comments.

Campbell, Oscar James, and Edward G. Quinn, eds. *The Reader's Encyclopedia of Shakespeare* (1966). Old, but still the most useful single reference work on Shakespeare.

Cercignani, Fausto. *Shakespeare's Works and Elizabethan Pronunciation* (1981). Considered the best work on the topic, but remains controversial.

Dent, R. W. *Shakespeare's Proverbial Language: An Index* (1981). An index of proverbs, with an introduction concerning a form Shakespeare frequently drew on.

Greg, W. W. *The Shakespeare First Folio* (1955). A detailed yet readable history of the first collection (1623) of Shakespeare's plays.

Harner, James. *The World Shakespeare Bibliography*. See headnote to Suggested References.

Hosley, Richard. *Shakespeare's Holinshed* (1968). Valuable presentation of one of Shakespeare's major sources.

Kökeritz, Helge. *Shakespeare's Names* (1959). A guide to pronouncing some 1,800 names appearing in Shakespeare.

———. *Shakespeare's Pronunciation* (1953). Contains much information about puns and rhymes, but see Cercignani (above).

Muir, Kenneth. *The Sources of Shakespeare's Plays* (1978). An account of Shakespeare's use of his reading. It covers all the plays, in chronological order.

Miriam Joseph, Sister. *Shakespeare's Use of the Arts of Language* (1947). A study of Shakespeare's use of rhetorical devices, reprinted in part as *Rhetoric in Shakespeare's Time* (1962).

The Norton Facsimile: The First Folio of Shakespeare's Plays (1968). A handsome and accurate facsimile of the first collection (1623) of Shakespeare's plays, with a valuable introduction by Charlton Hinman.

Onions, C. T. *A Shakespeare Glossary*, rev. and enlarged by R. D. Eagleson (1986). Definitions of words (or senses of words) now obsolete.

Partridge, Eric. *Shakespeare's Bawdy*, rev. ed. (1955). Relatively brief dictionary of bawdy words; useful, but see Williams, below.

Shakespeare Quarterly. See headnote to Suggested References.

Shakespeare Survey. See headnote to Suggested References.

Spevack, Marvin. *The Harvard Concordance to Shakespeare* (1973). An index to Shakespeare's words.

Vickers, Brian. *Appropriating Shakespeare: Contemporary Critical Quarrels* (1993). A survey—chiefly hostile—of recent schools of criticism.

Wells, Stanley, ed. *Shakespeare: A Bibliographical Guide* (new edition, 1990). Nineteen chapters (some devoted to single plays, others devoted to groups of related plays) on recent scholarship on the life and all of the works.

Williams, Gordon. *A Dictionary of Sexual Language and Imagery in Shakespearean and Stuart Literature*, 3 vols. (1994). Extended discussions of words and passages; much fuller than Partridge, cited above.

6. Shakespeare's Plays: General Studies

Bamber, Linda. *Comic Women, Tragic Men: A Study of Gender and Genre in Shakespeare* (1982).

Barnet, Sylvan. *A Short Guide to Shakespeare* (1974).

Callaghan, Dympna, Lorraine Helms, and Jyotsna Singh. *The Weyward Sisters: Shakespeare and Feminist Politics* (1994).

Clemen, Wolfgang H. *The Development of Shakespeare's Imagery* (1951).

Cook, Ann Jennalie. *Making a Match: Courtship in Shakespeare and His Society* (1991).

Dollimore, Jonathan, and Alan Sinfield. *Political Shakespeare: New Essays in Cultural Materialism* (1985).

Dusinberre, Juliet. *Shakespeare and the Nature of Women* (1975).

Granville-Barker, Harley. *Prefaces to Shakespeare*, 2 vols. (1946–47; volume 1 contains essays on *Hamlet, King Lear, Merchant of Venice, Antony and Cleopatra*, and *Cymbeline*; volume 2 contains essays on *Othello, Coriolanus, Julius Caesar, Romeo and Juliet, Love's Labor's Lost*).

————. *More Prefaces to Shakespeare* (1974; essays on *Twelfth Night, A Midsummer Night's Dream, The Winter's Tale, Macbeth*).

Harbage, Alfred. *William Shakespeare: A Reader's Guide* (1963).

Howard, Jean E. *Shakespeare's Art of Orchestration: Stage Technique and Audience Response* (1984).

Jones, Emrys. *Scenic Form in Shakespeare* (1971).

Lenz, Carolyn Ruth Swift, Gayle Greene, and Carol Thomas Neely, eds. *The Woman's Part: Feminist Criticism of Shakespeare* (1980).

Novy, Marianne. *Love's Argument: Gender Relations in Shakespeare* (1984).

Rose, Mark. *Shakespearean Design* (1972).

Scragg, Leah. *Discovering Shakespeare's Meaning* (1994).

————. *Shakespeare's "Mouldy Tales": Recurrent Plot Motifs in Shakespearean Drama* (1992).

Traub, Valerie. *Desire and Anxiety: Circulations of Sexuality in Shakespearean Drama* (1992).

Traversi, D. A. *An Approach to Shakespeare*, 2 vols. (3rd rev. ed, 1968–69).

Vickers, Brian. *The Artistry of Shakespeare's Prose* (1968).

Wells, Stanley. *Shakespeare: A Dramatic Life* (1994).

Wright, George T. *Shakespeare's Metrical Art* (1988).

7. The Comedies

Barber, C. L. *Shakespeare's Festive Comedy* (1959; discusses *Love's Labor's Lost, A Midsummer Night's Dream, The Merchant of Venice, As You Like It, Twelfth Night*).

Barton, Anne. *The Names of Comedy* (1990).

Berry, Ralph. *Shakespeare's Comedy: Explorations in Form* (1972).

Bradbury, Malcolm, and David Palmer, eds. *Shakespearean Comedy* (1972).

Bryant, J. A., Jr. *Shakespeare and the Uses of Comedy* (1986).

Carroll, William. *The Metamorphoses of Shakespearean Comedy* (1985).

Champion, Larry S. *The Evolution of Shakespeare's Comedy* (1970).

Evans, Bertrand. *Shakespeare's Comedies* (1960).

Frye, Northrop. *Shakespearean Comedy and Romance* (1965).

Leggatt, Alexander. *Shakespeare's Comedy of Love* (1974).

Miola, Robert S. *Shakespeare and Classical Comedy: The Influence of Plautus and Terence* (1994).

Nevo, Ruth. *Comic Transformations in Shakespeare* (1980).

Ornstein, Robert. *Shakespeare's Comedies: From Roman Farce to Romantic Mystery* (1986).

Richman, David. *Laughter, Pain, and Wonder: Shakespeare's Comedies and the Audience in the Theater* (1990).

Salingar, Leo. *Shakespeare and the Traditions of Comedy* (1974).

Slights, Camille Wells. *Shakespeare's Comic Commonwealths* (1993).

Waller, Gary, ed. *Shakespeare's Comedies* (1991).

Westlund, Joseph. *Shakespeare's Reparative Comedies: A Psychoanalytic View of the Middle Plays* (1984).

Williamson, Marilyn. *The Patriarchy of Shakespeare's Comedies* (1986).

8. The Romances (*Pericles, Cymbeline, The Winter's Tale, The Tempest, The Two Noble Kinsmen*)

Adams, Robert M. *Shakespeare: The Four Romances* (1989).

Felperin, Howard. *Shakespearean Romance* (1972).

Frye, Northrop. *A Natural Perspective: The Development of Shakespearean Comedy and Romance* (1965).

Mowat, Barbara. *The Dramaturgy of Shakespeare's Romances* (1976).
Warren, Roger. *Staging Shakespeare's Late Plays* (1990).
Young, David. *The Heart's Forest: A Study of Shakespeare's Pastoral Plays* (1972).

9. The Tragedies

Bradley, A. C. *Shakespearean Tragedy* (1904).
Brooke, Nicholas. *Shakespeare's Early Tragedies* (1968).
Champion, Larry. *Shakespeare's Tragic Perspective* (1976).
Drakakis, John, ed. *Shakespearean Tragedy* (1992).
Evans, Bertrand. *Shakespeare's Tragic Practice* (1979).
Everett, Barbara. *Young Hamlet: Essays on Shakespeare's Tragedies* (1989).
Foakes, R. A. *Hamlet versus Lear: Cultural Politics and Shakespeare's Art* (1993).
Frye, Northrop. *Fools of Time: Studies in Shakespearean Tragedy* (1967).
Harbage, Alfred, ed. *Shakespeare: The Tragedies* (1964).
Mack, Maynard. *Everybody's Shakespeare: Reflections Chiefly on the Tragedies* (1993).
McAlindon, T. *Shakespeare's Tragic Cosmos* (1991).
Miola, Robert S. *Shakespeare and Classical Tragedy: The Influence of Seneca* (1992).
———. *Shakespeare's Rome* (1983).
Nevo, Ruth. *Tragic Form in Shakespeare* (1972).
Rackin, Phyllis. *Shakespeare's Tragedies* (1978).
Rose, Mark, ed. *Shakespeare's Early Tragedies: A Collection of Critical Essays* (1995).
Rosen, William. *Shakespeare and the Craft of Tragedy* (1960).
Snyder, Susan. *The Comic Matrix of Shakespeare's Tragedies* (1979).
Wofford, Susanne. *Shakespeare's Late Tragedies: A Collection of Critical Essays* (1996).
Young, David. *The Action to the Word: Structure and Style in Shakespearean Tragedy* (1990).

————. *Shakespeare's Middle Tragedies: A Collection of Critical Essays* (1993).

10. The Histories

Blanpied, John W. *Time and the Artist in Shakespeare's English Histories* (1983).

Campbell, Lily B. *Shakespeare's "Histories": Mirrors of Elizabethan Policy* (1947).

Champion, Larry S. *Perspective in Shakespeare's English Histories* (1980).

Hodgdon, Barbara. *The End Crowns All: Closure and Contradiction in Shakespeare's History* (1991).

Holderness, Graham. *Shakespeare Recycled: The Making of Historical Drama* (1992).

————, ed. *Shakespeare's History Plays: "Richard II" to "Henry V"* (1992).

Leggatt, Alexander. *Shakespeare's Political Drama: The History Plays and the Roman Plays* (1988).

Ornstein, Robert. *A Kingdom for a Stage: The Achievement of Shakespeare's History Plays* (1972).

Rackin, Phyllis. *Stages of History: Shakespeare's English Chronicles* (1990).

Saccio, Peter. *Shakespeare's English Kings: History, Chronicle, and Drama* (1977).

Tillyard, E. M. W. *Shakespeare's History Plays* (1944).

Velz, John W., ed. *Shakespeare's English Histories: A Quest for Form and Genre* (1996).

11. *The Winter's Tale*

For discussions of the play within the context of Shakespeare's other late romances, see the items listed above in Section 8. For accounts of productions, see the bibliographic references in *The Winter's Tale* on Stage and Screen, above, pages 206–7.

Bryant, J. A., Jr. "Shakespeare's Allegory: *The Winter's Tale*." *Sewanee Review* 63 (1955): 202–22.

Coghill, Nevill. "Six Points of Stage-Craft in *The Winter's Tale.*" *Shakespeare Survey* 11 (1958): 31–41.

Colie, Rosalie. *Shakespeare's Living Art* (1974).

Draper, R. P. *"The Winter's Tale": Text and Performance* (1985).

Erikson, Peter. *Patriarchal Structure in Shakespeare's Dramas* (1985).

Ewbank, Inga-Stina. "The Triumph of Time in *The Winter's Tale.*" *Review of English Literature* 5 (April 1964): 83–100.

Frye, Northrop. *Fables of Identity* (1963).

Hunt, Maurice, ed. *"The Winter's Tale": Critical Essays* (1995).

Knight, G. Wilson. *The Crown of Life* (1947). Part of this material is reprinted above.

Male, David A. *"The Winter's Tale" [Shakespeare on Stage Series]* (1984).

McDonald, Russ. "Poetry and Plot in *The Winter's Tale.*" *Shakespeare Quarterly* 36 (1985): 315–29.

Mowat, Barbara A. "Rogues, Shepherds, and the Counterfeit Distressed: Texts and Infracontexts of *The Winter's Tale* 4.3." *Shakespeare Studies* 22 (1994): 58–76.

Muir, Kenneth, ed. *Shakespeare: "The Winter's Tale": A Casebook* (1969).

Overton, Bill. *"The Winter's Tale"* (1989).

Sokol, B. J. *Art and Illusion in "The Winter's Tale"* (1994).

Tillyard, E. M. W. *Shakespeare's Last Plays* (1938). Part of this material is reprinted above.

Traub, Valerie. *Desire and Anxiety: Circulations of Sexuality in Shakespearean Drama* (1992).

Traversi, D. A. *Shakespeare: The Last Phase* (1955).

The Signet Classics Shakespeare Series:

The Histories

Extensively revised and updated expert commentary provides
more enjoyment through a greater understanding of the texts

HENRY IV: PART I, Maynard Mack, ed.

HENRY IV: PART II, Norman Holland, ed.

HENRY V, John Russell Brown, ed.

HENRY VI: PARTS I, II, & III, Lawrence V. Ryan,
Arthur Freeman, & Milton Crane, ed.

RICHARD II, Kenneth Muir, ed.

RICHARD III, Mark Eccles, ed.

Available wherever books are sold or at
penguin.com

facebook.com/signetclassics

The Signet Classics Shakespeare Series:

The Tragedies

Extensively revised and updated expert commentary provides
more enjoyment through a greater understanding of the texts

ANTONY AND CLEOPATRA, Barbara Everett, ed.

CORIOLANUS, Ruben Brower, ed.

HAMLET, Sylvan Barnet, ed.

JULIUS CAESAR, William and Barbara Rosen, ed.

KING LEAR, Russell Faser, ed.

MACBETH, Sylvan Barnet, ed.

OTHELLO, Alvin Kernan, ed.

ROMEO AND JULIET, J.A. Bryant, Jr., ed.

TROILUS AND CRESSIDA. Daniel Seltzer, ed.